Human Rights in the States

Recent Titles in
Contributions in Legal Studies
Series Editor: Paul L. Murphy

HUMAN RIGHTS IN THE STATES

New Directions in
Constitutional Policymaking

Edited by

Stanley H. Friedelbaum

CONTRIBUTIONS IN LEGAL STUDIES,
NUMBER 43

Greenwood Press

NEW YORK • WESTPORT, CONNECTICUT • LONDON

AAW0971

JAN 2 9 1990

Library of Congress Cataloging-in-Publication Data

Human rights in the states : new directions in constitutional
   policymaking / edited by Stanley H. Friedelbaum.
      p.   cm. — (Contributions in legal studies, ISSN 0147–1074 ;
   no. 43)
      Bibliography: p.
      Includes index.
      ISBN 0–313–25451–6 (lib. bdg. : alk. paper)
      1. Civil rights—United States—States.   2. Courts—United States
   —States.   3. Federal government—United States.   I. Friedelbaum,
   Stanley H. (Stanley Herman), 1927–   .   II. Series.
   KF4750.Z95H86 1988
   342.73′ 085—dc19
   [347.30285]   88–3094

British Library Cataloguing in Publication Data is available.

Library of Congress Catalog Card Number: 88–3094
ISBN: 0–313–25451–6
ISSN: 0147–1074

First published in 1988

Greenwood Press, Inc.
88 Post Road West, Westport, Connecticut 06881

Printed in the United States of America

The paper used in this book complies with the
Permanent Paper Standard issued by the National
Information Standards Organization (Z39.48–1984).

10   9   8   7   6   5   4   3   2   1

Contents

Preface

The past two decades have witnessed a remarkable revival of interest in the work of the state courts. As the U.S. Supreme Court continued to retreat from the unusual activism of the Warren years, so judges in a number of states moved beyond federal guarantees by creating significant bodies of law independently derived. This is not to say that state constitutional provisions have generally diverged from the federal text. To the contrary, a linguistic identity suggested parallel lines of reasoning looking toward the attainment of similar results. Yet the end products did not undeviatingly convey like meanings; and, in fact, a number of state courts came to assert an autonomy that served to shield their findings from federal review.

Such an effort to preclude Supreme Court intervention would hardly have been persuasive during the 1960s when the prevailing majority, with Justice Hugo Black serving as its principal architect, achieved an almost complete "nationalization" of the Bill of Rights. The assumption was that nothing less than the extension of the full panoply of federal constitutional safeguards would be effective as a deterrent against state abuses. By contrast, recent opinions, representing a broad cross-section of views, acknowledge the desirability of state participation in expanding the scope of human rights. This new-found recognition has not led the Court to relinquish its role as an ultimate preserving agency responsible for the establishment and maintenance of minimal requirements. What has changed is the notion of national exclusivity and its replacement by a formula of sharing that reaffirms the historic functions of each state in securing the rights of its citizens.

A variety of contemporary case studies reveals topical patterns coupled with a diversity that defies easy categorization. Not unexpectedly, the intensity of any court's responses may be measured by reference to familiar criteria: the judges' perceptions of the review function, the tradition of activism or restraint that has developed, the interplay of federal-state standards, and the permissiveness or rigor of the guidelines devised to gauge exercises of the police power. All the same, an emphatic interventionism and a variety of interpretational techniques present departures from accustomed norms, especially in California, New Jersey, Hawaii, and Alaska. The studies are indicative of a reinvigorated sense of social awareness and of sensitivity to the preservation and enlargement of individual rights. While the states of the Old Confederacy remain conservative in outlook, notable exceptions continue to appear as the effects of an advancing urbanism have begun to intrude.

Many of the essays that follow reflect the excitement and innovative spirit associated with the opening of a new era. Although the temptation is strong to limit selections to the novel products of the state judiciaries, a penchant for experimentation, long attributed to the federalism of yesteryear, is apparent in other contexts as well. It is always difficult to arrive at a consensus describing a core of subjects as analytic exemplars. The range of activities peculiar to fifty states makes agreement on such a selection an elusive goal at best. What reasonably may be expected to result is a representative choice—one that illustrates both the similarities and the diversification of substance and style associated with an assemblage of political entities that ostensibly comprise a single nation.

Expressions of gratitude are in order to those who assisted in the preparation of this work. As in any collaborative effort, the success of the venture ultimately depended on the cooperation and performance of the contributors. It is a pleasure to note that on all occasions, each responded to my requests for changes, additions, and deletions with exceptional good humor and in the best tradition of collegiality. The Rutgers University Research Council, as in the past, provided generous support in facilitating the preparation of the manuscript. The staffs of the Rutgers University libraries on the several campuses extended many courtesies along the way. My colleagues in the Department of Political Science helped more than they knew in serving as sounding boards for my steady stream of declamation concerning state constitutional cases and issues. Sheila Friedlander and Phyllis Moditz offered capable typing and kindred services when they were most needed. Mildred Vasan of Greenwood Press first encouraged me to undertake this book and, at several critical points, she furnished useful advice and reassurance. Finally, my wife, Claire, and daughter, Barbara, as always, suffered through extensive time spans with characteristic forbearance and understanding as still another research project took more of my time than I could have anticipated.

Stanley H. Friedelbaum

Introduction

STANLEY H. FRIEDELBAUM

Judicial Activism in Retreat: The Uncertain Outlook for "New" Federal Rights

With the close of the Burger Court era and a renewed emphasis on judicial restraint, the U.S. Supreme Court cannot always be looked upon as an inviting forum for litigants intent on advancing human rights. Expansive readings of federal guarantees of constitutional liberty seem increasingly unlikely, especially as these may be expected to elaborate on definitions of personal autonomy. Perhaps the most notable decisions of the Burger Court touched on the fashioning of a limited right of heterosexual, conjugal privacy. The opinions were marked by a willingness to reembrace the remnants of substantive due process, albeit within carefully delineated boundaries, in affirming personal discretion in matters of procreation, marriage, and family living. Such cases as *Roe v. Wade*,[1] *Eisenstadt v. Baird*,[2] and *Carey v. Population Services International*[3] attest to the Court's recognition of the importance of intimate associations not only in enhancing the lives of human beings but also in ensuring the continued vibrancy of a free and open society. Whether such goals remain a part of the Court's design is doubtful even if the votes are still wanting to overturn the basic rights that have been sanctioned.

A majority made plain in *Bowers v. Hardwick*[4] its disinclination to extend the concept of liberty beyond what had been protected throughout the nation's "history and tradition." There is a reluctance to describe new rights that require ventures across unexplored borders into an uncharted doctrinal terrain. Although the Court admits that the cases in which due process rights have been given substantive content are "legion," it disavows any expansion of "judge-made" constitutional law because, in doing so, the judiciary is "most vulnerable and comes nearest to illegitimacy."[5] Thus, it appears, the articulation of rights not finding textual support in the Constitution is unlikely; heightened judicial protection will be limited to what has already been identified.

In many respects, the *Hardwick* decision parallels Justice Benjamin Cardozo's dicta of half a century ago distinguishing segments of the Bill of Rights applicable to the states by reference to a standard of what is "implicit in the concept of ordered liberty." The line of division permitted the absorption of no more than that which had previously controlled state action. There emerged a "rationalizing principle" that grounded liberty in the social and moral values of the past. It reflected a philosophy of restraint linking constitutional principles to an incrementalism imbedded in history. The role of the national government was a circumscribed one, though Cardozo, like current members of the Court, had to concede, however grudgingly, that the "domain of liberty, withdrawn by the Fourteenth Amendment from encroachment by the states, had been enlarged by latter-day judgments."[6]

If the narrow construction placed on the amendment, then and now, accurately depicts the status of human freedoms, it follows that significant responsibilities fall to the states in preserving the rights of their citizens. Admittedly such an account of the Fourteenth Amendment's effects is exaggerated, intended largely to add to an ongoing debate concerning the Court's role.[7] It is not likely to be taken seriously even by the most extravagant proponents of a return to the "original intentions" of the framers of the Constitution or of the post–Civil War amendments.[8] The judicial record of past decades cannot be so heedlessly erased. Since a major reversal of precedents requires more than vacuous declamation, it is reasonable to assume that most of the provisions of the Bill of Rights will continue to be applicable to the states. Yet the Court's reluctance to move beyond the explicit language of the Constitution or to discover new rights in the amorphous wording of the Fourteenth Amendment's due process clause ought not to be dismissed as pointless rhetoric. If opportunities for a revival of state constitutional law have been pursued to good effect during the years of the Burger Court, an even more productive era may lie ahead as personnel changes reshape the Supreme Court.

Historical Patterns: State Constitutional Law in Perspective

In the first stages of American constitutionalism, the states played significant initiatory roles. A number of state constitutions preceded the

national constitution, and, in many ways, state charters provided pro-
totypes for the creation of what subsequently came to be viewed as the
federal model. More than a century of colonial experimentation with
governing forms resulted in the emergence of an ill-defined but dis-
cernible system of provincial self-rule. The state constitutions that took
shape during the era of independence and state building took much of
their content and distinguishing structural features from British tradition, from practices developed during decades of neglect under an antiquated and poorly functioning imperial system, and from indigenous
efforts, often hobbled but strikingly persistent, that promoted a remarkable measure of local autonomy.[9]

It was this unconventional and varied heritage that, during the early
years of the Republic, passed to the state courts as they assumed primacy
in the review of federal and state questions. Although the First Congress
established national tribunals, their jurisdiction was narrowly limited to
avoid incursions on the authority of the state courts.[10] The Supreme
Court, despite its constitutional status, occupied a far less exalted position
than that which it holds today. Its major function was to oversee the
protection of federal rights, but its role, a modest one by any measure,
was not free from challenge by state judges whose reputations often
surpassed those of the Supreme Court justices. So pervasive were state
influences that Justice Joseph Story, a disciple of John Marshall, took
pains to admonish state judges of their responsibility to comply with
holdings of the Supreme Court.[11] His assertions did little to dispel the
doubts of courts, as well as legislatures, in a number of states. During
the antebellum years, several state courts openly took issue with Story,
seriously questioning his efforts to fix a national locus of appellate authority.

James Madison's efforts to secure approval of a Bill of Rights in the
First Congress had also raised divisive questions of federalism. From the
outset, differences existed concerning the need for the inclusion of a
Bill of Rights in the national constitution and, more significant, its possible displacement of counterpart guarantees in the state charters. There
were undeniable elements of redundancy in a recital of safeguards found
in state declarations. Another of Madison's proposals, suggesting a selective list of rights to be guarded against state action, carried in the
House of Representatives[12] but failed to command a majority in the
Senate. It is likely that the Senate's willingness to accept an expansive
First Amendment was prompted by assurances that its provisions would
not be directed to the states, especially in the area of church-state separation where steps to effect disestablishment proved to be both controversial and slow moving. Interestingly, the Supreme Court did not
construe the religion clauses of the First Amendment for almost a century.[13]

That the state courts would continue to retain primary authority in local matters was confirmed by the Supreme Court's disposition of Fifth Amendment claims in the 1833 case of *Barron v. Baltimore*.[14] At issue was a damage action brought by the owner of a wharf against the city for street construction projects that had rendered his property useless for commercial purposes. Barron invoked the Fifth Amendment, which prohibits the taking of private property for public use without just compensation. Chief Justice John Marshall,writing for the court, rejected Barron's pleas for lack of jurisdiction. The provisions of the Bill of Rights, Marshall made clear, were not applicable to the legislation of the states. They were, as the chief justice perceived them, "limitations of power granted in the instrument itself; not of distinct governments, framed by different persons and for different purposes."[15] It resulted that one of the leading nationalists of the day had acquiesced in, if he had not formally established, a model of dual federalism that was as effective in preserving state interests as it was disarmingly simplistic in design.

Antebellum judicial review, at both the state and national levels, remained at a rudimentary stage when measured against modern practices. A central concern of the courts of the 1820s was to protect against untoward legislative measures that undermined the confidence of the people in their elected representatives. It was only in succeeding decades that the judiciary recognized a duty to defend minority rights against an overreaching majoritarianism and to resolve social conflicts. The state courts sought to redress wrongs in a limited number of areas, principally in relation to the distribution and use of alcoholic beverages, public grants to railroads and other utilities, and the protection of the rights of married women.[16]

An emphasis on public policy issues began to command the interest of judges, but it is easy to overstate the role of state courts. Plainly, the competition among special interest groups, when it occurred, was not comparable to contemporary clashes. Nor were there crises over the reach of judicial review resembling those that, in subsequent years, came to threaten the independence of the judiciary. Almost a half-century passed following Marshall's controversial discourse in *Marbury v. Madison* before a second act of Congress was held unconstitutional. The latter, occurring in the *Dred Scott* case[17] with its unfortunate consequences, cast so long and dismal a shadow on judicial decisionmaking as to eclipse the power of the Supreme Court during the years of the Civil War and Reconstruction. Whether the state courts could have flourished as major instruments of change, with the former Confederate states in disarray and dominated by outside interests, is open to serious doubt in any case.

Not surprisingly, the turbulent era of the Civil War and Reconstruction had given rise to an upsurge of federal power. On the one hand, the

notion of state primacy remained in disfavor after decades of acrimonious debate that had ended in armed conflict over the nature of the
Union. On the other hand, dramatic economic growth brought urgent
demands for a new centralization. Congress responded, in part, by en-
larging the authority of the federal courts. The ensure some measure
of protection for the recently freed slaves, legislation enacted in the 1870s
established the federal courts as alternative guardians of the civil rights
of citizens.[18] The writ of habeas corpus was extended, in specified circumstances, to state prisoners who claimed violations of their rights.
Concomitantly, the jurisdiction of the federal courts was gradually enlarged to accommodate the needs of an increasingly national economy.
That the Supreme Court declined to extend the federal judicial power
to its permissible limits reflected not only a respect for the state courts
but also an almost nostalgic attachment to a bygone era of federalism.

If the state courts continued to participate significantly in the affairs
of a nation traditionally prone to litigation, their functions lay principally
in a redefinition of commercial and property law. The disputes were
largely of a private character, primarily in the areas of debt collection,
contracts, and real property. The issues were complex, reflecting the
instability of the marketplace and financial institutions. They required
judges to adjust diverse claims of debtors and creditors, as well as to
protect the interests of other parties less directly linked to their transactions.[19] Judicial intervention in the shaping of public law, particularly
constitutional law, remained infrequent, though the review function
doubtless encompassed such inquiries.

The adoption of the Fourteenth Amendment and its anticipated implementation in the courts opened a new era, giving rise to expanded
views of nationalism. In what had previously been referred to as the
"compound republic of America,"[20] access to the federal trial courts was
often dependent on the accident of state citizenship under the diversity
clause of the Constitution. Not only had the federal judiciary now been
invested with greatly expanded authority; the bases for a suit had also
been far more broadly conceived. The Fourteenth Amendment itself
enjoined the states from abridging the privileges and immunities of
citizens, from depriving persons of life, liberty, or property without due
process of law, and from denying them the equal protection of the laws.

All the same, the narrow construction initially accorded these provisions recalled the debate over Madison's proposal to apply selected
provisions of the Bill of Rights to the states. The Reconstruction amendments apparently had not eliminated uncertainty concerning the nationalization process despite an elaboration of the privileges and
immunities of citizens of the United States. In the *Slaughterhouse Cases*,[21]
the Supreme Court declined to concede broad scope to the privileges
and immunities clause even as a majority tersely rejected claims premised

upon a "new" due process. It was the latter clause that subsequently was utilized to achieve Madison's goals. Yet in an arduous step-by-step progression, little was achieved without considerable rancor marked by recurring skirmishes over the "original" intent of the Fourteenth Amendment.[22]

During the second half of the nineteenth century, the caseloads of the state supreme courts rose dramatically. Population growth and related factors contributed to a flood of litigation that threatened to overwhelm personnel. Despite efforts to assign a limited number of appeals to panels or specially designated commissioners, the volume of cases continued to multiply. The establishment of intermediate appellate courts seemed an obvious means of alleviating some of the pressure. A second alternative lay in affording discretion in the selection of cases rather than in ensuring an appeal "as of right" to all who sought one. Neither of these reforms became widespread until the middle of the twentieth century. It was only then that greater attention was directed to significant cases, that a "formalistic" style gave way to an emphasis on judicial creativity, and that separate concurring and dissenting opinions became more frequent in the decisionmaking process.[23]

Any lingering doubts concerning the breadth of federal jurisdiction were put to rest early in the twentieth century. The protective mantle of the Eleventh Amendment, effectively immunizing the states from suit, was lost in 1908 when the Supreme Court held state officials accountable if they sought to act under unconstitutional state statutes.[24] Even more dramatic was the Court's adoption of rigorous standards of review in assessing a burgeoning body of state economic and social legislation. An infusion of federal judicial negativism, by way of substantive due process, threatened the power of the states to provide for the well-being of their citizens.[25]

A plethora of judicial inventions, at best peripherally tied to the text of the Constitution and hitherto unknown in the interpretive lexicon, posed such formidable tests as a requirement of liberty of contract (between employers and employees)[26] and the notion of an affectation with the public interest[27] as measures of the validity of the states' exercise of the police power. Economic laissez faire became the order of the day, while Herbert Spenser's *Social Statics* served as the prevailing philosophy of the Court. For almost half a century, a narrow majority of the justices held sway as a "superlegislature," weighing the merits of an impressive array of state regulatory schemes. In determining the "reasonableness" of legislation, they displaced the will of popularly elected representatives with a new-found activism and a widespread resort to confining gauges of the public welfare. Clearly established canons of deference to legislative policy choices had been subordinated to novel criteria that were linked, almost inextricably, to the achievement of negative results.[28]

In the face of a proliferation of far-reaching federal statutes and administrative regulations stemming from the New Deal, the Supreme Court startled many observers by the abrupt and pervasive nature of its retreat from substantive due process. Perhaps the trauma of the institutional crisis of 1937–1938 had been decisive in inaugurating an era of judicial self-abnegation. National legislative dominance in the initiation of "cooperative" economic and social programs remained undiminished as recurring centripetal pressures continued to multiply.[29] At the same time, the Court's renunciation of its supervisory role in economic affairs restored some semblance of balance to federal-state judicial relations and opened the way to meaningful review by the state courts. Modified versions of substantive due process survived in the states where federal standards, in effect, had ceased to exist.[30]

Events of World War II, marked by an emphasis on strong national leadership and the imposition of a broad spectrum of federal controls, eclipsed the role of the states. A disquieting flurry of suggestions, looking toward the replacement of traditional states by regional units, provided a strong impetus for the introduction of long-overdue reform proposals. Following the end of the war, a number of states launched major revitalization projects that by any measure ranged beyond piecemeal constitutional and administrative alterations. The admission of Alaska and Hawaii as states also did much to dispel the notion of a hopeless provincialism. Plainly the survival of the states as political entities, apart from any redefinition of their actual functions, was no longer in question. Although federal supremacy remained the dominant theme, constitutional revision, particularly as it effected an updating of antiquated judicial systems, fostered the establishment of viable state courts, possessed of the capability, if not always the willingness, to take on expanded responsibilities.[31]

As the Supreme Court's abandonment of active economic review continued unabated, judicial activism took an unaccustomed turn, though hardly one without historic roots. The progressive application of most of the guarantees of the federal Bill of Rights to the states, a process that ranks among the most remarkable examples of improvisation in the annals of the Court, reached fulfillment in the late 1960s. If nationalization initially had been anticipated by the adoption of the Fourteenth Amendment, it came to fruition during the years of the Warren Court. The oft-repeated identification of individual liberties took as its predicate the due process clause, which in turn served as the catalytic agent of "absorption." If anything, the nationalization of the Bill of Rights reinforced a preexisting reluctance to rely on state constitutional provisions as libertarian instruments. The assumption was that state bills paled by comparison with the federal model, that the states could not or would not provide adequate levels of protection, and that if the potential existed for a continuing elaboration of the concept of liberty, it was tied to a growing rather than a dwindling catalog of federal safeguards.[32]

The momentum for a widespread commitment to national standards flowed from the lack of vigor long attributed to state courts. Among the factors that were said to have contributed to untoward state results were judgmental and stylistic deficiencies, subtle inadequacies in technique and procedure, and a general outlook oriented toward restraint.[33] By contrast, the federal Supreme Court of the 1960s served as the center of activity for an eclectic collection of private pressure groups and, on occasion, for the solicitor general as the national protector of the public interest.[34] Significant advances in human rights were achieved by both the Warren Court and the lower federal courts serving as integral parts of what some critics later termed an imperial judiciary. All the same, the supposed dormancy of the state courts proved to be illusory. In California[35] and New Jersey,[36] among other states, a renewed judicial activism was in progress, though it was virtually ignored by commentators, who directed little attention to defining or even exploring the scope of state constitutional rights.

Before the Burger Court had begun to take on a distinctive identity, dire predictions of a massive retreat from the gains of the Warren era appeared repeatedly in the professional journals and in popular accounts. While the fears expressed proved to have been exaggerated, the prospects were remote that the range of rights and freedoms enunciated would closely parallel, either in volume or in thematic content, those that had achieved prominence during the late 1950s and 1960s. If the early decisions revealed little that was dramatically different, the introduction of new doctrines remained notably sparse. As judicial initiatives slowed and the feverish pace of the past decade moderated, the justices moved toward a posture of restraint, if not of outright quiescence, in the formulation of public policy. The Court no longer could be looked upon as a continuing or even a reliable source of libertarian activism, though, in an unexpected display of positive decisionmaking, a majority resurrected an attenuated version of substantive due process as the basis for a fledgling right of personal autonomy.[37] But even with respect to this new-found offshoot of a claim to privacy, restrictive measures of elaboration and implementation reflected the essentially conservative tenor of the Court.

The turn away from Warren Court rulings was best exemplified by limitations imposed on the access of litigants to the federal courts and by the paucity of readily available federal remedies. To a limited degree, the majority's record was vulnerable to charges of successive denials of claims under provisions of civil rights legislation dating from Reconstruction. Perhaps the most notable departures lay in the Court's restatement of the criminal law. If the Warren Court, in effect, had established an unwonted federal code of criminal procedure, the new majority reverted to more traditional guidelines that assured a more active role for the states. Cases reexamining the meanings previously assigned to the Fourth, Fifth, and Sixth amendments reflected a pronounced narrowing of precedents. In particular, judicial debates over the controversial exclusionary rule of evidence reached new heights.[38]

A halting return to the state courts is of recent origin. In part it was prompted by a studied restraint, if not a marked reluctance, on the part of the Burger Court to create additional rights by judicial fiat. An unlikely consensus has developed among the justices, avowing the desirability and efficacy of state constitutional predicates. The liberal bloc has proceeded without enthusiasm and, more often than not, accompanied by condemnation of the Court's inaction. By contrast, the conservatives have embraced a new judicial federalism as a positive article of constitutional faith. Whether, in either event, policy choices derive from acts of desperation or from conscious exercises in protective intervention, the authority of the state courts to extend rights beyond minimal federal standards has never been in doubt.[39]

Rising levels of expectation regarding the quality of state court products have led state judges, in turn, to consider alternative decisional routes. Assuming that threshold questions of subject matter jurisdiction have been resolved, the range of options open to the judges is tied largely to anticipated results. The topical studies that follow provide a sampling of some of the salient factors that have played a part in their ordering of priorities. In assessing each, readers will find it helpful to weigh one or more questions that, while not determinative, may be suggestive of possible motivating sources and of judicial efficacy in advancing human rights. Has the treatment of the issues in the state courts led to an outcome materially different from comparable determinations in the federal courts? Are the essential elements examined of the same order and intensity in the courts of the state and of the nation? Do the nature and terms of state decisionmaking parallel or depart from what may reasonably be expected to flow from the construction of counterpart provisions of the Constitution? In short, does review in the state courts serve as an effective or an intrusive mode of intervention?

Notes

1. Roe v. Wade, 410 U.S. 113 (1973).
2. Eisenstadt v. Baird, 405 U.S. 438 (1972).
3. Carey v. Population Services International, 431 U.S. 678 (1977).
4. Bowers v. Hardwick, 54 L.W. 4919 (1986).
5. Id. at 4921.
6. Palko v. Connecticut, 302 U.S. 319 (1937).

7. The issues raised provoked an unprecedented rhetorical cross-fire in the fall of 1985 between Attorney General Edwin Meese and Associate Justices William Brennan and John Paul Stevens of the Supreme Court. See William J. Brennan, "The Constitution of the United States: Contemporary Ratification" (text and teaching symposium, Georgetown University, Washington, D.C., October 12, 1985), and address of John Paul Stevens, luncheon meeting of the Federal Bar Association, Chicago, October 23, 1985.

8. For a thoughtful review of contemporary constitutional theory, see Michael J. Perry, *The Constitution, the Courts, and Human Rights* (New Haven: Yale University Press, 1982).

9. See Willi P. Adams, *The First American Constitutions* (Chapel Hill: University of North Carolina Press, 1980.)

10. Paul M. Bator et al., Hart and Wechsler's *The Federal Courts and the Federal System* (Mineola, N.Y.: Foundation Press, 1973), p. 418.

11. Martin v. Hunter's Lessee, 1 Wheat. 304 (1816).

12. *Annals of Congress*, 1st Cong., 1st sess., I, 435, 441 (1789). See also Robert A. Rutland, *The Birth of the Bill of Rights, 1776–1791* (New York: Collier Books, 1962), pp. 212ff.

13. Reynolds v. United States, 98 U.S. 145 (1879).

14. Barron v. Baltimore, 7 Pet. 243 (1833).

15. Id. at 247.

16. William E. Nelson, "Changing Conceptions of Judicial Review: The Evolution of Constitutional Theory in the States, 1790–1860," *University of Pennsylvania Law Review* 120 (1972): 1166, 1179–85.

17. Dred Scott v. Sandford, 19 How. 393 (1857).

18. An excellent review, updating data on the early statutes, is provided in *"Developments in the Law—Section 1983 and Federalism," Harvard Law Review* 90 (1977): 1133.

19. Robert A. Kagan et al., "The Business of State Supreme Courts, 1870–1970," *Stanford Law Review* 30 (1977): 121, 137–41.

20. Federalist No. 51.

21. Slaughterhouse Cases, 16 Wall. 36 (1873).

22. As the debate gained momentum, the principal protagonists were Justices Felix Frankfurter and Hugo Black. See, e.g., Adamson v. California, 332 U.S. 46 (1947).

23. Kagan et al., "The Business of State Supreme Courts," pp. 121, 128–32.

24. Ex parte Young, 209 U.S. 123 (1908).

25. A succinct review is provided in Robert L. Stern, "The Problems of Yesteryear—Commerce and Due Process," *Vanderbilt Law Review* 4 (1951): 446.

26. The classic test was announced in Lochner v. New York, 198 U.S. 45 (1905).

27. See Walton H. Hamilton, "Affectation with a Public Interest," *Yale Law Journal* 39 (1930): 1089. Among the principal cases was New State Ice Co. v. Liebmann, 285 U.S. 262 (1932).

28. The oft-noted details are recounted in Benjamin F. Wright, *The Growth of American Constitutional Law* (Chicago: University of Chicago Press, Phoenix ed., 1967), chaps. 8–10 *passim*.

29. A thoughtful inquiry may be found in Robert G. McCloskey, "Economic

Due Process and the Supreme Court: An Exhumation and Reburial," *Supreme Court Review 1962*: 34.

30. Monrad G. Paulsen, "The Persistence of Substantive Due Process in the States," *Minnesota Law Review* 34 (1950): 91; John A. C. Hetherington, "State Economic Regulation and Substantive Due Process of Law," *Northwestern University Law Review* 53 (1958): 13.

31. See Charles R. Adrian, "Trends in State Constitutions," *Harvard Journal on Legislation* 5 (1968): 311; W. Brooke Graves, "State Constitutional Law: A Twenty-five Year Summary," *William and Mary Law Review* 8 (1966): 1.

32. Henry J. Abraham, *Freedom and the Court* (New York: Oxford University Press, 1982), chaps. 3, 4.

33. Nevertheless, as early as 1951, a commentator complained that state decisions were too frequently ignored when civil liberties issues arose. Monrad G. Paulsen, "State Constitutions, State Courts and First Amendment Freedoms," *Vanderbilt Law Review* 4 (1951): 620.

34. An excellent study, one that reflects the spirit of the period from the perspective of the Justice Department, is Victor S. Navasky, *Kennedy Justice* (New York: Atheneum, 1971).

35. The Supreme Court of California had acted innovatively even during the Warren years. See, e.g., Perez v. Lippold, 198 P.2d 17 (Cal. 1948), holding an antimiscegenation statute unconstitutional.

36. The New Jersey Supreme Court moved to compel legislative redistricting prior to Baker v. Carr, 369 U.S. 186 (1962). See Asbury Park Press, Inc. v. Woolley, 161 A.2d 705 (N.J. 1960).

37. Stanley H. Friedelbaum, "A New Bill of Rights: Novel Dimensions of Liberty and Property," in Stephen L. Wasby, ed., *Civil Liberties* (Lexington, Mass.: D. C. Heath, 1976), chap. 9.

38. An evaluation by a member of the Court is contained in William J. Brennan, Jr., "Guardians of Our Liberties—State Courts No Less Than Federal," in Mark W. Cannon and David M. O'Brien, eds., *Views from the Bench* (Chatham, N.J.: Chatham House Publishers, 1985), chap. 21.

39. An excellent series of survey articles and books, in addition to individual, specialized studies, has appeared in recent years. See, e.g., "Project Report: Toward an Activist Role for State Bills of Rights," *Harvard Civil Rights–Civil Liberties Law Review* 8 (1973: 271; A. E. Dick Howard, "State Courts and Constitutional Rights in the Day of the Burger Court," *Virginia Law Review* 62 (1976): 873; "Developments in the Law—The Interpretation of State Constitutional Rights," *Harvard Law Review* 95 (1982): 1324; Mary Cornelia Porter and G. Alan Tarr, eds., *State Supreme Courts: Policymaking in the Federal System* (Westport, Conn.: Greenwood Press, 1982).

Human Rights in the States

Judicial Federalism: The Interplay of National-State Standards

STANLEY H. FRIEDELBAUM

The traditional dualism associated with American federalism has come to serve as an effective instrument for litigants and state judges alike. A range of policy alternatives, more often than not linked to presumed outcomes, has figured prominently in the selection of courts and adjudicatory techniques. Yet such discretion in the decisionmaking process is of recent origin. For much of our history, the opportunities for flexibility were less numerous. Case law, deriving from a bifurcated judicial system, developed along parallel but notably separate lines. In fact, the potential for choice that inheres in judicial federalism remained no more than a remote possibility, if not a fanciful vision, until the early 1970s.

During the Warren years, there was a tendency to resort to a federal court whenever the option was available. The notion that state courts could be relied on to safeguard federal interests was not taken seriously. Even less credibility was accorded actions initiated solely on the basis of guarantees found in the state constitutions. It was widely assumed that counterpart state provisions were less effective, by reason of failings in the state judiciaries, than were relevant sections of the national Bill of Rights. In the circumstances, the selection of a federal district court as the tribunal of choice proved to be a perfunctory exercise for most advocates and their clients. It mattered little that a number of states had undertaken major constitutional revision efforts following World War II; nor was it looked upon as significant that an impressive array of "new" rights had been fashioned.

The rediscovery of state courts and state constitutions arose out of necessity, not because of a conscious return to a bygone provincialism and surely not as a result of attachments to the traditional values of federalism. The Burger Court emerged as a less dependable source of judicial activism than its predecessor, though it hardly effected the dramatic change of course that many of its critics had predicted. In retrospect, the Court came to be associated with a spirit of moderation, a limited range of innovations, and a less intrusive posture in judicial policymaking. All the same, the Court could no longer be relied on to serve as the nation's agenda setter. Perhaps in response to such altered conditions and attitudes, the justices displayed a new willingness to defer to the state courts. The attention of several of these courts, for whatever reasons, turned increasingly to expansive definitions of privacy, to the extension of the rights of the criminally accused, to the problems of public education and to redressing the effects of exclusionary zoning.

What was being pursued, intentionally or unwittingly, resembles a textbook model of judicial federalism, one that draws selectively on the products of state courts while ensuring that national minimum standards will be observed. An affinity among courts advances the broad objectives of American constitutionalism; at least in theory, it obliges all judges to share responsibility for the system's continued durability and its ability to adapt to the requirements of successive generations. It represents at once a variable force for progress and stability in a pluralistic society.

Whether such exalted goals have been achieved is problematic. That sharp intercourt differences occasionally arise, that outcomes may be acutely and grievously dissimilar from state to state and from nation to state, and that judicial performance is not always consistent or even principled need not detract from a noteworthy catalog of accomplishments. As the case studies in this chapter demonstrate, both the nation and the states serve as fruitful laboratories. To what extent the interplay of standards has strengthened specific liberties remains an open question, one that must be considered and reevaluated periodically. But it is undeniable that a number of courts encourage a variety of solutions, affording opportunities not available in a unitary judicial system.

Private Property, Expressional Freedom, and State Action

When, in the early 1970s, the Supreme Court sanctioned the right of a privately owned shopping center to prohibit the distribution of handbills,[1] several state courts moved to protect free speech guarantees. Judicial intervention occurred in response to the changing nature of commercial as well as community activities. Shopping malls, often located adjacent to major highways, had largely replaced downtown business districts previously used by demonstrators and others who sought to influence public opinion. In the 1940s, the Court had compared a company town to a municipality, sustaining expressive activities on its streets under the First Amendment.[2] Such a functional equivalency test was applied to a shopping center two decades later when the Court protected the right to picket in a labor-management dispute.[3] However, the subsequent imposition of limitations,[4] followed by the outright rejection of the test's underlying rationale,[5] encouraged a number of state courts to create their own remedies.

The Supreme Court of California assumed a characteristic position of leadership in safeguarding rights of speech and petition. In *Robins v. PruneYard Shopping Center*,[6] the court relied on provisions of the state constitution that it took to be of more extensive scope than federal analogues. By doing so, it overruled a previous state decision that had resulted in contrary findings.[7] The center's owners appealed to the federal Supreme Court, asserting a right to exclude premised on the Fifth Amendment's ban on a taking of property without just compensation and the Fourteenth Amendment's proscription of a deprivation of property without due process of law.

Justice William Rehnquist, who wrote for the Court in *PruneYard*, denied that the taking clause had been violated; nor did he find merit in the claimed assault on property interests. Instead, he affirmed the state court's authority to extend protection to state constitutional rights of expression and petition.[8] That the Supreme Court, by its ruling, had substantially added to the stature of judicial federalism is incontestable. There were explicit references to the exercise of the state's police power and its sovereign right to preserve the liberties of its citizens. In the majority's view, the federal property claims advanced did not rise to the level of infringements sufficient to outweigh state-created rights.

Notably wanting in the state court's exposition had been consideration of the state action concept, often regarded as a significant threshold factor for jurisdictional purposes. In the absence of governmental action, the question recurs, are courts free to intervene in private disputes? Are they privileged to act as if they hold roving commissions to preserve individual rights against invasion by nonstate actors? At the federal level, a state action requirement has long been exacted, and the standards applied often have served as measures of judicial activism or restraint.[9] By comparison, several state courts have adopted relaxed criteria, permitting intervention on state constitutional grounds where federal inquiries would be precluded. Whether such a judgment reflects the state text or serves merely as a pretext for judicial activism is not always apparent.[10]

The Supreme Court of Washington, in a plurality opinion, dismissed the state action requirement in applying state constitutional guarantees to a group collecting initiative signatures at a shopping center.[11] To justify the imposition of restrictions on private property, the court invoked the police power in defense of expressive freedom. An explicit demonstration of state action was said to be unnecessary in view of the permissive nature of state procedures as distinguished from federal guidelines. More recently, New York's highest court disassociated itself from this effort with strong denunciations of what it looked upon as constitutional license.[12] Regardless of the nature of the issues, the precedents suggest, the results sought to be achieved will weigh heavily, and perhaps conclusively, in resolving state action questions.

If doubt ever existed concerning the applicability of the First Amendment to restrictions on expressive activities in "special-purpose" public places, it was removed when the federal Supreme Court, in *Widmar v. Vincent*,[13] rejected a state university's attempt to prevent the use of its facilities for religious worship or teaching. Justice Lewis Powell, who wrote for the Court, explored the application of free speech principles, noting that the Constitution forbids a state to enforce exclusions from a "forum generally open to the public, even if it was not required to create the forum in the first place."[14] In this instance, it was clear, the content-based discrimination against religious speech was explicitly attributable to state action. The Court disavowed any intention to question the university's right to make academic judgments or to provide for the allocation of its resources.

Conceivably a private educational institution may be treated differently though it possesses many of the same characteristics as its state counterpart. Whether, apart from the First Amendment, state constitutional safeguards obtain as, in some cases, they do in regard to private shopping centers is debatable. Access to campus facilities or grounds has never been held to be equal for students and nonstudents alike.[15] But the point at which the line is to be drawn is not always easy to determine when a campus is open to the public and is constantly exposed to outside influences.

Prior to the federal Supreme Court's ruling in *Widmar*, such issues were considered in a case that arose in the New Jersey courts. A trivial incident, the unauthorized distribution of political handbills on the campus of Princeton University, touched off a series of events and led to subsequent appeals that ultimately reached the U.S. Supreme Court. The canvasser's conviction of criminal trespass caused him to challenge the constitutionality of the exclusionary regulations and, collaterally, to question the controversial shopping center cases that in part had presented doctrinal parallels. Initially, the threshold issue of state action had to be resolved. Beyond this barrier lay familiar questions relating to the design of judicial federalism, the reach of the First Amendment, the meaning of the taking clause of the Fifth Amendment, and the scope of protection against state deprivations of property under the Fourteenth Amendment.

In *State v. Schmid*,[16] the New Jersey Supreme Court resorted to the speech and assembly provisions of the state constitution following an ineffectual examination of federal precedents. In large measure, this was facilitated by the national Supreme Court's indulgent view of the role of state courts in *PruneYard*.[17] It was clear that Justice Rehnquist had virtually invited state judges to identify individual rights of expression and petition that exceeded federally recognized standards when measured against private property interests. For New Jersey's highest court to move assertively in this area occasioned few surprises in view of the court's past ventures. In *State v. Shack*,[18] decided a decade earlier, the court had determined not to pursue a constitutional route because, in the wording of the prevailing opinion, a holding cast in "nonconstitutional terms" more adequately served the libertarian interests of the litigant. What distinguished *Schmid* was a return to constitutional principles. Whether the New Jersey court would be able to fashion a cohesive opinion within this more confining framework, still marked by a generous interspersing of federal precedents, remained uncertain.

Justice Alan Handler, who prepared the prevailing opinion, initially examined traditional tests of state action in the light of Schmid's First Amendment challenge. Despite an impressive array of indicators that demonstrated the university's continuing relationship with the state, he concluded, the degree of public involvement did not establish a sufficiently close nexus. Nor did a resort to the trespass laws create a defensible state identity. Although a persuasive "congeries of facts" had been marshaled, the court found that Princeton remained essentially autonomous and private; therefore, restraint was required in any resolution of competing First Amendment values. This course was particularly advisable, the majority pointed out, since the case presented "strong crosscurrents of policy that [had to]...be navigated with extreme care."[19]

Setting aside the issue of federal constitutional rights, Justice Handler moved to examine Schmid's claims founded on the state bill of rights and privileges. Did the lack of restrictions arising out of considerations of federalism and a consequent easing of state action requirements facilitate more permissive scrutiny of the conduct of private parties? Were the complementary state guarantees of free speech and assembly available to prevent "unreasonably restrictive or oppressive conduct on the part of private entities that have otherwise assumed a constitutional obligation not to abridge the individual exercise of such freedoms because of the public use of their property"?[20] There were, the court noted, societal obligations associated with public enjoyment of private property. A balance had to be struck between expressional and property interests premised on a scale measuring the extent of public use. Recognizing that Princeton University has provided an open campus while deferring to its institutional integrity and independence, Justice Handler determined that Schmid's state constitutional rights had been violated because of the absence of a "reasonable" regulatory scheme governing protected speech and association.[21]

Despite the New Jersey Supreme Court's ruling on state constitutional grounds, Princeton University took an appeal to the federal Supreme Court, alleging a deprivation of its rights under the First, Fifth, and Fourteenth amendments. The university claimed an invasion of its academic freedom and of its autonomy to control expressive activities by outsiders. The state joined in seeking review, but it declined to present an opinion on the merits of the arguments advanced. Because of this inadequate record, the Supreme Court dismissed for want of jurisdiction. Had the Court concluded on this cryptic note, a routine basis for non-intervention could readily have been sustained. Instead the justices went on to attach an unsigned statement. The state's reluctance to take a position on the merits was said to have resulted in the absence of a case or controversy in a proceeding that raised "difficult constitutional issues." Furthermore, the Court found mootness in the effort to have it review a regulatory scheme governing solicitations that the university itself had seen fit to replace, if not to repudiate, while the case was pending on appeal. Nor was there federal standing, the justices avowed, with respect to a judgment that did not preclude the university from a ruling on the validity of its new regulations in a subsequent action.[22]

Even in the absence of a critical inquiry into the reasons that the Court assigned, questions remain. Why was it necessary for an opinion to be submitted? Would not the obscure statements of the past have sufficed? And if a rationale had to be supplied, did it need to range so conspicuously into complex jurisdictional issues? During the past decade, similar appeals of cases decided on independent state grounds have been disposed of perfunctorily.

Sunday Closing Revisited

If the effort to delineate the boundaries of expressional freedom proved difficult for a state court, cases associated with antiquated Sabbath or blue laws promised to raise equally vexatious questions. The federal Supreme Court's Sunday closing law decisions of 1961[23] had rejected establishment and free exercise challenges tied to a lengthy record of acrimonious debate. A divided Court upheld the state's police power to ensure a uniform day of rest and relaxation. Ancillary problems of equal protection were shunted aside with brief allusions to the sufficiency of legislative classifications that, in the majority's view, met a reasonableness test and revealed no invidious discrimination. During the two decades that followed, the state courts dealt more rigorously with statutory dis-

tinctions but not with the divisive issues of religious liberty that, whether referred to directly or impliedly, could hardly be ignored.

Two cases, one arising in the New Jersey courts and the other in Pennsylvania, offered insights into adjudicatory techniques that served in the achievement of predetermined goals. To the chagrin of the dissenters in the New Jersey case, an otherwise activist majority adhered to traditional lines of inquiry, citing federal precedents as the bases for sustaining restrictions on Sunday sales long since abandoned elsewhere. By contrast, the Pennsylvania court treated the issues by way of state predicates. The results were no more satisfying, though at least the public policy objective of setting aside the laws had been achieved. A critical examination of the opinions reveals much concerning judicial motives and the use of result orientation in giving effect to them.

The revival of enforceable Sunday closing laws in the 1950s occurred largely in response to the widespread establishment of highway shopping centers intent upon unrestricted sales of goods traditionally confined to weekdays. Such aggressive merchandising, contrary to time-honored observations of Sunday as a day of rest or of religious devotion, adversely affected city merchants accustomed to a more leisurely pace. Indeed it was the deteriorating economic status of the urban merchants that proved to be decisive in reawakening interest in Sabbath laws long thought to be archaic. Defunct issues were raised, linked less to religious interests than to the survival of sales practices of a bygone era.

In *Vornado, Inc. v. Hyland*,[24] the New Jersey Supreme Court set aside objections premised on a denial of equal protection guarantees, the sole issue reserved for review two decades earlier.[25] The court elected to follow federal guidelines in dismissing charges of an arbitrary categorization of articles that could and could not be sold on Sunday. There were references to such anomalies as the permitted sale of sneakers but not of shoes, to the issue of selective enforcement, and to the uneven effects of county-by-county referenda resulting in unlimited retail selling in half the state. To these complaints, the majority responded, as had the U.S. Supreme Court in 1961, that the validity of Sunday closing statutes, admittedly beset by numerous and varied exemptions, was sustainable on social and economic grounds; that deference had to be accorded legislation intended to ensure a day of rest and relaxation despite the inconvenience claimed by would-be Sunday shoppers; and that no more than a minimum rationality test need be applied.

The dissenters in *Vornado* berated the court for being "at odds with the realities of the commercial and consumer worlds" and for ignoring the primacy of individual autonomy. One of the opinions attacked the majority for having failed to strike an appropriate balance between the regulatory power of the state and personal free choice, for vague proscriptions of conduct, for uneven administration, and for a rational basis test that lacked an exacting standard of review.[26] Another dissent included persistent references to the equal protection clause of the state constitution as an independent source not limited to the meanings associated with counterpart federal provisions. If, as here, the nature of the restraint was not matched by an adequate governmental goal, the court was admonished, indulgent national standards ought not to be followed in weighing legislation that is "distinctly a matter of unique and special local concern."[27]

In a tribunal long associated with judicial activism and concern for social causes, *Vornado* pointed to result orientation as pervasive as that found in agenda-setting cases. An ostensible deference to federal standards and to legislative prerogatives did little to disguise the court's effort to avoid an open clash with the political branches. Why a court that had shown little hesitation in confronting the issue of congressional districting prior to *Baker v. Carr*[28] and in launching an unprecedented campaign to eliminate exclusionary zoning[29] chose to avoid controversy over Sunday closing remains uncertain. Perhaps the question was not sufficiently compelling to warrant a major thrust; or the incursions upon personal autonomy were viewed as minimal in view of the availability of open counties; or the relative ease of a resort to referendum procedures seemed to require less by way of judicial intervention. For whatever reasons, the selection of federal precedents served the purpose that a majority sought to achieve: a policy of restraint in approaching problems that ultimately could be expected to disappear as unrequited relics alien to the dynamics of contemporary business.

By contrast, the Supreme Court of Pennsylvania, in *Kroger Co. v. O'Hara Township*,[30] premised a contrary holding on the state constitution's equal protection clause subsumed, within the context of this case, under the guise of a provision forbidding special laws regulating trade. A majority pointed to the current law's unacceptable hodgepodge of exceptions. As the court viewed it, the scheme bore no fair and substantial relationship to the purported aim of affording citizens a uniform day of rest and recreation, an objective that was not questioned. The act's failings could be remedied, the court noted, but any changes had to be compatible with constitutional mandates.[31]

One of the dissenters in *Kroger* took exception to the majority's characterization of the blue laws as arbitrary and confusing. A critique of the prevailing opinion made much of the federal Supreme Court's support for Sunday closing laws and of the need to adhere to the criteria applied. To hold otherwise, a minority declared, had the effect of converting the court into a superlegislature assessing the wisdom of legislation. The negative outcome announced had come to pass, it was charged, because the state court had resorted to a heightened standard of scrutiny at variance with the rational basis criteria that traditionally sustained deferential review.[32]

In retrospect, equal protection claims, debated at length in the New Jersey and Pennsylvania courts, furnished no more than a specious basis for the different results reached. If common ground existed, it lay in a firm resolve to avoid any decision linked to the religion clauses of the federal or state constitutions. Yet it was difficult for either of the majority blocs to pass over central issues relating to the distinctive character and meaning of Sunday in meeting a "rest and relaxation" objective. The Pennsylvania court assiduously refrained from any reliance on an equal protection test other than one calling upon the state to demonstrate a "fair and substantial" relation to the object of the legislation. It was untenable to require more unless, as one of the dissenting opinions noted, an interest akin to a suspect classification or a fundamental right had been identified.

To the contrary, the majority in the New Jersey court proceeded in full awareness of the need to defer to the legislature and in the absence of any willingness to reexamine the merits of Sunday closing. Yet the simplistic nature of the prevailing opinion failed to take into account economic realities, if not changing public attitudes and standards of morality. Almost two decades had passed since the federal Supreme Court's redundant essay in "family togetherness" had been foisted upon a nation even then skeptical of such a feeble justification for the exercise of the state's police power. To assume that so tenuous a rationale would be acceptable a generation later, in the light of intervening events, suggested naiveté or an indifference to social change. The future of closing restrictions, if one existed, lay in narrow classifications of proscribed sales and permissiveness in the designation of a day or days of rest designed to meet compelling free exercise claims. Despite repeated judicial disclaimers, such charges of narrow sectarianism had not disappeared, no matter how adroit the reasoning to divest Sunday of its religious significance.

The New Jersey court dissenters' introduction of personal autonomy as an issue imparted an air of modernity to the Sunday closing debate. If, as still seems doubtful, establishment and free exercise questions can be successfully shunted aside, the right of the individual to shop if and when he or she chooses to do so may be utilized as a convincing alternative. To whatever degree, an emphasis on a new-found libertarianism should suffice to trigger a heightened level of scrutiny, surely one adequate to sustain a holding of invalidity. Since, however, the votes of no more than two justices out of a seven-member court could be mustered in support of this position, the divisive question of Sunday closing in New Jersey was left to the electorate, which in county-by-county referenda abolished Sunday sales restrictions in all but two counties. What the state's highest court had refused to concede, opting instead for a leaden reworking of federal precedents, the people accomplished by a persistent, well-organized resort to the democratic process assisted in no small measure by the powerful commercial interests involved. If the dissenters had sought vindication, the ultimate victory was theirs, but hardly by the traditional means with which they had long been conversant.

Reverse or Benign Discrimination

Plainly among the most controversial remedies pursued in the quest for racial equality, preferential programs have been some of the last accommodative tools to be explored by American appellate courts. The constitutional dilemma posed when such schemes are challenged is formidable and, at times, conflicting values and well-nigh insoluble problems emerge within the time-honored framework of judicial decisionmaking. Does the guarantee of equality before the law, so often cited as part of a proud heritage, permit a reversal of form because of the egregious treatment of minorities over much of the nation's history? Is there sufficient ambiguity in the phrasing of the Fourteenth Amendment's equal protection clause or counterpart state provisions to warrant any measure of discrimination, albeit well intentioned? May the present generation be held accountable for the discriminatory acts of their forebears, and, if so, to what extent may those living today be expected to make the necessary sacrifices? Does preferential treatment, viewed in terms of its possible effects, serve to advance the cause of minority rights, or is it merely another way of drawing distinctions, admittedly more subtle but no less invidious? These questions suggest a profile of the great national debate that has raged during the past decade. The leading cases expand on these themes, introduce others, and raise important issues of public policy throughout.

As the central focus of a vast array of interest groups, the now-famous *Bakke* case[33] has few, if any, equals. The federal Supreme Court had had an earlier opportunity to pass upon the principle of reverse discrimination in *DeFunis v. Odegaard*,[34] but a majority of five elected to postpone a substantive decision on grounds of mootness. It was in *Bakke* that the Court finally agreed to confront the issue on the merits, though the doubtfulness of the results was painfully apparent. In this case of first impression, the justices were so divided that no majority opinion was submitted. Justice Powell, who announced the judgment of the Court, went no further than to affirm the order to admit Bakke to the Medical School of the University of California at Davis and to invalidate the special admissions program in question under the Fourteenth Amendment but to reverse the holding that race might never be taken into account in subsequent admissions decisions.

How, then, did *Bakke* ever reach the U.S. Supreme Court, and why did the Court agree to plenary review in the light of the fractious responses that the several opinions disclosed? As the opinions in the Supreme Court of California reveal, the stratagem to ensure a final disposition by the nation's highest court seems to have been purposeful. The California court's decision to premise its holding of invalidity of Bakke's exclusion on the Fourteenth Amendment was unusual in a tribunal known not only for its activism but also for its widespread reliance on independent state grounds. Clearly the U.S. Supreme Court, in a political sense, could have exercised little discretion in the granting of review in a case that had become a cause célèbre.

Equally intriguing is *De Ronde v. Regents of the University of California*,[35] where, in the aftermath of *Bakke*'s several phases, the Supreme Court of California went on to sustain a preferential program despite its decisive rejection just five years earlier. Had the federal Supreme Court's equivocal opinions been so pervasive as to effect a major doctrinal turnabout? Had the shaky precedents established succeeded in rendering a majority averse to any meaningful resort to the state's equal protection clause? Altered public policy objectives, implemented by a continuing emphasis on result orientation, once again figured prominently in the resolution of these and kindred questions.

Justice Stanley Mosk, who wrote for a near-unanimous court in *Bakke*, had resorted to the Fourteenth Amendment's equal protection clause as the basis for unaccustomed results. In an opinion closely linked to traditional attitudes, he denounced the revival of racial percentages as harmful rather than benevolent—"a dangerous concept fraught with potential for misuse." A quota is no less offensive, Mosk declared, "when it serves to exclude a racial majority."[36] Preferential admission policies thus were held to be unconstitutional on majoritarian grounds, clearly a departure from the California court's usual solicitude for minority concerns. Despite this unorthodox approach to an issue that had long been divisive, only one member of the court dissented.

Just three years following the federal Supreme Court's ambivalent performance in *Bakke*, the Supreme Court of California sustained a race-conscious admissions program strikingly similar to that which it had previously set aside. There were indications in *De Ronde* that the state court had "reached out" to decide the case. The doctrine of mootness could readily have been invoked to avoid a ruling on the merits. The plaintiff, a white male, had been graduated from a law school other than the state institution to which he had sought entry and in fact had been admitted to the bar. Yet the court chose not to dismiss the case while conceding that the questions raised were of no concern to the initiating party. The issues were said to be of "continuing statewide interest" and therefore appropriate for resolution as a matter of public policy.[37]

The majority made much of the U.S. Supreme Court's several opinions in *Bakke*. As Justice Frank Richardson viewed it, the decision, though predicated on differing rationales, provided "clear guidance" and "for practical and policy reasons" ought not to be disregarded.[38] Adherence to uniform standards was held to be desirable in the area of educational opportunity, and to this end the court premised its holding on the Fourteenth Amendment's equal protection clause. By contrast, De Ronde's arguments, tied to the California Supreme Court's reasoning in *Bakke*, were rejected cavalierly. His pleas, relying on equal protection guarantees of the state constitution, were dismissed with the bland observation that no greater protection is provided than that contained in the federal charter. Notably missing was the fervor for a ruling on independent state grounds that had become characteristic of the California court in extending the reach and content of personal rights beyond those specified in the Constitution. Once again, the results sought to be achieved dominated the decisionmaking process.

Alone in dissent, Justice Mosk urged that the admissions scheme in *De Ronde* be declared unconstitutional for its failure to meet a strict scrutiny test required by the state constitution's equal protection clause. He went on to denounce the majority's "radical departure" from accepted state norms. The new role, Mosk asserted, represented a return to the "medieval notion of government by status."[39] He branded such a basis for the distribution of benefits a form of racism—discrimination premised upon a "misguided social homeopathy."[40] Yet the strength of his polemic evidently had little effect in persuading the majority to alter course.

Personal Autonomy and Sexual Preference: Redefining Legislative Prescriptions of Morality

If pivotal shifts of premises had served, though not always convincingly, to facilitate a dramatic change of direction from *Bakke* to *De Ronde*, a contemporaneous ruling by New York's highest court revealed a similar inclination to resort to the varied techniques of result orientation. The case of *People v. Onofre*[41] raised disturbing issues of privacy centered about acts of deviate sexual behavior customarily subject to the penalties of the criminal law. For a state court to defy conventional morality by finding an antisodomy statute invalid is unusual under any circumstances. Even more exceptional in this instance was the majority's reliance on federal precedents during an era when new and bold initiatives had failed to emerge from the Burger Court. Within the framework of judicial federalism, a choice of state constitutional provisions could have been expected when a majority sought to achieve innovative results. Such an alternative apparently was rejected, and, in this light, the court's pithy performance in construing expansively meager federal precedents proved all the more surprising.

What prompted one of the nation's most respected common law courts to delve so boldly into an area of law often avoided by tribunals better known for their activism? Had the Supreme Court's return to substantive due process, albeit relied upon in a limited and selected number of cases, encouraged such an approach to controversial issues? There are intimations in the prevailing opinion that federal standards need not be restricted to the precise holdings of the Court; that the construction of the national Constitution by state courts may serve to elaborate upon what previously have been established precedents; and that a resort to state constitutions is not the only or even the preferable way of achieving innovative results. Perhaps, it may have been inferred, a continuing development of national standards of personal autonomy, painstaking and slow moving though the process is, offers prospects for the most durable end products of a creative judicial federalism.

Nevertheless, the revival of substantive due process remains one of the most volatile and unreliable bases on which to premise libertarian advances. The subjectivity traditionally associated with judicial value choices is enhanced where, as here, constitutional moorings are few and disconcertingly vague. If the contemporary Supreme Court has created segments of a new bill of rights by judicial fiat, it has also drawn lines restricting additions, if any, to definitions of "normal" heterosexual relations. Clearly what New York's Court of Appeals attempted in *Onofre* falls outside the federal Court's announced guidelines. It was not likely that the state court's teachings would be persuasive and that, if the challenges were pressed, that they would survive searching federal review.

Judge Hugh Jones, writing for the court in *Onofre*, made reference to a "penumbral" right of privacy announced in *Griswold v. Connecticut*,[42] a 1965 case that contributed to the creation of a "zone of privacy." The zone subsequently was expanded to encompass a cluster of rights protective of family life, matrimony, and procreation. More troublesome was the decision at hand, involving acts of "individual gratification" that bore little or no relation to practices traditionally held immune from state intervention. It mattered little that the majority sought to limit its holding to the narrow question of whether the federal Constitution permits a recourse to the criminal law to prohibit consensual sodomy. Nor was it doctrinally significant that the right claimed was described as one of "independence," not to be impeded by governmental restraint. Less trivial, though clearly not critical, were the majority's caveats against commercialization, the need to ensure the noninvolvement of minors, and a cordoning process to guard against any intrusion upon public sensibilities.[43] In view of the Supreme Court's recent pronouncements in *Bowers v. Hardwick*,[44] it would no longer be tenable for the New York court to allude, as it did in *Onofre*, to a growing federal right of privacy with its outer limits still undefined.

An enigma remains concerning the choice of adjudicatory techniques despite the New York court's efforts to explain away its decision by way of *Griswold* and its progeny. It was questionable, then and now, for the court to have resurrected federal substantive due process as a barrier in defense of personal autonomy. Adequate state constitutional analogues could have served if, in fact, the conduct in question was considered deserving of judicial protection. Even if it is assumed that the marital relationship does not provide the ultimate criterion of sexual freedom for adults, a renewed resort to courts as superlegislatures is a radical step, reviving the specter of the *Lochner* doctrine[45] and the controversies to which it had given rise. It is doubtful that the need for rejection of the state's antisodomy statute could be demonstrated to be so compelling as to justify establishment of a newly crafted, federally based precedent. To be sure, the decision was only in the state courts of New York, but it was capable of adoption elsewhere within the current contours of horizontal judicial federalism.

The Abortion Imbroglio

During the past decade, Congress has approved a series of measures curtailing federal contributions to state programs funding abortions for the indigent. Such actions have encouraged state legislatures to revise downward state counterpart benefits, thus reflecting a newly established national model. Any hope that the federal Supreme Court could be relied upon to protect the interests of the needy was shattered when, in *Harris v. McRae*,[46] a majority made clear that, while a woman's right to an abortion was preserved, assurances of financial support lay beyond the ken of the Constitution. If substantive due process had given rise to a new-found right, it had not progressed to the point of prescribing the only means by which, in many instances, the right could be realized.

How, then, might public funding of abortions be required and made binding upon a state legislature? Plainly, a resort to the national Constitution, as in *Onofre*, would have proved to be a futile exercise in reexamining the Supreme Court's views. The only channel for judicial restoration appeared to lie with the states. Though *Harris* might have been disappointing as a doctrinal support, the permissive language of the majority opinion did not preclude such a choice.

It remained for the Supreme Judicial Court of Massachusetts, among others, to establish the necessary framework. In reviewing the constitutional predicates available, the justices centered their attention about such familiar safeguards as due process, equal protection, and the state equal rights amendment. It was an artful treatment of due process that emerged as decisive in achieving the court's much-sought objective of redressing the balance.

In *Moe v. Secretary of Administration*,[47] the Massachusetts court considered state laws that barred the payment of Medicaid funds for abortions not required to prevent the death of the mother. Pseudonymous plaintiffs, representing the class of Medicaid-eligible pregnant women, had challenged the restrictions by means of the Massachusetts Declaration of Rights. Justice Francis Quirico, who wrote for a majority, initially disposed of jurisdictional issues and threshold considerations claimed to have precluded judicial intervention.[48] Then, moving to the merits, he premised a holding of unconstitutionality on a state version of due process to which he extended a substantially broader scope and reach than federal counterpart provisions had been given in *Harris*.

The state's highest court condemned the imposition of a discriminatory burden upon the exercise of a fundamental right. Justice Quirico acknowledged that the legislature need not subsidize the costs of childbearing or of health care generally. Once the state elected to do so, however, he asserted, it was no longer at liberty to weigh the options in the allocation of public funds. Instead it was obliged to follow a course of "genuine indifference" rather than one of selectivity in the granting of benefits. A resort to interest balancing, the court noted, yielded the same result. The state's interest in the preservation of life was outweighed by the magnitude of the individual right involved.[49]

Chief Justice Edward Hennessey, dissenting, rejected this mode of analysis. A financial inducement to encourage full-term childbirth, he averred, could not be equated with the removal of impediments to a woman's choice of an abortion. The finding of invalidity was inappropriate when, in reality, the argument should have been addressed to the legislature in its policymaking role. The chief justice did not deny the court's freedom to apply a more rigorous standard of due process than that derived from its federal analogue. But he was not persuaded that his colleagues should elect to do so in this case where judicial intrusiveness was palpably improper.[50]

When, in *Committee to Defend Reproductive Rights v. Myers*,[51] comparable issues arose, the Supreme Court of California set aside a selective withdrawal of benefits limited to indigent pregnant women. Justice Matthew Tobriner cited guarantees that protected women's rights in the circumstances—rights that, he claimed, could not be impaired through a discriminatory public funding scheme. In particular, he made reference to a constitutionally sanctioned right of privacy and to a judicially invented right of procreative choice. While the state charter remained the principal, if not the sole, source of such provisions, critical guidelines more closely associated with the 1950s and 1960s were revived to strike down the legislature's exclusion of funds for elective abortions. By pursuing this course, the court departed strikingly (and more directly) from the federal Supreme Court's reasoning than had the Massachusetts supreme court.

Justice Tobriner selected as the fulcrum of decisionmaking the doctrine of unconstitutional conditions. The notion of conditioned spending had found its most persistent applications during the McCarthy era when access to public employment, housing, welfare, and unemployment benefits was often made contingent on avowals of loyalty and of nonassociation with subversive organizations.[52] To thwart such practices, the doctrine of unconstitutional conditions, essentially an offshoot of non-economic due process, was invoked to prohibit any restriction of benefits linked to a would-be recipient's waiver of a constitutional right or to the exercise of the right in a manner favored by government. It was in this context that the California Supreme Court set aside what it took to be the conditioning of benefits upon a sacrifice by poor women of their right to an abortion. Should the court sanction such coercion, Tobriner declared, the Bill of Rights might "eventually become a yellowing scrap of paper."[53]

Justice Richardson's dissent centered about familiar charges of judicial usurpation of legislative prerogatives. He denied that the privacy amendment, approved by the voters in 1972, went further than to restrict the distribution of record information and data; it was intended primarily to shield the private affairs of individuals from undue state intrusion. An extension of the clause to sustain the funding of abortions, Richardson asserted, represented a "speculative jump in reasoning... of Olympian proportions."[54] Recognition of a woman's constitutional right to abort did not oblige the legislature to provide public monies to ensure its full and unrestricted effectuation. Taking issue with the majority's recounting of discriminatory treatment, Justice Richardson characterized the prevailing opinion as "semantic legerdemain."[55]

If the California court had expanded procreative choice with unusual breadth, the New Jersey Supreme Court embraced a less extravagant posture but one that ranged well beyond the legislature's funding of abortions necessary to preserve the woman's life. A majority, though unwilling to affirm a constitutional right to health, nevertheless set aside the statute as excessively narrow—a violation of state equal protection, albeit tied to language that, in its cumulative impact, had been used to protect a right of privacy. Justice Stewart Pollock, who wrote for the court in *Right to Choose v. Byrne*,[56] found that the state could not limit funding solely to what was necessary to secure life. All the same, the state was not required to subsidize elective, nontherapeutic abortions. If the state constitution served as a supplemental source of liberty, it did not impose on government a positive duty to fund all abortions. This midspectrum distinction, Justice Pollock averred, was consistent with the state's responsibility to proceed "in a neutral manner"[57] and conformed to a conventional balancing test.[58]

Two separate opinions exemplify the divergent views expressed in the New Jersey case. Justice Morris Pashman, concurring in part and dissenting in part, took exception to the court's presumption that health need be accorded no more than a "high priority" under the state constitution. To him, no significant distinction could be drawn between a right to health and a right to life. Consequently health took on the attributes of a fundamental individual right, not to be jeopardized unless a compelling state interest required it. Freedom to choose an abortion, according to Justice Pashman, was part of one's "personhood," deserving of the "highest protection."[59] In dissent, Justice Daniel O'Hern conceded, as had all of his colleagues, that a concept of equal protection was implicit in the New Jersey Constitution's avowals of natural and inalienable rights. Yet he firmly rejected charges that a woman's right to abort would be infringed in the absence of an affirmative funding program. To convert the right "to be let alone" in an area of personal choice into a requirement of public subsidization, Justice O'Hern charged, would produce an "unprecedented result."[60]

Conclusion

Implicit in the resurgence of state judicial activism are notions of accommodation and comity in the federal system. In practical terms, advocates often link a choice of forums to projected outcomes, which, in turn, are dependent on precedents previously announced, as well as a particular court's perceptions of public policy. With the end of the Warren years and the opening of an era of diminished intrusiveness on the part of the federal Supreme Court, an identifiable selection of state appellate courts has expanded the scope of state-derived individual rights. It has become almost obligatory for members of the trial bar to include references to state charters, wherever relevant, if client interests are to be served. A widespread nationalization of American law, still reflected in familiar claims of denials of First or Fifth Amendment rights and *Miranda* warnings, has begun to recede as the Supreme Court reassumes its historic role as a guardian of institutional values rather than an instrument in the vanguard of social change.

All the same, it is possible to exaggerate an accommodation that requires no more than an easy shifting of decisional predicates. A resort to state constitutions solely to evade distasteful Supreme Court judgments or to achieve preconceived objectives will not long escape the scrutiny of critics. Ephemeral decisions contribute little to meaningful analysis or argument. If anything, they denigrate state constitutional law and threaten to undermine the constructive developments of the past two decades. The fruits of a principled jurisprudence, not those attributed to an unabashed result orientation, offer the best prospects of producing a lasting, definitive impact on the constitutional mainstream. It is from such products that state constitutions increasingly gain respect and stature as discrete sources of fundamental rights.

Perhaps in response to an excessive and, at times, a confusing intermingling of state and federal predicates, the U.S. Supreme Court has imposed more rigorous standards for decisions premised on independent state grounds. The turning point occurred in a 1983 case, *Michigan v. Long*,[61] where the justices reached a remarkable consensus in establishing new guidelines.[62] Justice Sandra Day O'Connor, writing for the Court, called for a "plain statement" by a state court that a decision is based on an interpretation of its own constitution. Otherwise the Court will assume that it has jurisdiction to review when a state decision is primarily determined by federal law, when it is interwoven with federal law, when national precedents are cited other than for purposes of guidance, or when such precedents are said to "compel" the result reached.[63] That state courts have become increasingly wary of the effects of *Michigan v. Long* is evident in recent decisions preserving results independently derived.[64]

If, in fact, the Supreme Court's insistence on bona-fide state constitutional predicates has served to diminish the ardor of some state judges, there is no suggestion that current trends will be precipitously reversed or even appreciably slowed. State courts may still make reference to federal guidelines and reasoning so long as the opinion includes a disavowal that federal cases determinately influenced the outcome.[65] Alternatively a state court may openly rely on federal precedents while construing them in such a way as to break new ground. New York's highest court elected to pursue the latter course in *People v. Onofre*[66] and, more recently, in a federal equal protection context, it dealt creatively with significant gender-related issues.[67] In either case, the momentum for innovation need not be lost even if, as seems likely, the Supreme Court's decision in *Michigan v. Long* reflects less enthusiasm than previously existed for the experimental activism of a number of state courts. A vibrant judicial federalism requires close attention to the means as well as the ends of decisionmaking. Regardless of the Court's more exacting criteria, any reversion to the national Bill of Rights as a virtually exclusive basis for preserving human freedoms is neither necessary nor desirable. The diversity of sources associated with constitutional federalism is to be preferred in promoting the goals of a pluralistic society and, perhaps more pointedly, in fostering the American experiment in statecraft.

Notes

1. Lloyd Corp. v. Tanner, 407 U.S. 551 (1972).

2. Marsh v. Alabama, 326 U.S. 501 (1946).

3. Amalgamated Food Employees Union v. Logan Valley Plaza, 391 U.S. 308 (1968).

4. Lloyd Corp. v. Tanner, 407 U.S. 551 (1972).

5. Hudgens v. NLRB, 424 U.S. 507 (1976).

6. 592 P.2d 341 (Cal. 1979).

7. Diamond v. Bland, 521 P.2d 460 (Cal. 1974).

8. PruneYard Shopping Center v. Robins, 447 U.S. 74 (1980).

9. Stanley H. Friedelbaum, "Reprise or Denouement: Deference and the New Dissonance in the Burger Court," *Emory Law Journal* 26 (1977): 337, 364–67.

10. With respect to the shopping center and associated cases, see "Developments in the Law—The Interpretation of State Constitutional Rights," *Harvard Law Review* 95 (1982): 1324, 1423–26.

11. Alderwood v. Washington Environmental Council, 635 P.2d 108 (Wash. 1981).

12. Shad Alliance v. Smith Haven Mall, 488 N.E.2d 1211 (N.Y. 1985).

13. Widmar v. Vincent, 454 U.S. 263 (1981). Congress passed an equal access act in response to *Widmar*. P.L. 98–377, 20 U.S.C. secs. 4071 et seq.

14. 454 U.S. at 268.

15. The Court in *Widmar* had affirmed the university's authority to impose "reasonable regulations compatible with [its] mission upon the use of its campus and facilities." Id. at 268, n. 5.

16. State v. Schmid, 423 A.2d 615 (N.J. 1980).

17. PruneYard Shopping Center v. Robins, 447 U.S. 74 (1980).

18. State v. Shack, 277 A.2d 369 (N.J. 1971).

19. State v. Schmid, 423 A.2d 615, 624 (N.J. 1980).

20. Id. at 628.

21. Id. at 633.

22. Princeton University v. Schmid, 455 U.S. 100, 102–3 (1982).

23. McGowan v. Maryland, 366 U.S. 420 (1961); Two Guys from Harrison–Allentown v. McGinley, 366 U.S. 582 (1961); Braunfeld v. Brown, 366 U.S. 599 (1961); Gallagher v. Crown Kosher Super Market, 366 U.S. 617 (1961).

24. Vornado, Inc. v. Hyland, 390 A.2d 606 (N.J. 1978).

25. Two Guys from Harrison, Inc. v. Furman, 160 A.2d 265 (N.J. 1960).

26. Vornado, Inc. v. Hyland, 390 A.2d 606, 615ff. (Justice Morris Pashman, dissenting).

27. 390 A.2d at 620ff. (Justice Alan Handler, dissenting).

28. Baker v. Carr, 369 U.S. 186 (1962). The New Jersey Supreme Court had acted previously in Asbury Park Press, Inc. v. Woolley, 161 A.2d 705 (N.J. 1960).

29. Southern Burlington County NAACP v. Township of Mt. Laurel, 336 A.2d 713 (N.J. 1975) and subsequent cases.

30. Kroger Co. v. O'Hara Township, 392 A.2d 266 (Pa. 1978).

31. Id. at 274–75.

32. Id. at 279–80. See also People v. Abrahams, 353 N.E.2d 574 (N.Y. 1976).

33. Regents of the University of California v. Bakke, 438 U.S. 265 (1978).

34. DeFunis v. Odegaard, 416 U.S. 312 (1974).

35. De Ronde v. Regents of the University of California, 625 P.2d 220 (Cal. 1981).

36. Bakke v. Regents of the University of California, 553 P.2d 1152, 1171 (Cal. 1976).

37. De Ronde v. Regents of the University of California, 625 P.2d 220, 222 (Cal. 1981).

38. Id. at 229.

39. Id. at 238.

40. Id. at 239.

41. People v. Onofre, 415 N.E.2d 936 (N.Y. 1980).

42. Griswold v. Connecticut, 381 U.S. 479 (1965).

43. People v. Onofre, 415 N.E.2d 936, 940–41 (N.Y. 1980).

44. Bowers v. Hardwick, 54 L.W. 4919 (1986).

45. Lochner v. New York, 198 U.S. 45 (1905).

46. Harris v. McRae, 448 U.S. 297 (1980).

47. Moe v. Secretary of Administration, 417 N.E.2d 387 (Mass. 1981).

48. Id. at 395.

49. Id. at 399–404.

50. Id. at 406–8.

51. Committee to Defend Reproductive Rights v. Myers, 625 P.2d 779 (Cal. 1981).

52. See Stanley H. Friedelbaum, *Contemporary Constitutional Law: Case Studies in the Judicial Process* (Boston: Houghton Mifflin, 1972), pp. 144–53.

53. Committee to Defend Reproductive Rights v. Myers, 625 P.2d 779, 798 (Cal. 1981).

54. Id. at 811.

55. Id. at 807.

56. Right to Choose v. Byrne, 450 A.2d 925 (N.J. 1982).

57. Id. at 935.

58. "A woman's right to choose to protect her health by terminating her pregnancy outweighs the State's asserted interest in protecting a potential life at the expense of her health." Id. at 937.

59. Id. at 951.

60. In agreement with Justice O'Hern's position, see Fischer v. Department of Public Welfare, 502 A.2d 114 (Pa. 1985).

61. Michigan v. Long, 463 U.S. 1032.

62. Only Justice Blackmun, concurring, and Justice John Paul Stevens, dissenting, expressed disagreement over what Blackmun termed the Court's "new presumption of jurisdiction over cases coming ... from state courts." Id. at 1054.

63. Id. at 1040–41.

64. See, e.g., State v. Jewett, 500 A.2d 233 (Vt. 1985).

65. State v. Coe, 679 P.2d 353, 361–62 (Wash. 1984).

66. People v. Onofre, 415 N.E.2d 936, cert. den. sub nom. New York v. Onofre, 451 U.S. 987 (1981).

67. People v. Liberta, 474 N.E.2d 567 (N.Y. 1984).

2

State Constitutionalism and "First Amendment" Rights

G. ALAN TARR

It is customary today to think of the U.S. Supreme Court as the primary protector of civil liberties and to seek the parameters of the freedoms of religion, speech, and the press in its rulings on the First Amendment. Certainly the defense of those liberties has afforded the Court some of its finest hours and called forth some of its most eloquent opinions.[1] Yet the identification of these freedoms with the federal Constitution and the U.S. Supreme Court is actually comparatively recent. For over a century after its ratification, the Bill of Rights was viewed as protecting these rights only against federal infringement, and relatively few First Amendment cases came before the Court.[2] Indeed it was not until 1927 that the Court first invalidated governmental action under the First Amendment and not until 1931 that it struck down a state law as violating the freedom of the press.[3] Thus, until the twentieth century, state constitutions and state courts provided the primary protection against infringements on the freedoms of religion, speech, and the press.

With the advent of selective incorporation, the roles of federal and state law—and federal and state courts—changed dramatically.[4] By ruling that the federal Constitution afforded protection against state infringements of the freedoms of religion, speech, and the press, the Supreme Court multiplied its opportunities to address "First Amend-

Research on this chapter was conducted under a fellowship from the National Endowment for the Humanities. Further research support was provided by the Rutgers University Research Council. The author gratefully acknowledges this invaluable support.

ment" issues. At the same time, the preference of litigants for federal forums diverted many claims from state courts, thus curtailing opportunities for the development of a state constitutional jurisprudence. Even when issues arose in state tribunals, attorneys typically ignored state bills of rights or treated the state and federal provisions as interchangeable, relying on the U.S. Supreme Court for doctrine and precedent. Yet even during the era in which federal constitutional law was overwhelmingly predominant—roughly from the 1930s to the mid–1970s—a few state courts continued to rely on their own constitutions to develop independent positions on selected "First Amendment" issues. More recently, with the development of the new judicial federalism, judges in several states have rediscovered their state bills of rights and have used them to forge new protections and to develop their own constitutional doctrines.[5]

This study examines the development of the freedoms of speech, press, and religion under state constitutions. Several fundamental questions provide the focus for this analysis. What are the differences between the state and federal constitutional protections? How have these differences affected state courts' development of constitutional doctrine and their resolution of particular cases? Have the states sought to develop independent constitutional positions, or have they tended to follow the lead of the Supreme Court? What do the findings on state courts' protection of the freedoms of speech, press, and religion indicate about the states' role in protecting human rights?

Religion under State Constitutions

Although federal and state constitutions safeguard religious liberty and enforce some degree of separation between church and state, comparison of the language in the state and federal provisions, as well as in those of the various states, reveals significant differences in both specificity and substance. Insofar as these variations reflect different understandings of the nature and legitimate scope of religious liberty and of the appropriate degree of church-state separation, they suggest that the interpretation of state guarantees may yield different results from those secured under the First Amendment.

The Free Exercise of Religion under State Constitutions

Religious freedom encompasses freedom of belief and freedom of action in accordance with one's beliefs. Government can interfere with freedom of belief by proscribing or prescribing certain beliefs or by penalizing those who profess them.[6] Several of the original states, in their initial constitutions, recognized a "natural and unalienable right to

worship Almighty God according to the dictates of [one's] own conscience," and similarly emphatic language can be found in most subsequent
constitutions.[7] Nevertheless, full freedom of belief was achieved only
gradually. Most of the original states did not eliminate their religious
tests for office, instituted in colonial times, until the nineteenth century,
and some continued to require that officeholders profess a belief in God
as late as the twentieth century.[8] Indeed, in 1959 the Maryland Court
of Appeals upheld the denial of public office to an atheist, a ruling the
U.S. Supreme Court reversed a year later.[9] Similarly, until the mid–
nineteenth century, all states followed the common law rule requiring
a belief in God and in a future state of rewards and punishments as a
qualification for witnesses.[10] Although some anomalous provisions remain in state constitutions, many states during the nineteenth century
adopted constitutional provisions that eliminated these religious tests.[11]
Thus, a developing appreciation in the states of the requirements of
religious liberty has led to strong constitutional safeguards for freedom
of belief.

Whereas the freedom to believe may be absolute, the freedom to act
in accordance with one's religious beliefs cannot be. Controversy may
arise when a state, in meeting its constitutional responsibility to protect
the health, safety, welfare, and morals of its citizens, adopts regulations
that impinge on believers' freedom of action. Neither the First Amendment nor those state provisions, which were modeled on it, provide
explicit guidance on how to reconcile the claims of free exercise with
the state's legitimate exercise of its police power. But some state constitutions do deal with the problem directly. Several, for example, specifically take account of religious scruples involving military service,
exempting conscientious objectors from service in the state militia.[12]
More generally, twenty state constitutions have attempted to resolve
potential conflicts by expressly including a police power qualification on
the free exercise of religion. Typical is the Connecticut Constitution,
which, after mandating that "the exercise and enjoyment of religious
profession and worship . . . shall forever be free," provides that this right
"shall not be so construed as to excuse acts of licentiousness, or to justify
practices inconsistent with the peace and safety of the state."[13] Relying
on such constitutional language, which seems to afford less protection
for religiously motivated conduct than is now available under the federal
Constitution, state courts have generally sustained state laws challenged
as violative of religious liberty.[14]

In upholding the laws, state courts during the late nineteenth century
developed what has become known as the secular regulation rule. *Commonwealth v. Plaisted*, in which the Massachusetts Supreme Judicial Court
sustained the conviction of a member of the Salvation Army who had
violated a law requiring a license for street parading, exemplifies the

dominant approach. Although Plaisted insisted that his actions constituted religious worship, the Massachusetts court maintained that the
motives for his action were irrelevant. Instead, it noted that "the provisions of the constitution which are relied on, securing freedom of
religious worship, were not designed to prevent the adoption of reasonable rules and regulations for the use of streets and public places," and
it concluded that the Salvation Army was subject to the same restrictions
as any secular body engaging in similar actions.[15]

In incorporating the free exercise clause in *Cantwell v. Connecticut*, the
U.S. Supreme Court first adopted the secular regulation rule pioneered
by the state courts.[16] It applied the rule more stringently than had its
state counterparts, however, particularly when appellants' freedom of
speech was also affected by state regulations, overturning several state
rulings that upheld restrictions on door-to-door proselytizing and on
the distribution of religious literature.[17] During the 1960s the Court
abandoned the secular regulation rule altogether, requiring instead that
states demonstrate a compelling state interest to justify laws that im-
pinged on religiously motivated conduct.[18]

The Supreme Court's incorporation and subsequent reinterpretation
of the free exercise clause has not prompted state courts to take a fresh
look at their state guarantees of religious liberty. On the contrary, these
courts have tended to ignore state bills of rights and to look to federal
doctrine and precedent for direction.[19] This has held true whether they
were confronting familiar free exercise questions, like the withholding
of medical treatment on religious grounds, or novel issues, like the deprogramming of cult members or the use of drugs in religious worship.[20]
The advent of the new judicial federalism has not altered this pattern.

The failure of most state courts to develop state constitutional law may
reflect a judgment that, given the police power exception found in many
state constitutions and the body of precedent developed in the states,
state bills of rights offer less protection to religiously motivated conduct
than does the First Amendment. Alternatively, it may indicate a judicial
unwillingness to block state programs or to carve out exceptions to their
coverage. But, whatever the cause, in the protection of religious liberty,
state courts over the past forty years have played a distinctly subsidiary
role, applying federal constitutional principles rather than developing
state law.

The Establishment of Religion under State Constitutions

The apparent vagueness of the First Amendment's ban on laws "respecting an establishment of religion" has allowed Supreme Court justices to disagree fundamentally over the meaning of the clause and even
when they have professed a common understanding of its purposes, to

differ sharply over how the clause applied in specific cases.[21] Many contemporary state constitutions, by contrast, contain specific and detailed provisions governing the relationship between church and state. Although the clarity of the constitutional language does not preclude disagreement on sensitive issues of church and state, it does, when considered in conjunction with the controversies that led to its adoption, offer the basis for an independent state jurisprudence in a field where the Supreme Court has failed to provide consistent direction.[22]

The initial issue of church-state relations that the states confronted was whether to maintain existing religious establishments. At the outbreak of the American Revolution, four states had exclusive establishments of religion in the European sense, and five had dual or multiple establishments.[23] Although the states' original constitutions did not eliminate the existing religious establishments, independence did trigger a movement toward disestablishment, best exemplified by the famous campaign against religious establishment in Virginia. Equally important were the replacement of exclusive with multiple establishments in four states and the substitution of multiple for dual establishments in two others.[24] No subsequently admitted state created a religious establishment, and by the 1830s pressure from dissenting churches, such as the Baptists, as well as the federal example, had led the original states to remove the last vestiges of their official establishments. As new constitutions were adopted in the original states, they usually eliminated constitutional language recognizing state religious establishments.[25]

Although the states ended their official establishments, many continued to provide unofficial support for religion in general and for Protestant Christianity in particular. Given the relative religious homogeneity of the American population at the beginning of the nineteenth century,, this is hardly surprising. State courts, for example, continued to recognize Christianity as part of the common law and to sustain convictions for blasphemy when speakers disparaged Christian beliefs.[26] Similarly, despite acknowledging the religious character of Sunday closing laws, state courts consistently upheld them, noting in one case that "the Christian religion may be protected from desecration by such laws as the legislature in its wisdom may deem necessary."[27]

The states' tacit support of Protestantism was most manifest in the operation of the public schools established during the nineteenth century. In view of their responsibility in providing for the moral education of their students, most of these schools adopted religious means to achieve this purpose, such as instituting compulsory programs of daily prayers and of readings from the King James version of the Bible. In addition, the teaching of history in the public schools—particularly when it dealt with sensitive subjects such as religious conflict during the Reformation—tended, at least in the view of Catholics, to be highly one-sided, fostering prejudice against Catholics and hostility toward the Catholic church.[28]

With the immigration of large numbers of Catholics to the United States during the nineteenth century, controversy intensified over the alleged "Protestantizing" of public education. In New York and other states, the Catholic hierarchy charged that the states were actually operating a system of Protestant sectarian schools; it demanded the elimination of the objectionable practices of the public schools and, more to the point, the provision of public support for Catholic schools. In several states, the dispute over the schools escalated into violent conflict.[29] Even more important, at least for present purposes, the demand by Catholics for state funding of their schools and for the elimination of Protestant religious practices in public schools spurred a constitutional response.[30] Several states instituted or strengthened their constitutional bans on aid to religious institutions and their mandates that school funds be expended only for public schools. Other states responded to the controversy by adopting similar provisions in their constitutions. Finally, several states, which were settled later or where religious conflict was less intense, borrowed the strict constitutional language from their sister states. As a result, most state constitutions record a considered constitutional judgment on what remains today a highly contentious issue of church-state relations. Thus, attention needs to be directed to how state courts have interpreted their constitutions in dealing with state aid to religious institutions—particularly sectarian schools—and their clients, and with governmental sponsorship of religious practices.

Aid to Religious Institutions. Given the specificity of state constitutional prohibitions, it is hardly surprising that few cases have arisen involving direct aid to religious schools and that state courts have almost unanimously struck down such aid as unconstitutional.[31] The sole exception to this pattern, a 1913 Massachusetts ruling upholding aid to sectarian colleges and universities, was promptly overturned by a constitutional amendment outlawing such aid.[32] State cases since World War II have focused on indirect aid to religious schools and their students, such as the provision for transportation and textbooks to children attending those schools. The U.S. Supreme Court has ruled that these programs do not violate the First Amendment.[33] In so ruling, however, it initially distinguished between aid to students and aid to sectarian schools, relying on the "child-benefit theory" originally developed by the Louisiana Supreme Court, and in later cases asserted that the programs' primary effect was not to further the religious mission of the schools.[34] Thus, when these forms of indirect aid were challenged in state courts, the basis for challenge was typically the state constitution.

State courts have divided over the constitutionality of these programs of indirect aid. A number of state constitutions expressly provide for such programs. In 1947, after the New Jersey Supreme Court upheld a program of bus transportation for parochial school students in *Everson v. Board of Education*, the state incorporated authorization for such programs in its new constitution.[35] And after the Wisconsin and New York courts struck down school transportation programs, amendments were adopted in those states that authorized their reinstitution.[36] On the other hand, the Alaska Supreme Court concluded that, given the constitution's broad prohibitory language, if the state's founders had wished to permit such a program, they would have included a provision similar to those of New York and New Jersey.[37]

More generally, the differing outcomes in the states seemed to depend on whether the justices have been willing to read the applicable state provisions as independent constitutional judgments on the permissibility of aid to religious institutions. State courts that have upheld the challenged programs have usually assumed, often without supporting analysis, that the relevant state provisions imposed no greater restriction than did the First Amendment.[38] In contrast, courts that have invalidated the challenged programs have been more attuned to differences in constitutional language and to the historical experiences that produced them.[39] *Gaffney v. State Department of Education*, which examined the constitutionality of Nebraska's textbook loan law, provides a model of independent constitutional analysis.[40] The Nebraska Supreme Court, eschewing the tripartite analysis developed by the U.S. Supreme Court, focused instead on Nebraska's constitutional prohibition of any "appropriation in aid of any sectarian institution or any educational institution not owned and controlled by the state."[41] The clarity of this language, the court insisted, made interpretation unnecessary, and its broad sweep admitted of no exceptions. Indeed the records of the convention that drafted the provision indicated that a major aim was to devise a precise prohibition that would prevent sectarian conflict over the funding of church-related schools. The court therefore concluded that the law was unconstitutional.

Other state courts have focused on the precise language of their state constitutions in justifying the development of an independent constitutional position. The California Supreme Court, for example, concluded that the state constitution's ban on expenditures for "any sectarian purpose" was designed to prevent the state from providing benefits to sectarian schools that furthered their educational purpose, and on that basis, it struck down a textbook loan program.[42] Similarly, the Idaho Supreme Court, in striking down a state law authorizing the transportation of students to nonpublic schools, reasoned that the emphatic character of the prohibitory language of the state's constitution was designed to impose even more stringent restrictions than had the First Amendment.[43] Finally, the Massachusetts high court, noting that a challenged textbook loan program aided sectarian schools in carrying out their essential educational function, held that it violated the amendment, adopted following its 1913 decision, that ruled out the "use" of money for "maintaining or aiding" sectarian schools.[44]

Public Sponsorship of Religious Practices. Most state constitutions contain strong prohibitions on governmental expenditures for sectarian religious purposes. In addition, largely in response to Catholic efforts to secure funding for parochial schools, many also expressly forbid sectarian control or influence in schools supported by state funds. Several others guarantee absolute freedom of worship and forbid government from compelling attendance at a place of worship. The constitution of Washington is representative: it safeguards "absolute freedom of conscience in all matters of religious sentiment, belief, and worship," provides that "no public money or property shall be appropriated for or applied to any religious worship, exercise or instruction," and requires that "all schools maintained or supported wholly or in part by the public funds shall be forever free from sectarian control or influence."[45]

It is difficult to reconcile the unofficial support for religion in the states, particularly the pervasive practices of Bible reading and prayer in public schools, with these constitutional provisions. As a result, during the nineteenth century, litigants began to challenge these and similar practices under their state constitutions. Five state courts anticipated the Supreme Court's analysis in *School District of Abington Township v. Schempp* and struck down Bible reading in the schools under their state constitutions.[46] In addition, the Florida and New Jersey supreme courts, despite upholding Bible-reading programs, ruled that the distribution of copies of the Gideon Bible to students involved an unconstitutional preference for a particular religious sect; the New Mexico Supreme Court forbade distribution of other religious literature on similar grounds.[47]

All the same, most state courts rejected constitutional challenges to Bible reading and other sectarian observances in the public schools.[48] To do so, they were forced to deny that the Bible was sectarian, arguing that its "adopt[ion] by one or more denominations as authentic ... or inspired, cannot make it a sectarian book."[49] Similarly, they were obliged to maintain that use of a version of the Bible favored by a particular sect did not constitute governmental endorsement of or preference for a particular religion. Finally, they had to deny that school prayer and Bible reading transformed the classroom into a place of worship, insisting that the constitutional ban on compelled attendance at a place of worship applied only to places where people met for that express purpose.[50] These assertions, unconvincing though they are, demonstrate the commitment of many state courts to upholding Bible reading in the schools.[51] Indeed, even after the U.S. Supreme Court struck down the practice under the federal Constitution, the Florida Supreme Court continued to insist that Bible reading was not a religious exercise.[52] Paradoxically, the courts' opinions also underline the strength of state constitutional strictures on governmental sponsorship of religious practices. The clarity and forcefulness of the provisions precluded interpreting them in an accommodative fashion, and state courts were thus forced to misrepresent the situations that they confronted in order to uphold the practices that they favored.

A related issue, which has emerged in state courts over the past two decades, is the constitutionality of maintaining religious displays on public property. Prior to 1984, when the U.S. Supreme Court ruled that the inclusion of a nativity scene in a Christmas display on public property did not violate the establishment clause, courts in five states had addressed the issue.[53] In complex and protracted litigation, the Oregon Supreme Court initially upheld and then invalidated the erection in a city park of a permanent fifty-one-foot-high Latin cross that would be illuminated during the Christmas and Easter seasons, only to reverse itself once again when the cross was designated as a war memorial and illuminated only on patriotic holidays.[54] The Oklahoma Supreme Court has upheld erection of a similar cross in a public park, and the Florida Supreme Court has endorsed the display of a lighted cross on the county courthouse each December.[55] On the other hand, the Colorado Supreme Court has reversed the dismissal of a suit challenging the inclusion of a crèche in Christmas decorations displayed on the steps of the city and county building, and the California Supreme Court in *Fox v. City of Los Angeles* has struck down the display of a lighted cross on the city hall to commemorate Christmas and Easter.[56]

In only three cases did the courts consider the displays in the light of state bills of rights. The Colorado Supreme Court, maintaining that the state and federal guarantees "embod[ied] similar values," relied on the tripartite test developed by the Supreme Court in *Lemon v. Kurtzman* in interpreting the state guarantee and concluded that the appellants had shown a prima facie case of constitutional violation. Yet because this ruling was linked so closely to the application of federal doctrine, there is some question as to its continuing viability in the wake of the Supreme Court's contrary decision in *Lynch v. Donnelly*. In contrast, the Oklahoma and California supreme courts undertook independent interpretation of their state guarantees, albeit with conflicting results. Acknowledging that expenditures to support or to benefit a religious sect would violate the state constitution, the Oklahoma Supreme Court insisted that despite the city's maintenance and illumination of the cross, no public monies were used. Furthermore, the court continued, the display of the cross did not entail forbidden governmental support for religion since the commercial setting of the cross "stultif[ied] its symbolism and vitiate[d] any use, benefit, or support for any sect, church, denomination, system of religion, or sectarian institution as such."[57] Considerably more convincing was the California Supreme Court's opinion in *Fox*. The court pointed out that the sectarian religious character of the display in question was apparent in both the selection of the cross, a symbol particularly pertinent to the Christian religion, and in the efforts of Greek Orthodox Christians to ensure that the cross would be displayed on their Easter. It thus concluded that the state's special recognition of one religion, at least where others were not similarly recognized, violated the state's constitutional ban on preference for religious sects.

Conclusions

There appears to be substantial justification for the development of an independent state jurisprudence in the realm of religious liberty and church-state relations. State constitutional guarantees differ markedly in language and form from their federal counterparts. For many states, these differences reflect the process of constitutional development in which provisions were adopted over time to resolve or to prevent conflicts over such contentious issues as the maintenance of religious establishments and aid to sectarian schools. For others, they reflect a borrowing of provisions from sister states. Yet whatever the basis for the differences, the result has been that the states have developed a distinctive constitutional perspective on the claims of religious liberty and on the separation of church and state. Insofar as the guarantees of religious liberty in state constitutions incorporate police power exceptions, they afford less protection than the free exercise clause, at least as currently interpreted by the U.S. Supreme Court. On the other hand, because the prohibitions on aid to religious institutions are more detailed, more precise, and—given the controversies that engendered them—more far-reaching than the establishment clause, they fully justify a strongly separationist reading. Thus, reliance on state constitutions should yield different results from those obtained under the First Amendment.

Since incorporation, however, state courts have generally grounded their rulings in federal rather than state constitutional law. In free exercise cases, this may reflect a belief that consideration of state provisions is irrelevant since no laws upheld under the First Amendment would be struck down under state guarantees and some that survived state constitutional scrutiny would nonetheless be invalidated under the First Amendment. In the area of church-state relations, where some courts have pursued an independent course, the explanation for state reliance on federal doctrine and precedent, even in interpreting state provisions, is less clear. Perhaps this reliance reflects deference based on the stature of the Supreme Court and the quality of its analyses. If so, this deference may be forfeited, and at least one state court has justified its recent shift to a reliance on state provisions by noting the inconclusiveness and va-garies of federal precedent.[58] Alternatively, reliance on federal prece-dent may reflect judicial dissatisfaction with the results that would be obtained from a rigorous application of state constitutional principle. Whatever the cause, it can be expected that as the Supreme Court moves toward a more accommodationist stance on establishment issues, litigants will increasingly call upon the state courts to uphold the separation of church and state under state constitutional provisions.

Speech and Press under State Constitutions

The colonists' vigorous exercise of their rights to speak and to publish their sentiments was vital to the Revolutionary movement. Thus, it is hardly surprising that when the original state constitutions were drafted, their declarations of rights guaranteed the freedoms of speech and/or of the press.[59] By the 1840s, all the original states, as well as all those subsequently admitted, had established constitutional protections for the freedoms of speech and of the press. Because the First Amendment restricted only the federal government, these guarantees provided the sole protection against state infringements of "First Amendment" rights during the nineteenth century, and in view of the infrequency of federal litigation, the rulings interpreting them were the main source of judicial doctrine on the freedoms of speech and of the press.[60]

Despite some interstate variation in constitutional language, exami-nation of these provisions reveals two common aspects. First, the state constitution makers evidently viewed the freedoms of speech and of the press as important primarily for the contributions that they made to self-government. In some instances, the constitutional language makes this connection explicitly. The North Carolina Constitution of 1776, for ex-ample, stated: "The freedom of the press is one of the great bulwarks of liberty, and therefore ought never to be restrained."[61] In other in-stances, the framers' concern with this connection can be inferred from their treatment of the right to trial by jury. In recognition of the fact that prosecutions for seditious libel might be used to stifle dissent, some early constitutions combined the freedom of the press and the protection of trial by jury in a single provision.[62] Others took specific steps to prevent governmental harassment of critics, establishing truth as a defense in "prosecutions for the publication of papers investigating the official con-duct of officers, or men in public capacity," and safeguarding the jury's right to determine both the law and the facts in such cases.[63] Second, state guarantees of the freedoms of speach and the press were not de-signed to produce an absolute protection. This is reflected in the Penn-sylvania Constitution of 1790, which stated: "The free communication of thoughts and opinions is one of the invaluable rights of man; and every citizen may freely speak, write, and print on any subject, *being responsible for the abuse of that liberty.*" [64] This distinction between liberty and its abuse, with liability for irresponsible speech and publications, was incorporated into most state constitutions during the late eighteenth and early nineteenth centuries.

The same distinction between freedom and license, between expression that did and did not threaten the general welfare, underlay most state judicial rulings on the freedoms of speech and of the press during the nineteenth and early twentieth centuries. [65] Like the "bad tendency test" employed by the U.S. Supreme Court during the early 1900s, to which it bears a strong resemblance, this distinction lent itself to conservative results. Thus, most state courts upheld state power against constitutional challenges in cases involving restrictions on unpopular political advocacy, the regulation of obscenity, limits on labor picketing, and the unauthorized use of public property to convey messages. [66] Occasionally, it is true, state courts did draw the line between individual rights and the public welfare in ways that safeguarded speech and the press. [67] Nonetheless, the period of state ascendancy was characterized by rulings and doctrinal developments inimical to the vigorous exercise of speech and press freedoms.

This period of state ascendancy lasted until the early twentieth century, when the Supreme Court began its first serious consideration of the freedoms of speech and of the press. Initially the Court cited state court rulings to buttress its decisions. [68] Quite rapidly, however, the doctrinal debate on the Court assumed a life of its own, detached from the body of state cases, pursuing arguments and directions unanticipated by the state courts. As the Court's elaboration of First Amendment law proceeded, affording protections for speech and press beyond those available under state law, interest in state constitutional protections—on the part of both litigants and state courts—receded, and the state courts came to operate like lower federal courts, applying the doctrines and precedents developed by the Supreme Court. [69]

To the extent that state courts did play an independent role from World War I to the early 1970s, their role was largely a negative one, circumscribing the freedoms of speech and of the press. A survey of state court rulings during the period reveals an eagerness to follow Supreme Court rulings that placed restrictions on speech or the press; a reluctance to follow expansive Court rulings that at times shaded into noncompliance; and a tendency to interpret First Amendment rights narrowly in the absence of immediately applicable Court precedents. In relation to the free exercise of religion, these tendencies were evident in state decisions restricting the rights of Jehovah's Witnesses. They were also apparent in state judicial rulings involving unpopular political speech, labor picketing, and associational rights.[70] When faced with First Amendment claims in these areas, state courts often chose to follow the more restrictive federal precedents, such as *Gilbert v. Minnesota* and *Gitlow v. New York*, rather than subsequent rulings more solicitous of speech and press.[71] In some instances, the courts secured the desired results of upholding restrictions on speech and press by blithely distinguishing clearly applicable precedents.[72] Frequently the Supreme Court had to intervene and uphold First Amendment freedoms on appeal. The reluctance of state courts to provide adequate protection of press and speech freedoms led one commentator, writing in 1951, to conclude that "the record of state court guardianship of 'First Amendment Freedoms' is disappointing" and that "if our liberties are not protected in Des Moines, the only hope is in Washington."[73]

During the 1970s, state courts again began to look to their state constitutions in resolving questions about freedom of expression. The Oregon Supreme Court's return to the state's bill of rights was part of a more general campaign to resuscitate state constitutional law, and thus the court sought to chart an independent constitutional course even in cases where federal doctrine was already available.[74] Other state courts looked to their state constitutions only infrequently, when distinctive features of state constitutional guarantees seemed to offer protection for press and speech rights not available under the federal Constitution. The two areas in which state courts have made their most notable contributions are in securing press (and public) access to judicial proceedings and in protecting speech against private abridgement.

Access to Judicial Proceedings

If the press is to perform adequately its function of informing the public, it must be able to gather and to publish newsworthy information. Some governmental regulations, however, even if adopted for legitimate purposes and applicable to all citizens, have the effect of restricting reporters' access to information and thereby limit the press's ability to serve as the eyes and ears of the public. During the 1970s, several cases arose in federal and state courts concerning the constitutional status of the press's news-gathering function.[75] Of particular concern were judicial orders that excluded the press from trials and pretrial proceedings. When the U.S. Supreme Court initially confronted the issue in *Gannett v. DePasquale*, it sustained a judge's order, issued with the consent of both parties, excluding the press and public from a pretrial hearing.[76] The Court concluded that the Sixth Amendment did not require that courts always be open to the public and that, if the public was excluded, the First Amendment did not require that the institutional press be granted access superior to that of the general public. A year later, the

Court apparently reconsidered its position and struck down a judicial order closing a trial to the general public, suggesting that the First Amendment does offer some protection for news gathering.[77] Nonetheless, the Court's failure to unite behind a majority opinion and the variety of rationales offered by the justices made conclusions about the scope of the press's right of access difficult.

The Court's decision in *Gannett* prompted the media to turn to state constitutions to bolster their claims of a right of access to judicial proceedings. In contrast to the Sixth Amendment, the constitutions of twenty-six states either mandate that the administration of justice be "open" or forbid "secret" courts.[78] Relying on this language in conjunction with state guarantees of the freedom of the press, the courts in several states have recognized a right of access to judicial proceedings for the press. The contours of that right, however, have varied from state to state. In a pre-*Gannett* case, the Arizona Supreme Court, although striking down a judicial order excluding the public and the news media from a preliminary hearing on a multiple homicide, took a narrow view. According to the court, the language of the constitution could not be interpreted literally because of its potential conflict with "the equally important constitutional right to a fair trial by an impartial jury."[79] Rather, the court—looking to federal doctrine and precedent—chose to apply the clear-and-present-danger test in determining when the press and public could be excluded and pointedly noted that its ruling did not extend to preliminary hearings at which potentially inadmissible evidence might be presented.[80]

More recent rulings have gone further in ensuring access for the public and the press. The North Dakota Supreme Court, for example, has expanded the range of proceedings to which access is guaranteed, requiring that the press and public be admitted not only to courtroom proceedings but also to a quasi-judicial inquiry by the state's attorney.[81] Other courts have set stringent standards for exclusion of the public and the press from trials and pretrial hearings. A prime example is *State ex rel. Herald Mail Co. v. Hamilton* (1980), in which the West Virginia Supreme Court, relying on the state constitution's open courts provision, struck down a judicial order barring the press and public from portions of a pretrial hearing in a murder case.[82] Noting that other courts had interpreted analogous provisions as securing an independent right of access for the public, the court asserted that the same right must be accorded the press both as a part of the public and as a surrogate for it. It further maintained that the right extended not only to trials but to other judicial proceedings as well, expressly endorsing the reasoning of dissenting justices in *Gannett* on this point.[83] Although it acknowledged that the right was not absolute, the court warned that closure was permissible only when there was "a clear likelihood that there [would] be irreparable damage to the defendant's right to a fair trial"; it urged that the traditional techniques for insulating the jury from publicity be used whenever possible.[84]

At least one court—the Oregon Supreme Court—seems to have read its constitutional guarantee as absolutely barring closed proceedings. In *State ex rel. Oregonian Publishing Co. v. Deiz*, the court struck down a statute that permitted exclusion of the public and press from juvenile court proceedings.[85] Complicating this case was the fact that the state legislature, contemporaneously with the adoption of the constitution, had enacted a statute authorizing closure of judicial proceedings under certain circumstances. The court, however, rejected the contention that this law meant that the constitutional guarantee was not to be interpreted literally. Rather, it distinguished sharply between legislation and constitution making, maintaining that laws adopted in response to an immediate problem could not vitiate the force of a constitutional principle.

If some state courts after *Gannett* seized upon their guarantees of open courts to afford access for the press, others not only failed to do so but also showed a marked hostility to demands for access. In *Globe Newspaper Co. v. Superior Court*, the Supreme Judicial Court of Massachusetts sustained a law requiring the closure of trials during testimony by minors who had been rape victims, and in *San Jose Mercury News v. Municipal Court*, the California Supreme Court upheld a statute that allowed the exclusion of the press and public from preliminary hearings without a case-by-case showing that closure was necessary to ensure a fair trial.[86] The Massachusetts court largely ignored the state constitution's open courts provision, claiming that the plaintiffs had not adequately addressed it in their brief.[87] The California court did consider the state claim, but it read the records of the constitutional convention that framed the provision to indicate that the public trial guarantee was to be interpreted narrowly.[88] Even after the U.S. Supreme Court overturned the *Globe Newspaper* ruling on First Amendment grounds, the California court continued to reject constitutional challenges to the law, until it was eventually struck down by the Supreme Court.[89]

In reversing the decision of the California Supreme Court in this case, the U.S. Supreme Court announced federal standards for resolving access claims similar to those that had been developed by state courts in the wake of *Gannett*. Thus litigation on access to judicial proceedings has come full cycle. Recourse to state constitutions was stimulated initially by concern about the adequacy of protection under the First Amendment. By equating federal protection with that available under state constitutions, the Court removed the incentive to look to state provisions and in effect ensured that future litigation would proceed on federal

rather than state grounds. Thus, what at the outset looked like an opportunity for state constitutions to play an independent role ended as
an episode of state initiative followed by federal occupation of the field.

Speech Rights on Private Property

By its very terms, the First Amendment safeguards the freedom of
speech only against governmental abridgement; litigants seeking relief
under the federal Constitution usually must demonstrate the presence
of state action. The U.S. Supreme Court, however, has held that private
entities engaged in public functions are also covered by the amendment.
Relying on this public function theory, the Court in *Marsh v. Alabama*
struck down restrictions on speech imposed by a corporation within a
company town.[90] Beginning in the late 1960s, litigants sought to extend
this public function analysis to privately owned shopping centers, contending that they, like company towns, served a public function and
therefore should be subject to the strictures of the First Amendment.[91]
After some initial indecision, the Court rejected this claim and ruled
that the owners of shopping centers, like other property owners, could
restrict or forbid speech on their private property.

Significantly, many state constitutional provisions do more than merely
proscribe governmental infringements of free speech. New Jersey's provision is representative: "Every person may freely speak, write, and publish his sentiments on all subjects, being responsible for the abuse of that
right. No law shall be passed to restrain or abridge the liberty of speech
or of the press."[92] Whereas the second sentence, like the First Amendment, bars governmental inference with the freedoms of speech and
press, the first sentence does not mention government at all but rather
announces a positive right of free expression, albeit one subject to regulation in the public interest. This express constitutional commitment
to promoting the free exchange of ideas among the state's citizens, one
going beyond the mere prohibition of governmental infringements on
the right to speak, provides a clear basis for extending protection beyond
what is available under the federal Constitution, and a number of state
courts have relied on such provisions to act against private abridgements
of free speech.

The seminal case is *Robins v. PruneYard Shopping Center*, in which the
California Supreme Court upheld Robins's right to collect signatures in
a privately owned shopping center for a petition protesting the United
Nations' anti-Zionism resolution.[93] The court initially observed that the
due process clause, as interpreted in the Supreme Court's shopping
center cases, did not preclude the states from regulating the uses of
private property in the public interest. The affirmative endorsement of
freedom of speech in the state constitution, it noted, signaled a strong

public interest, which could, at least in some circumstances, override the claims of property owners. More specifically, the court observed that Robins's solicitation of signatures for his petition neither interfered with the normal business operations of the mall nor diluted property rights. Consequently it concluded that Robins was entitled to protection under the state's constitution.

When the U.S. Supreme Court unanimously upheld the California court's ruling in *PruneYard*,[94] similar cases were brought before a number of other state supreme courts. Because the affirmative recognition of speech rights in state constitutions is accompanied by an "abuse" limitation, these courts—like the California court in *PruneYard*—had to consider whether speakers had interfered with the legitimate claims of property owners. Thus, the cases that they confronted promised an opportunity to develop independent state doctrine interpreting distinctive state guarantees. Indeed some courts made impressive strides in that direction. For example, in overturning the trespass conviction of a member of the U.S. Labor party who distributed leaflets on the campus of Princeton University without permission, the New Jersey Supreme Court in *New Jersey v. Schmid* carefully considered both the nature of the private property on which Schmid intruded and the extent to which Schmid's expression interfered with or, as in this case, promoted the purposes to which the property was dedicated.[95] Similarly, the Washington Supreme Court, in upholding an environmental group's right to collect signatures and demonstrate in a shopping mall, noted that the right depended on whether "state law confers such a right" and thoughtfully addressed the issues.[96]

State courts' enthusiasm for staking out an independent position has been far from unanimous, however. The rulings permitting speakers access to private property—particularly shopping centers—to present their views have given rise to sharp dissents from justices who found a state action requirement implicit in their state bills of rights.[97] Since 1984 the supreme courts of Connecticut, Michigan, and New York have endorsed this position, and no supreme court has read its constitution to require property owners to allow speakers access to their premises.[98] Moreover, commentators have identified several problems that courts still must resolve in delineating the scope of speech rights on private property.[99] It is too early to tell whether most state courts will find independent protection for free speech in the distinctive language of their constitutions and adequately resolve the complex problems encountered in balancing the claims of free speech and property rights.

Conclusions

Certain common features mark the development of state constitutional law on media access to judicial proceedings and on speech rights on private property. On both issues, the recourse to state constitutional law resulted from unfavorable federal rulings (on press access, *Gannett*; on speech rights, the shopping center cases) that prompted litigants—and hence state courts—to address themselves to the guarantees in state bills of rights. On both issues, the willingness of some state courts to accord greater protection depended on the distinctive language of state constitutional protections rather than on a sustained theoretical treatment of free expression. Indeed the state courts seemed to be self-consciously eschewing broad doctrinal formulations in favor of pronouncements tied to specific issues and specific constitutional language. Furthermore, on both issues, the response of state courts to litigants' claims was mixed. Despite similarities among the states' constitutional provisions, no court was able to present an interpretation that commanded the assent of all other courts. Finally, the long-run contribution of state constitutional law on both issues must be considered problematic. On the issue of access to judicial proceedings, the U.S. Supreme Court, by retreating from *Gannett*, has made federal law the more attractive alternative for litigants. On the issue of speech rights on private property, the recent trend in state decisions has been to accept the federal state action requirement as applicable to state guarantees, thereby undermining claims of private abridgement of speech rights and aligning state law with federal law. Certainly the record of state courts on these issues cannot make one sanguine about the prospects for a flowering of state civil liberties law during the era of the new judicial federalism.

Retrospect and Prospect

The division of labor between federal and state constitutions (and federal and state courts) in protecting "First Amendment" rights has changed dramatically over time. For over a century following the ratification of the Bill of Rights, state courts, relying on state constitutional guarantees, had primary judicial responsibility for safeguarding those rights. During this period, they established precedents and devised legal doctrines that influenced the initial development of federal constitutional law. With the incorporation of First Amendment liberties, however, the locus of litigation and of judicial creativity shifted. The U.S. Supreme Court supplanted its state counterparts, developing its own body of First Amendment doctrine and precedent, and state courts came to rely almost exclusively on federal law and doctrine in protecting the liberties of speech, press, and religion. Within the last two decades and with the emergence of the new judicial federalism, state courts have once again begun to address themselves to state guarantees of "First Amendment" rights.

It is still unclear whether the rediscovery of state guarantees portends a significant shift in the locus and focus of litigation in this area. Thus far, despite the hopes of the most fervent advocates of the new judicial federalism, the resurgence of state protections for "First Amendment" rights has not restored state courts and state protections to the centrality that they enjoyed in the nineteenth century. Instead, state rulings during the past two decades have continued to reflect the assumption that consideration of these issues should begin and, in most instances, end with federal precedent. When addressing issues on which the Supreme Court has already ruled, state supreme courts have largely relied on its precedents and doctrinal formulations, even when litigants have presented claims under both federal and state charters. The same tendency to base decisions on the First Amendment, as construed by the Supreme Court, is evident even when the Court has not directly ruled on an issue. When state courts have based their rulings on their state constitutions, they have characteristically relied on federal precedent and doctrine in interpreting the state provisions. Finally, when state courts have departed from the Supreme Court's rulings and developed independent positions, they have often justified their departures by pointing to distinctive language or provisions in state bills of rights. (This mode of justification is prominent in state judicial opinions supporting independent rulings on aid to sectarian education, on access to judicial proceedings, and on speech rights on private property.) In taking this approach, however, state courts have implicitly recognized that, given the availability of federal precedent, departures from it, even in the interpretation of state guarantees, require justification.[100] Moreover, as the diversity of state rulings on these issues illustrates, even significant differences in constitutional language have not always been sufficient to persuade state courts to pursue an independent constitutional course.

What accounts for the persistence of patterns of thought and practice established before the advent of the new judicial federalism? In part, state courts' deference to the Supreme Court's rulings is explicable in terms of the conservation of scarce judicial resources of time and effort: why address anew questions that have already been resolved or pretend to doctrinal amnesia when there is so much useful material on which to build? In part, too, it suggests a lack of self-confidence on the part of state courts, borne perhaps of the contrast between the Supreme Court's experience in developing First Amendment law and their own relative inexperience in dealing with complex issues in this field. Related to this is the habit, common to both state judges and the counsel arguing before them, of treating state guarantees as mere analogues of federal protections. Finally, state courts' failure to afford independent protections for 'First Amendment' rights may reflect a judicial reluctance to expand individual rights, particularly when such protection requires the invalidation of ongoing governmental programs.[101]

Nonetheless, despite a disappointing record over the last two decades, there is some basis for predicting that when state courts interpret state constitutions, they will come to play a more active role in safeguarding 'First Amendment' rights. First, in its interpretation of the Bill of Rights (including the First Amendment), the U.S. Supreme Court, by argument and example, has not only provided a justification for judicial activism in support of civil liberties; it has also supplied state courts with a model to emulate in developing state civil liberties law. At least some courts have consciously modeled their approach to civil liberties on that of the U.S. Supreme Court, and it is possible that over time they will extend their activity to First Amendment issues.[102] Second, through its rulings and the commentary that they have generated, the Supreme Court has stimulated legal thinking on civil liberties and sensitized judges to civil liberties claims. Over time, this too should affect how state courts respond to First Amendment claims brought under state constitutions.

Finally, the deluge of legal commentary on the new judicial federalism can be expected over time to promote judicial awareness of the distinctive character of state constitutional guarantees. Most state provisions are not mere analogues of the First Amendment. Some provisions antedate their federal counterparts and thus must be understood independently of them. (Furthermore, states that subsequently modeled their guarantees on early state provisions must be viewed as having consciously chosen between the federal and state models.) Other state provisions have no federal counterparts at all. Still others are couched in language different from the federal guarantees, reflecting the distinctive political perspectives and unique historical experiences of the various states. Taken together, then, a substantial basis exists for the development of a state constitutional jurisprudence of First Amendment rights. As state judges become educated to the distinctive historical experiences and legal perspectives that underlie state constitutional guarantees, they can be expected to become more sympathetic to First Amendment claims advanced under those guarantees. In a sense, then, advocates of the new judicial federalism, by applauding state judges' new sensitivity to state constitutional rights, are helping to create the very phenomenon that they claim to be describing.

Notes

1. See, for example, Abrams v. United States, 250 U.S. 616 (1919); New York Times v. Sullivan, 376 U.S. 254 (1964); and West Virginia Board of Education v. Barnette, 319 U.S. 624 (1943).

2. The U.S. Supreme Court ruled that the First Amendment was not applicable to the states in Permoli v. First Municipality, 3 How. 589 (1845). For a survey of the Court's rulings on freedom of speech and of the press during the

nineteenth and early twentieth centuries, see David B. Rabban, "The First Amendment in Its Forgotten Years," *Yale Law Journal* 90 (1981): 514–95; for a survey of its early religion rulings, see Philip B. Kurland, *Religion and the Law* (Chicago: University of Chicago Press, 1961), pp. 19–79.

3. The initial Supreme Court ruling invalidating governmental action as a violation of First Amendment freedoms was Fiske v. Kansas, 274 U.S. 380 (1927); however, this ruling involved the application of the law rather than its substance. The first rulings invalidating state laws on First Amendment grounds occurred four years later in Stromberg v. California, 283 U.S. 359 (1931), and Near v. Minnesota, 283 U.S. 697 (1931).

4. For the incorporation of the First Amendment's speech and press guarantees, see Gitlow v. New York, 268 U.S. 652 (1925). For the incorporation of the free exercise and establishment clauses, see Cantwell v. Connecticut, 310 U.S. 296 (1940), and Everson v. Board of Education, 330 U.S. 1 (1947).

5. The "new judicial federalism" refers to state courts' renewed attention to and reliance on state bills of rights to offer greater protections than are available under the federal Constitution. For surveys of the relevant literature and cases, see "Developments in the Law—The Interpretation of State Constitutional Rights," *Harvard Law Review* 95 (1982): 1324–1499, and Bradley D. McGraw, ed., *Developments in State Constitutional Law* (St. Paul, Minn., West: 1985).

6. Two state constitutions also protect against certain private abridgements of religious liberty. See Louisiana Const., Art. I, sec. 12, and Montana Const., Art. II, sec. 5.

7. See, for example, the declaration of rights in the 1776 Pennsylvania Constitution, sec. 2, and in the Delaware Constitution, sec. 2, as well as the 1776 New Jersey Constitution, Art. XVIII. For a compilation of state constitutional guarantees, see Ronald K. L. Collins, "Bills and Declarations of Rights Digest," in *The American Bench*, 3d ed. (Sacramento: Reginald Bishop Forster & Associates, 1985), pp. 2483–2523.

8. For a discussion of these religious tests, see Chester J. Antieau, Phillip M. Carroll, and Thomas C. Burke, *Religion Under State Constitutions* (Brooklyn: Alpert Press, 1965), chap. 5.

9. Torasco v. Watkins, 162 A.2d 438 (Md. 1960), rev'd, 367 U.S. 488 (1961).

10. Representative cases include Curtis v. Strong, 4 Day 51 (Conn. 1809), and Jackson ex rel. Tuttle v. Gridley, 18 Johns. R. 98 (N.Y. 1820). For discussions of religious tests for witnesses and the use of religious beliefs as a basis for impeaching witnesses' credibility, see Antieau, Carroll, and Burke, *Religion under State Constitutions*, chap. 5, and William G. Torpey, *Judicial Doctrines of Religious Rights in America* (Chapel Hill: University of North Carolina Press, 1948), chap. 10.

11. New York in 1846 became the first state to adopt a constitutional prohibition on religious tests for witnesses. New York Const., Art. I, sec. 3. For a survey of current constitutional provisions, see Collins, "Bills and Declarations," p. 2501.

12. See, for example, Colorado Const., Art. XVII, sec. 5; Idaho Const., Art. XIV, sec. 1; and Illinois Const., Art. XII, sec. 6.

13. Connecticut Const., Art. I, sec. 3. Some other early constitutions included the state's reservation of the police power as a separate element of the declaration

of rights. For a listing of current provisions incorporating police power limitations, see Collins, "Bills and Declarations," pp. 2496–99.

14. For a review of early state rulings upholding police power limitations on religiously motivated conduct, see Antieau, Carroll, and Burke, *Religion under State Constitutions*, chap. 4, and Torpey, *Judicial Doctrines*, chap. 2.

15. Commonwealth v. Plaistead, 19 N.E. 224, 226 (Mass. 1889).

16. Cantwell v. Connecticut, 310 U.S. 296 (1940).

17. See, for example, Lovell v. City of Griffin, 303 U.S. 444 (1938); Murdock v. Pennsylvania, 319 U.S. 105 (1943); and Martin v. City of Struthers, 319 U.S. 141 (1943).

18. See Braunfeld v. Brown, 366 U.S. 599 (1961); Sherbert v. Verner, 374 U.S. 398 (1963); and Wisconsin v. Yoder, 406 U.S. 205 (1972).

19. It is noteworthy in this regard that the review of developments in state civil liberties law in the *Harvard Law Review* did not even bother to mention state judicial initiatives in the religion area. For recent efforts to resuscitate the relevant provisions of the Oregon Constitution, see Salem College v. Employment Division, 695 P.2d 25 (Ore. 1985), and Cooper v. Eugene School District No. 4J, 723 P.2d 298 (Ore. 1986).

20. On the withholding of medical treatment, see Mitchell v. Davis, 205 S.W.2d 812 (Tex. 1947), and Kennedy Memorial Hospital v. Heston, 279 A.2d 670 (N.J. 1971); on deprogramming, see Katz v. Superior Court, 141 Cal. App. 3d 952 (Calif. 1977); and on religious use of drugs, see People v. Woody, 394 P.2d 813 (Calif. 1964).

21. For differences among the justices on the aims of the establishment clause, compare the opinion of Justice William Rehnquist in Wallace v. Jaffree, 105 S. Ct. 2479 (1985), with those of Justices Hugo Black and Wiley Rutledge in Everson v. Board of Education, 330 U.S. 1 (1947). For differences on the application of establishment clause tests, see, inter alia, Mueller v. Allen, 463 U.S. 388 (1983).

22. Even the justices themselves have noted the lack of consistent direction from the Court. As Justice Thurgood Marshall observed in Witters v. Washington Department of Services for the Blind, 106 S. Ct. 748 (1986): "The Establishment Clause has consistently presented the Court with difficult questions of interpretation and application." For a more caustic assessment of the Court's difficulties, see the opinion of Justice William Rehnquist in Wallace v. Jaffree, 105 S. Ct. 2479 (1985).

23. For a discussion of state religious establishments at the outbreak of the Revolution and during the early years of independence, see Arthur E. Sutherland, *Constitutionalism in America* (New York: Blaisdell, 1965), chap. 11; Thomas J. Curry, *The First Freedoms* (New York: Oxford University Press, 1986); and Leonard W. Levy, *The Establishment Clause* (New York: Macmillan, 1986), chaps. 1, 2.

24. For early developments, see Sutherland, *Constitutionalism in America*, and Levy, "No Establishment." For a detailed treatment of the struggles for disestablishment in particular states, see John W. Pratt, *Religion, Politics, and Diversity* (Ithaca: Cornell University Press, 1967); Thomas E. Buckley, *Church and State in Revolutionary Virginia, 1776–1787* (Charlottesville: University Press of Virginia,

1977); and Fletcher M. Green, *Constitutional Development in the South Atlantic States* (Chapel Hill: University of North Carolina Press, 1930).

25. Compare, for example, the 1776 New Jersey Const., Art. XIX, with the 1844 New Jersey Const., Art. I, sec. 4; the 1776 North Carolina Const., Art. XXXIII, with the 1835 amendment to Art. IV, sec. 2; and the 1777 New York Const., Art. XXXVIII, with the 1821 New York Const., Art. VII, sec. 3.

26. See, for example, Updegraph v. Commonwealth, 11 Serg. & R. 394 (Penn. 1832); and Commonwealth v. Kneeland, 20 Pick. 206 (Mass. 1838).

27. As a New York court put it in 1877, "The Christian religion may be protected from desecration by such laws as the legislature in its wisdom may deem necessary." See Neuendorff v. Duryea, 69 N.Y. 557, 563 (N.Y. 1877). More generally, see Antieau, Carroll, and Burke, *Religion under State Constitutions*, pp. 72–79.

28. For an unbiased assessment, see Leo Pfeffer, *Church State and Freedom* (Boston: Beacon Press, 1953), chap. 9.

29. For overviews of the conflict between Protestants and Catholics, see Ray A. Billington, *The Protestant Crusade 1800–1860* (New York: Macmillan, 1938), and Pratt, *Religion, Politics, and Diversity.*

30. See the Rhode Island Const., Art. 1, sec. 3, and Art. 12, sec. 4 (1842); the New York Const., Art. 9, sec. 1 (1846); the Ohio Const., Art. 6, sec. 2 (1851); the Massachusetts Const., Amendment 18 (1855); the Kansas Const., Art. 7, sec. 2 (1855); the Arkansas Const., Art. 9, sec. 1 (1868); the Pennsylvania Const., Art. 10, sec. 2 (1873); the Alabama Const., Art. 12, sec. 8 (1875); the Colorado Const., Art. 9, secs. 7 and 8 (1876); the Minnesota Const., Amendment, Art. 8, sec. 3 (1877); the California Const., Art. 9, sec. 8 (1879); and the Delaware Const., Art. 10, sec. 3 (1897).

31. Most cases have involved schools that, although nominally public, actually were Catholic parochial schools taught by members of religious orders. See, for example, State v. Taylor, 240 N.W. (Neb. 1932); Harfst v. Hoegen, 163 S.W.2d 609 (Mo. 1942); and Berghorn v. School District, 260 S.W.2d 573 (Mo. 1953).

32. Opinion of the Justices, 102 N.E. 464 (Mass. 1913), reversed by Massachusetts Const. Amend., Art. 46, sec. 2.

33. On bus transportation, see Everson v. Board of Education, 330 U.S. 1 (1947); and on the loaning of textbooks, see Board of Education v. Allen, 392 U.S. 236 (1968). The anomalous character of the *Allen* ruling is suggested by comparison with Meek v. Pittenger, 421 U.S. 349 (1975) and Wolman v. Walter, 433 U.S. 220 (1977).

34. The Supreme Court adopted the child benefit theory in *Everson*, and it relied on the distinction between direct and indirect effects in *Allen*. The origins of the child benefit theory can be found in Borden v. Louisiana State Board of Education, 123 So. 655 (La. 1929), and in Cochran v. Louisiana State Board of Education, 123 So. 664 (1929).

35. Everson v. Board of Education, 44 A.2d 333 (N.J. 1945), relying in part on New Jersey Const., Art. VIII, sec. 4, para. 3.

36. Reynolds v. Nusbaum, 115 N.W.2d 761 (Wisc. 1962), reversed by amendment, Wisconsin Const., Art. I, sec. 21; and Judd v. Board of Education 15 N.E.2d 576 (N.Y. 1938), reversed by amendment, New York Const., Art. XI, sec. 4.

37. Matthew v. Quinton, 362 P.2d 932 (Alas. 1961).

38. State rulings upholding the loan of textbooks to students in sectarian schools include: Board of Education v. Allen, 228 N.E.2d 791 (N.Y. 1967); Borden v. Louisiana State Board of Education, 123 So. 655 (La. 1929); Chance v. Mississippi State Textbook Rating & Purchasing Board, 200 So. 706 (Miss. 1941); Bowerman v. O'Connor, 247 A.2d 82 (R.I. 1968); and Opinion of the Justices, 258 A.2d 343 (N.H. 1969). State rulings upholding provision of transportation to students in sectarian schools include: Everson v. Board of Education, 44 A.2d 333 (N.J. 1945); Bowker v. Baker, 167 P.2d 256 (Cal. 1946); Snyder v. Newtown, 161 A.2d 770 (Conn. 1960); Board of Education v. Bakalis, 299 N.E.2d 737 (Ill. 1973); Nicholas v. Henry, 191 S.W.2d 930 (Ky. 1945); Americans United Inc. v. Independent School District No. 622, 179 N.W.2d 146 (Minn. 1970); Honohan v. Holt, 244 N.E.2d 537 (Ohio 1968); Rhoades v. School District of Abington Township, 226 A.2d 53 (Pa. 1967); and State ex rel. Hughes v. Board of Education of Kanawha, 174 S.E.2d 711 (1970).

39. State rulings striking down the loan of textbooks to students in sectarian schools include: California Teachers Association v. Riles, 632 P.2d 953 (Cal. 1981); Bloom v. School Committee of Springfield, 379 N.E.2d 578 (Mass. 1978); Advisory Opinion re Constitutionality of 1974 PA 242, 228 N.W.2d 772 (Mich. 1974); Paster v. Tussey, 512 S.W.2d 97 (Mo. 1974); Gaffney v. State Department of Education, 220 N.W.2d 550 (Neb. 1974); Dickman v. School District No. 62C, 366 P.2d 533 (Ore. 1961); McDonald v. School Board of Yankton, 246 N.W.2d 93 (S.D. 1976). State rulings striking down provision of transportation to students in sectarian schools, which have not been overturned by constitutional amendment, include: Matthews v. Quinton, 362 P.2d 932 (Alas. 1961); State v. Brown, 172 A.2d 835 (Del. 1934); Spears v. Honda, 449 P.2d 130 (Haw. 1969); Epeldi v. Engelking, 488 P.2d 860 (Id. 1971); Board of Education for Independent School District No. 52 v. Antone, 384 P.2d 911 (Okla. 1963); and Visser v. Nooksack Valley School District No. 506, 207 P.2d 198 (Wash. 1949).

40. Gaffney v. State Department of Education, 220 N.W.2d 550 (Neb. 1974).

41. The U.S. Supreme Court, in Lemon v. Kurtzman, 403 U.S. 602 (1971), announced a three-pronged test for determining whether a law violates the establishment clause: (1) does the law have a secular purpose? (2) is its primary effect to advance religion? and (3) does it foster an excessive entanglement between government and religion?

42. California Teachers Association v. Riles, 632 P.2d 953 (Calif. 1981).

43. Epeldi v. Engelking, 488 P.2d 860 (Id. 1971).

44. Bloom v. School Committee of Springfield, 379 N.E.2d 578 (Mass. 1978).

45. Washington Const., Art. IX, sec. 4.

46. School District of Abington Township v. Schempp, 374 U.S. 203 (1963). Rulings striking down Bible reading in public schools prior to *Schempp* include People v. Board of Education of District 24, 92 N.E. 251 (Ill. 1910); Herold v. Parish Board of School Directors, 68 So. 116 (La. 1915); State v. Scheve, 91 N.W. 846 (Neb. 1902); Weiss v. District Board, 44 N.W. 967 (Wis. 1890); and Board of Education v. Minor, 23 Ohio St. 322 (Ohio 1872).

47. Rulings striking down distribution of the Gideon Bible to students in public schools include Brown v. Orange County Board of Public Instruction, 128 So.2d 181 (Fla. 1960), and Tudor v. Board of Education, 100 A.2d 857

(N.J. 1954). In Miller v. Cooper, 244 P.2d 520 (N.M. 1952), the New Mexico Supreme Court forbade the distribution of Presbyterian religious literature in the state's public schools.

48. Rulings upholding Bible reading in public schools include: People ex rel. Vollmar v. Stanley, 255 P. 610 (Colo. 1937); Chamberlin v. Dade County Board of Public Instruction, 143 So.2d 21 (Fla. 1962); Wilkerson v. City of Rome, 110 S.E. 895 (Ga. 1921); Moore v. Moore, 20 N.W. 475 (Iowa 1884); Billard v. Board of Education, 76 P. 307 (Kan. 1904); Hackett v. Brookville Graded School District, 87 S.W. 792 (Ky. 1905); Donahoe v. Richards, 38 Me. 397 (Maine 1854); Spiller v. Inhabitants of Woburn, 12 Allen 127 (Mass. 1866); Pfeffer v. Board of Education, 118 Mich. 560 (Mich. 1898); Kaplan v. Independent School District, 214 N.W. 18 (Minn. 1927); Stevenson v. Hanyon, 7 Dist. 585 (Pa. 1898); Carden v. Bland, 288 S.W.2d 718 (Tenn. 1956); and Church v. Bullock, 109 S.W. 115 (Tex. 1908).

49. Hackett v. Brookville Graded School District, 87 S.W. 792, 794 (Ky. 1905).

50. Church v. Bullock, 109 S.W. 115 (Tex. 1908).

51. As Monrad G. Paulsen observed, "Instead of maintaining a 'wall of separation', many state courts have upheld enactments benefiting religion by narrow technical readings of their state constitutions." See Paulsen, "State Constitutions, State Courts, and First Amendment Freedoms," *Vanderbilt Law Review* 4 (1951): 642.

52. After the U.S. Supreme Court decided Schempp, the Florida Supreme Court continued to uphold the constitutionality of Bible reading in the state's schools, claiming that the practice was not religious but rather served the secular purpose of instilling moral values. See Chamberlin v. Dade County Board of Public Instruction, 160 So.2d 97 (Fla. 1964).

53. Lynch v. Donnelly, 465 U.S. 668 (1984).

54. Lowe v. City of Eugene, 451 P.2d 117 (Ore. 1969); reargued and rev'd, 459 P.2d 222 (Ore. 1969); reargued and aff'd, 463 P.2d 360 (Ore. 1969); and Eugene Sand & Gravel, Inc. v. City of Eugene, 558 P.2d 338 (Ore. 1976).

55. Meyer v. Oklahoma City, 496 P.2d 789 (Okla. 1972), and Paul v. Dade County, 202 So.2d 833 (Fla. 1967).

56. Conrad v. City and County of Denver, 656 P.2d 662 (Colo. 1983), and Fox v. City of Los Angeles, 587 P.2d 663 (Cal. 1978).

57. Meyer v. Oklahoma City, 496 P.2d 789, 792–93 (1972).

58. California Teachers Association v. Riles, 632 P.2d 953 (Cal. 1983).

59. Several of the original state constitutions—for example, those in New Jersey, Rhode Island, and South Carolina—either omitted declarations of rights or included only rudimentary listings.

60. Although state rulings were the major judicial source of doctrine on the freedoms of speech and the press, prestigious commentators such as James Kent, Joseph Story, and Thomas Cooley exercised considerable influence over legal developments in this field. For a discussion of their influence on state rulings and on the development of state constitutional guarantees, see Margaret A. Blanchard, "Filling in the Void: Speech and Press in State Courts prior to *Gitlow*," in *The First Amendment Reconsidered*, ed. Bill F. Chamberlin and Charlene J. Brown (New York: Longman, 1982), pp. 22–24. This essay is the best account of relevant

state legal developments during the nineteenth and early twentieth centuries, and I have relied heavily on it in my treatment of the period.

61. North Carolina Const., Declarations of Rights, sec. 15 (1776). The Virginia Const., Bill of Rights, sec. 12, added that this liberty would be restrained only "by despotic governments."

62. Georgia Const., Art. 4, sec. 3 (1789).

63. Tennessee Const., Art. 11, sec. 19 (1796).

64. Pennsylvania Const., Art. 9, sec. 7 (1790). Emphasis added.

65. The Supreme Court of New York summarized the state of the law in People v. Most, 64 N.E. 175, 178 (1902): "All courts and commentators contrast the liberty of the press with its licentiousness, and condemn as not sanctioned by the constitution of any state, appeals designed to destroy the reputation of the citizen, the peace of society, or the existence of the government."

66. For representative rulings on unpopular political advocacy, see In re Lithuanian Workers' Literature Society, 187 N.Y.S. 612 (N.Y. 1921), and Spies v. People, 12 N.E. 85 (Ill. 1887); on the regulation of obscenity, see Commonwealth v. Buckley, 86 N.E. 910 (Mass. 1909), and People v. Muller, 96 N.Y. 408 (N.Y. 1884); on the limitation of labor picketing, see Robinson v. Hotel and Restaurant Employees Local, 207 P. 132 (Id. 1922), and Cooks', Waiters', and Waitresses' Local Union v. Papageorge, 230 S.W. 1086 (Tex. 1921); and on restrictions on the use of public property, see People ex rel. Doyle v. Atwell, 188 N.Y.S. 803 (N.Y. 1921), and City of Duquesne v. Fincke, 112 A. 130 (Pa. 1920).

67. See, for example, People v. Johnson, 191 N.Y.S. 750 (N.Y. 1921), and Sillars v. Collier, 23 N.E. 723 (Mass. 1890).

68. See Gitlow v. New York, 268 U.S. 652, 667, 668 (1925), Whitney v. California, 274 U.S. 357, 372 (1927), and Near v. Minnesota, 283 U.S. 697, 715, 719 (1931).

69. Thus one commentator in the late 1960s noted the "pervasive influence of the Supreme Court in developing standards for the preservation of free expression." See "Note, Freedom of Expression under State Constitutions," *Stanford Law Review* 20 (1968): 318.

70. For an example of how state courts sought to narrow projections for political speech, see Thomas v. Casey, 1 A.2d 866 (N.J. 1938); for labor picketing, see Meadowmoor Dairies, Inc. v. Milk Wagon Drivers' Union, 21 N.E.2d 308 (Ill. 1939); and for associational rights, see Nelson v. Wyman, 105 A.2d 756 (N.H. 1954). For a useful overview of state rulings, see Carol E. Jenson, *The Network of Control* (Westport, Conn.: Greenwood Press, 1982).

71. Gilbert v. Minnesota, 254 U.S. 325 (1920), and Gitlow v. New York, 268 U.S. 652 (1925). For a discussion of this tendency, see Jenson, *Network of Control*, chap. 4.

72. See Gibson v. Florida Legislative Investigating Committee, 108 So.2d 729 (Fla. 1958), and Bates v. City of Little Rock, 319 S.W.2d 37 (Ark. 1958). For a more general discussion, see Jenson, *Network of Control*, chap. 5.

73. Paulsen, "State Constitutions," p. 642.

74. Under the leadership of Justice Hans Linde, the Oregon Supreme Court has played a major role in interpreting state bills of rights. For an elaboration of the court's position on state civil liberties law, see Hans A. Linde, "Without 'Due Process': Unconstitutional Law in Oregon," *Oregon Law Review* 49 (1970):

133–87. For examples of how the Oregon court has sought to develop an independent body of law on free expression, see State v. Spencer, 611 P.2d 1147 (Ore. 1980), and State v. Robertson, 649 P.2d 569 (Ore. 1982). Because no other states have followed Oregon's lead, this chapter centers about the general pattern of state court rulings rather than Oregon's efforts.

75. This chapter focuses on only one aspect of limitations on news gathering, the denial of access to judicial proceedings. For an overview of related issues, see David M. O'Brien, *The Public's Right to Know: The Supreme Court and the First Amendment* (New York: Praeger, 1981).

76. Gannett v. DePasquale, 443 U.S. 368 (1979).

77. Richmond Newspapers, Inc. v. Virginia, 448 U.S. 555 (1980); see also Globe Newspapers, Inc. v. Superior Court, 457 U.S. 596 (1982).

78. For a listing of state constitutions that have such open courts provisions, see Collins, "Bills and Declarations," pp. 2511–13.

79. Phoenix Newspapers Inc. v. Jennings, 490 P.2d 563, 565 (Ariz. 1971).

80. The Arizona court looked to the U.S. Supreme Court's rulings in Thomas v. Collins, 323 U.S. 516 (1945), and Bridges v. California, 314 U.S. 252 (1941), for direction.

81. KFGO Radio, Inc. v. Rothe, 298 N.W.2d 505 (N.D. 1980).

82. State ex rel. Herald Mail Co. v. Hamilton, 267 S.E.2d 544 (W. Va. 1980).

83. Id. at 550.

84. Id. at 551.

85. State ex rel. Oregonian Publishing Co. v. Deiz, 613 P.2d 23 (Ore. 1980).

86. Globe Newspaper Co. v. Superior Court, 423 N.E.2d 773 (Mass. 1981), and San Jose Mercury News v. Municipal Court, 638 P.2d 655 (Cal. 1982).

87. In its initial ruling in Globe Newspaper Co. v. Superior Court, the Massachusetts Supreme Judicial Court pointedly refused to reach the state constitutional issue because it had been relegated "to one cursory, conclusory footnote" in plaintiffs' brief (401 N.E.2d 360, 366 [Mass.1980]). After the case was remanded by the U.S. Supreme Court for consideration in the light of the ruling in *Richmond Newspapers*, the Massachusetts court never addressed the state constitutional issue.

88. 638 P.2d 655, 658–59 (1982).

89. The U.S. Supreme Court overturned the decision of the Massachusetts Supreme Judicial Court in Globe Newspaper Co. v. Superior Court, 457 U.S. 596 (1982). The California Supreme Court nonetheless upheld the state's law permitting closure of preliminary hearings in Press-Enterprise Co. v. Superior Court, 691 P.2d 1026 (Cal. 1984). The Supreme Court reversed in Press-Enterprise Co. v. Superior Court, 54 L.W. 4869 (1986).

90. Marsh v. Alabama, 326 U.S. 501 (1946).

91. The Supreme Court's three shopping center cases were Amalgamated Food Employees Union v. Logan Valley Plaza, 391 U.S. 308 (1968); Lloyd Corporation v. Tanner, 407 U.S. 551 (1972); and Hudgens v. NLRB, 424 U.S. 507 (1976).

92. New Jersey Const., Art. I, sec. 6.

93. Robins v. PruneYard Shopping Center, 592 P.2d 341 (Cal. 1979).

94. PruneYard Shopping Center v. Robins, 447 U.S. 74 (1980).

95. State v. Schmid, 423 A.2d 615 (N.J. 1980). For another ruling according

access to a private college campus, see Commonwealth of Pennsylvania v. Tate, 432 A.2d 1382 (Pa. 1981).

96. Alderwood Associates v. Washington Environmental Council, 635 P.2d 108, 112 (Wash. 1981). The views expressed in the plurality opinion are elaborated in Robert F. Utter, "The Right to Speak, Write, and Publish Freely: State Constitutional Protection against Private Abridgement," *University of Puget Sound Law Review* 8 (Winter 1985): 159–94. See also Batchelder v. Allied Stores International, 445, N.E.2d 590 (Mass. 1983).

97. The rulings recognizing the right of speakers to present their views in privately owned shopping centers were handed down by divided courts. The vote in *PruneYard* was 4–3, in *Alderwood* 5–4, with only a plurality opinion, and in *Batchelder* 4–3.

98. Cologne v. Westfarms Associates, 409 A.2d 1201 (Conn. 1984); Woodland v. Michigan Citizens Lobby, 378 N.W.2d 337 (Mich. 1985); and Shad Alliance v. Smith Haven Mall, 498 N.Y.S.2d 99 (N.Y. 1985). An earlier decision, which denied state constitutional protection after only cursory consideration, is State v. Felmet, 273 S.E.2d 708 (N.C. 1981).

99. For discussions of these problems and possible solutions to them, see Martin B. Margulies, "Westfarms' Unquiet Shade," *University of Bridgeport Law Review* 7 (1986): 1–45; and Sanford Levinson, "Freedom of Speech and the Right of Access to Private Property under State Constitutional Law," in McGraw, *Developments in State Constitutional Law.*

100. When state courts engage in independent interpretation of their constitutional guarantees, dissenting justices often argue for the importance of uniformity in federal and state constitutional interpretation. See, for example, the dissent of Justice Frank Richardson in Fox v. City of Los Angeles, 587 P.2d 663, 677 (Cal. 1983). For commentary that stresses the importance of uniformity in interpretation, see Paul S. Hudnut, "State Constitutions and Individual Rights: The Case for Judicial Restraint," *Denver University Law Review* 63 (1985): 85–103.

101. For a case study that supports this view, see Mary Cornelia Porter and G. Alan Tarr, "The Ohio Supreme Court and the New Judicial Federalism: An Anatomy of a Failure," *Ohio State Law Journal* 45 (1984): 143–59. For more general support of this point, see G. Alan Tarr, *Judicial Impact and State Supreme Courts* (Lexington, Mass.: Lexington Books, 1977), esp. chap. 6.

102. On this point generally, see Mary Cornelia Porter, "State Supreme Courts and the Legacy of the Warren Court: Some Old Inquiries for a New Situation," in Mary Cornelia Porter & G. Alan Tarr, eds. *State Supreme Courts: Policymakers in the Federal System* (Westport, Conn.: Greenwood Press, 1982), chap. 1.

3

Gender Issues in the States: The Private Sphere and the Search for Equality

SUE DAVIS

The civil law, as well as nature herself, has always recognized a wide dif-
ference in the respective spheres and destinies of man and woman. Man is,
or should be, woman's protector and defender. The natural and proper timidity
and delicacy which belongs to the female sex evidently unfits it for many of
the occupations of civil life. The constitution of the family organization which
is founded in the divine ordinance, as well as in the nature of things, indicates
the domestic sphere as that which properly belongs to the domain and functions
of womanhood.

Justice Joseph P. Bradley,
concurring in *Bradwell v. Illinois*, 16 Wall. 130 (1873)

American law in the nineteenth century reflected a separate spheres
ideology, according to which men occupy the public realm of politics
and the marketplace and women exist in the private realm of the home
and family. Legal means were used to preclude women's participation
in public life. For example, the U.S. Supreme Court upheld state laws
prohibiting women from practicing law, from voting, and from serving
on juries.[1] However, the law did not reach into the private sphere.
Women were isolated from the law and had no way to obtain legal relief
for problems that might arise in the domestic realm. Separating life into
two clearly defined spheres guaranteed that women would remain in a
subordinate position. Men, firmly in control in the public sphere, were
also able to dominate the private sphere, where they remained unres-
trained by legal sanctions.[2]

As women have sought and gained access to the public sphere, they have urged legal regulation of the formerly neglected private realm in the belief that genuine gender equality will not be possible until women achieve equality in their domestic lives. This chapter examines two private sphere issues to which state courts and legislatures have only recently begun to devote serious attention. The issues of marital rape and the property rights of unmarried cohabitants forcefully depict the impact on women of the legal system's neglect of the private sphere. Traditionally, marital rape was not considered a crime. Indeed, it was considered a legal impossibility under the common law. Sexual relations in marriage were private and beyond the reach of the law. The result was that no legal protection was available to women who were victims of rape and other sexual abuses by their husbands: "In this unregulated private sphere, men were free to oppress women. Specifically, they were free to rape their wives."[3] Similarly, courts stayed out of the private sphere by refusing to recognize property agreements between couples who lived together without marriage. The result of legal noninvolvement in that area was that, upon termination of such a relationship, the property would belong to the partner whose name was on the title—nearly always the man.[4]

An examination of developments in the law regarding marital rape and the property rights of unmarried cohabitants will demonstrate that the legal treatment of such issues has had and will continue to have a significant impact on the quest for gender equality.

Marital Rape: When a Woman Says "I Do," She Does Not Give Up Her Right to Say "I Won't"

The sanitary stereotype of marital rape depicts rape as a petty conflict—a disagreement over sex that the husband wins.[5] In a scene in the motion picture *Gone with the Wind*, Rhett Butler carries an unwilling Scarlett O'Hara up the stairs to her bedroom. Although the audience does not see what happens next, Scarlett appears the following morning, singing happily and primping before her mirror.[6] The sanitary stereotype, which romanticizes and trivializes marital rape, is belied by studies revealing that when a husband forces his wife to have sex with him, usually he is violent and brutal. Studies have also disclosed a surprising incidence of marital rape. One study, based on interviews with 930 women in San Francisco, found that 14 percent of the women who had ever been married had been raped by a husband or ex-husband.[7] Another inquiry, based on a survey of 323 Boston-area women, noted that 10 percent of the married or previously married women in the sample had said that their husbands had "used physical force or threat to try to have sex with them." That study found that sexual assault by husbands was the most common form of sexual assault that women experience. "Rape by husbands appears to be one of the forms of sexual coercion that a woman is most likely to experience in her lifetime."[8] Moreover, the studies also suggest that the psychological harm of rape is exacerbated when the rapist is the victim's husband: "When you are raped by your husband you [have to] live with your rapist."[9]

Typically rape statutes have provided an exemption for marital rape by specifying that a man commits a rape when he has "sexual intercourse with a female, not his wife, by force and against her will."[10] As recently as the mid-1970s, every state in the United States retained an exemption for a husband from prosecution for forcible rape of his wife.

The marital rape exemption in the United States is based on the common law rule that, as a matter of law, a husband cannot rape his wife. The origin of that rule has been traced to a statement made by Lord Matthew Hale, chief justice of England during the seventeenth century. In a book published posthumously in 1736, Hale wrote: "The husband cannot be guilty of a rape committed by himself upon his lawful wife, for by their mutual matrimonial consent and contract the wife hath given up herself in this kind unto her husband, which she cannot retract."[11] Hale's comments grounded the common law rule in the theory of contract and implied consent.[12]

Another rationale on which the common law rule was based was that women were the property of their husbands. Under that theory, marital rape became legally impossible because a man could not be prosecuted for using his own property. The common law rule was also based on the unity of person concept according to which the legal existence of a woman was suspended during marriage as her legal identity was merged with that of her husband.[13] Because the husband and wife were melded into one legal being, rape in marriage was a legal impossibility; the husband could not rape himself.

Modern developments in the law have undermined the notions on which the common law rule was based and have raised the question of whether the rule retains any validity.[14] Nevertheless, modern courts and commentators have found justifications for retaining the marital rape exemption. These justifications have been based on concerns that the abolition of a husband's immunity would lead to serious abuses of the law, would cause insurmountable evidentiary problems, would lead to fabricated charges, would encourage vindictive wives to use rape charges for revenge, and would thwart the reconciliation of estranged couples.

American courts, seemingly "incapable of conceiving other resolutions of the issue,"[15] adopted the common law rule.[16] For example, in 1905 a Texas court, in a case that involved a couple who had been denied a divorce and thereafter continued to live in the same house but did not share the same bedroom, held that the man could not be convicted of an assault with intent to rape his wife because "after a woman assumes the marriage relation the law will not permit her to retract her consent thus given."[17]

In the mid–1970s, states began to reform their rape statutes to modify and in some cases to eliminate the marital rape exemption, either by legislative action or by judicial decision. By 1986, ten states had abolished the exemption and expressly allowed prosecution for spousal rape under all circumstances.[18] Eleven states permitted prosecution in most cases of husbands who rape their wives during marriage and while living together.[19]

In contrast, twenty-eight states continue to have statutory or case law that prohibits the prosecution of a husband for the rape of his wife.[20] Several states have extended the marital rape exemption to unmarried cohabitants[21] or voluntary social companions.[22] Several states have a partial exemption based on the status of the marriage. A number of these states allow prosecution if the parties were living apart at the time of the incident[23]; others allow prosecution only if the parties at the time of the incident were separated by court order[24] or were living apart and one spouse had filed a petition for annulment, divorce, separation, or separate maintenance.[25] In Alabama, Illinois, and South Dakota, a husband is subject to prosecution for rape only if a final divorce decree existed at the time of the incident. Two states, Arkansas and Mississippi, have not addressed the marital rape exclusion in either statutory or case law.

While state legislatures have been responsible for most of the changes in rape laws, there has also been noteworthy judicial action. In 1978 a highly publicized marital rape case in Oregon—the first case instituted under the state's revised statute that eliminated the exemption—brought the spousal rape issue to the attention of the general public.[26] Greta Rideout accused her husband of raping her after "beating her into submission." There was conflicting testimony, and John Rideout was acquitted.[27] The couple reconciled but later divorced.[28]

The New Jersey courts have rejected the common law rule. In 1977 a trial court considered whether a husband could be prosecuted for raping his wife.[29] The judge held that the common law rule was codified in the rape statute and concluded that he lacked the authority to change that rule.[30] Nevertheless, the judge indicated his disapproval of the exemption:

How can one logically defend the result, that a husband has an unbridled right, protected by law, to force himself sexually upon [his wife] at any time he chooses no matter how far the marriage relationship has deteriorated between them. Truly, society should not suffer such a situation to continue upon so callous a basis as applications of contract law and the doctrine of consent.[31]

That decision was affirmed on appeal.[32] In 1981 the New Jersey Supreme Court held that the common law exemption did not apply when the couple was living apart.[33]

In 1981 the Massachusetts Supreme Judicial Court, relying in part on the New Jersey court's reasoning, interpreted the 1974 revision in the rape statute that deleted the word *unlawful* from the definition of proscribed sexual intercourse. The court found that the intent of the legislature was to eliminate the common law exclusion.[34]

New York's highest court abolished the exemption on constitutional grounds. In 1977, the court of appeals held that the marital rape exemption was an unconstitutional violation of the equal protection clauses of the Fourteenth Amendment and the state constitution. The court found that the distinction in the law based on marital status had no rational basis. Additionally it held that the law violated equal protection because it applied to males who forcibly rape females but exempted females from criminal liability for the forcible rape of males. The court asserted that the distinction between male and female did not meet the requirement that the classification be substantially related to the achievement of an important governmental objective. It found Hale's notion of implied consent irrational and absurd.[35]

In 1985 the Georgia Supreme Court also rejected the common law rule on state constitutional grounds. The common law exemption, the court held, not only violated the state constitution's equal protection clause but also conflicted with statutes regarding rights of personal security and marriage laws. The court concluded that the implied consent theory is "without logical meaning and *obviously conflicts* with our constitutional and statutory laws and our regard for all citizens of this State."[36]

In 1984 the Virginia Supreme Court declined to abandon the marital rape exemption entirely but held in *Weishaupt v. Commonwealth*:

A wife can unilaterally revoke her implied consent to marital sex where, as here, she has made manifest her intent to terminate the marital relationship by living separate and apart from her husband; refraining from voluntary sexual intercourse with her husband; and, in light of all the circumstances, conducting herself in a manner that establishes a de facto end to the marriage.[37]

If the wife revokes her implied consent, the husband can be found guilty of raping her. Six months following that decision, the Virginia high court had the opportunity to apply this reasoning.[38] Edward Kizer broke into his wife's apartment, ripped off her clothes, and beat and raped her. He was convicted of rape and sentenced to twenty years in prison. On appeal, a majority of the supreme court interpreted *Weishaupt* to require that a wife show that she has conducted herself in a manner that makes it clear to her husband that the marriage has ended. The court reversed Kizer's conviction on the basis of its finding that Mrs. Kizer's conduct had been "equivocal, ambivalent, and ambiguous."[39] Thus, according to the Virginia court, although the husband had filed suit to obtain custody of their child, the couple had not engaged in sexual relations for six months, and had lived apart for a month preceding the attack, Edward Kizer might not have been aware that his marriage had been terminated.[40]

Although during the past decade, legislatures and courts have instituted major reforms in the law of marital rape, twenty-eight states still retain the marital rape exemption. During the next few years, it is possible that additional states will be added to the list of those whose legislatures have expressly abolished the marital rape exemption. Where legislatures are reluctant to abandon the exemption, judicial action may bring about changes in the law. When statutes are silent on the exemption, courts may hold, as the New Jersey and Florida courts have done, that the common law rule no longer has any validity.

Activist-oriented state courts may invalidate rape laws that contain express exemptions. Such laws are vulnerable to constitutional challenge on both equal protection and privacy grounds. First, it may be argued that the marital rape exemption violates the equal protection clause of the Fourteenth Amendment, as well as counterpart state constitutional provisions. The exemption distinguishes between married and nonmarried women and denies the former the protection normally provided by the state against bodily violence. A classification based on marital status would be required to bear only the minimum scrutiny implicit in the rational basis test. Nevertheless, a court could easily find, as the New York Court of Appeals has held, that no rational basis exists for such a classification. Second, an equal protection argument could be premised on a fundamental rights analysis. The state, according to such an argument, infringes on the rights of bodily integrity, reproductive freedom, and individual autonomy by refusing to protect married women against rape by their husbands.[41] Third, the marital rape exemption may be challenged on gender discrimination grounds. Even a gender-neutral rape statute that exempts husbands, it may be claimed, constitutes intentional discrimination against women and fails to withstand the intermediate scrutiny required for gender classifications.[42] Gender discrimination arguments should apply with added force in states that have adopted equal rights amendments; courts could readily determine that the exemption violates the state constitutional provision.[43]

The existence of the marital rape exemption in twenty-eight states attests to the fact that women still occupy a subordinate position in American society. True gender equality remains unrealized. The exemption also constitutes a major obstacle to the achievement of equality.

It degrades women by denying them protection against brutal attack and renders the state an accessory to crimes of violence against women.

Property Rights of Unmarried Cohabitants

In the early 1970s, "living together" attracted a great deal of attention as it became increasingly common for young couples, many of whom were middle-class college students, to become involved in live-in relationships.[44] Although estimates of the extent and significance of unmarried cohabitation vary considerably, there is no question that the practice has increased greatly[45] and that, in the 1980s, it is widely accepted among Americans of all ages and classes.[46]

Nonmarital live-in relationships raise significant legal issues, including the question of whether an unmarried cohabitant may bring an action for loss of consortium and whether cohabitation constitutes grounds for termination of alimony from a previous marriage.[47] The property rights of unmarried couples upon separation have posed particularly difficult questions. Courts have been confronted with questions regarding the ability of a surviving partner to make a claim against a deceased partner's estate, how the property of separating partners should be divided, and whether one partner may be required to make support payments to the other.[48]

Traditionally, when unmarried cohabitants took property disputes to court either upon separation or after the death of one partner, judges left the parties as they found them. They deemed agreements between unmarried cohabitants to be unenforceable on the ground that, because sex without marriage was proscribed by fornication statutes, any contract that included an agreement to cohabit was based on an illegal consideration and was therefore illegal.[49] It was widely believed that enforcement of a contract between an unmarried couple would be tantamount to bestowing judicial approval on immoral behavior. Courts refused to acknowledge the contractual rights of unmarried cohabitants in the belief that such recognition would discourage marriage, thus contravening the public policy of promoting and protecting that institution. In part, perhaps, judicial nonrecognition may have been intended to punish people engaged in immoral conduct. The result was that when a couple separated, the man, who commonly held title to property, retained all the property accumulated during a nonmarital relationship.[50] When a man's death ended the relationship, the woman might be deprived of any share of the property; it might be awarded to the man's former wife or his children by that marriage.

The prevalence of the practice of living together among college students during the 1960s and 1970s may have contributed to a widespread belief that unmarried cohabitation offers an alternative life-style where traditional male-female roles are obliterated and where the parties are free to separate at will. In truth, it has been much more common for cohabiting couples to follow conventional patterns of marriage.[51] The woman often performs the duties of homemaking and child raising, while the man takes on the responsibilities of the breadwinner. What is more, the woman may work in her partner's business without salary, or, if employed, she may give her paychecks to her partner. These relationships have commonly been long term, and frequently the couple has had children.[52] The ties established clearly are not based on any notion of alternative life-styles. On the contrary, they approximate traditional marriage.[53] The property accumulated by the couple during the relationship has generally been held in the man's name. Thus, at the end of the relationship, the woman not only may lack a legal right to a share of the property, but she also may be unemployable, or at least she may have severely diminished her earning capacity.[54]

Michelle Triola Marvin and Los Angeles attorney Marvin M. Mitchelson brought the problem of the terminated dependent female cohabitant to the attention of millions of Americans. Michelle and actor Lee Marvin had lived together for seven years. All of the property that the couple had accumulated during this period was placed in Lee Marvin's name; at the time of their separation, the value of the property was estimated at more than $1 million. Lee Marvin was a well-known Hollywood film star; Michelle, who had at one time been an entertainer, had not pursued her career. Instead she had acted as Marvin's companion, homemaker, housekeeper, and cook.

After their relationship had ended, Michelle filed an action alleging that she was entitled to half the property acquired during the relationship and to support payments. The trial court granted judgment on the pleadings for Lee Marvin. An intermediate appellate court affirmed, stating in part that no rights are acquired in "meretricious relationships" without an agreement between the parties and that a contract made in contemplation of such a relationship is contrary to public policy and will not be enforced.[55]

The California Supreme Court reversed, holding that express contracts between unmarried partners are enforceable unless the contract is explicitly and inseparably based on sexual services.[56] Emphasizing that "adults who voluntarily live together and engage in sexual relations are . . . as competent as any other persons to contract respecting their earnings and property rights,"[57] the court also noted that an implied agreement may provide the basis for apportioning property. Additionally, the California court pointed to the possibility of relief on several other grounds.[58]

On remand, the Superior Court of Los Angeles considered the question of whether Michelle and Lee had an express or an implied contract to share property; it found that they had not.[59] Further, the court decided that there had been no mutual effort in the accumulation of property during the relationship. Although Michelle served as cook, homemaker, and companion to Lee, he spent $72,000 on her in less than six years. Moreover, on the occasions when Michelle had earned money, she had deposited it in her own separate account. Nevertheless, taking into account the fact that Michelle would be unable to resume a career in the entertainment industry, the court awarded her $104,000 for the purpose of rehabilitation.[60]

The saga of Michelle Marvin and Lee Marvin captured the attention of the public and introduced the misleading term *palimony* to the vocabulary of many Americans. The California Supreme Court's decision was exaggerated and distorted by the media.[61] The *Marvin* decision in 1976, despite the fanfare, was by no means the first judicial decision in California to recognize the property rights of unmarried cohabitants. In 1932, the California Supreme Court had held that a property agreement between unmarried cohabitants was not invalidated by their agreement to live together so long as the "immoral relation" was not a consideration for the agreement.[62] In 1973, a California appellate court had held that if there was "an actual family relationship with cohabitation and mutual recognition and assumption of all the usual rights, duties, and obligations attending marriage," property would be distributed according to the state's statutory provision for division of community property.[63] The court found support for its decision to divide the property in the state's no-fault divorce statute enacted in 1970. The court's reasoning was followed by one appellate court[64] and rejected by another.[65] It was subsequently set aside by the California Supreme Court in *Marvin*.[66]

By 1976, other states had also begun to recognize property rights of unmarried cohabitants. As early as 1928, the Oregon Supreme Court had noted that a contract to cohabit was valid because it could be carried out without performing any illegal act.[67] In 1976 the Oregon Supreme Court, in *Latham v. Latham*,[68] went further than the California court was to go a year later in *Marvin*. In *Marvin*, the California court held that contracts between unmarried cohabitants are enforceable unless they are based on an agreement for sexual services. Thus, where the contract may have been based in part on an agreement involving sex, if that portion of the agreement is severable from the rest, the contract is enforceable. In *Latham*, the Oregon court declined to use such an approach and held that a contract between unmarried cohabitants was not void as against public policy. In that case, the woman had performed the function of "caring for, keeping after (her partner), and furnishing and providing him all the amenities of married life" in return for half of all the properties accumulated by both parties. The justices found support for their decision in the legislature's repeal of the law proscribing "lewd and lascivious cohabitation."[69]

Courts in Washington also recognized property rights of cohabitating couples many years before the California courts encountered Michelle Marvin and Lee Marvin. The Washington Supreme Court announced in 1948 in *Creasman v. Boyle* the rule that property acquired by a man and a woman not married to each other belongs to the one in whose name the legal title to the property has vested. According to this rule, courts were to presume as a matter of law that the parties had disposed of their property as they had intended.[70] The *Creasman* presumption created an obstacle for the division of property in the absence of an express contract. Nevertheless, the Washington courts ordered the division of cohabitants' property on the basis of theories that were created as exceptions to the rule, such as implied partnership,[71] constructive trust,[72] and resulting trust.[73] In 1957 the Washington Supreme Court upheld a division of property between unmarried cohabitants based on the trial court's determination of the person who owned the property.[74] By the early 1970s, the Washington courts were explicitly questioning the considerably eroded *Creasman* presumption.

A Michigan appellate court in 1973 held that, based on an oral agreement, a woman was entitled to the house held in the name of her deceased cohabitant.[75] The Massachusetts Supreme Judicial Court in 1975 enforced a man's promise to leave a will bequeathing his entire estate to a woman in return for her domestic, social, and business services.[76] A New Hampshire statute provided that cohabitation for the preceding three years would allow the other party to be treated as the decedent's surviving spouse.[77]

In short, *Marvin* was not the first case to hold agreements of unmarried cohabitants to be enforceable. Its importance lay in the fact that it raised the level of awareness of millions of Americans and that it provided a catalog of remedies for cohabitants whose relationships were terminated. In so doing, the *Marvin* case encouraged more litigation, and it contributed to the subsequent development of the law in other states.

By late 1986, a majority of state courts had taken judicial notice of the unusual increase in the number of cohabitating couples and had resolved property disputes based on contract law.[78] Many courts have followed California's example by holding that contracts between unmarried cohabitants are enforceable so long as they are not based on an agreement for sexual services. The most widely used approach has been to order a division of property on the basis of an express contract. Such contracts have almost always consisted of an oral agreement either that the parties will share the property accumulated during a relationship or that the man will take care of the woman if she provides domestic services for him.[79] The New Jersey Supreme Court, at the forefront of the movement, held enforceable a man's oral promise to take care of a woman for the rest of her life.[80] The same court, in a subsequent case, sustained interim support payments ordered by a trial court to a woman after termination of a twenty-year cohabitation.[81] In the final resolution of that case, the New Jersey Supreme Court upheld the transfer of the home to the woman and a lump sum payment based on an annual support figure multiplied by the woman's life expectancy.[82] A number of other states have held express contracts to be enforceable as long as they did not involve compensation for sexual services.[83]

Courts in several jurisdictions have declined to recognize implied agreements and have required an express contract. For example, the New York Court of Appeals in 1980 held that express unwritten contracts between unmarried cohabitants are enforceable, but a contract may not be implied by a live-in arrangement.[84] Courts in Michigan,[85] New Hampshire,[86] and Iowa[87] have adopted the same approach to allocating the assets of unmarried cohabitants.

A number of other state courts have relied on the language of *Marvin* and permitted recovery based on an implied agreement. In 1978, for example, the Oregon Supreme Court ruled that, absent an express agreement, courts should examine the facts to determine the terms to which the parties had implicitly agreed. The court noted that cohabitation itself can be relevant evidence of an agreement to share incomes during continued cohabitation.[88] In 1984, the Nevada Supreme Court held that each case would be considered on its own merits, with consideration given to the purpose, duration, and stability of the relationship and the expectations of the parties. If it is alleged and proved that there was an agreement to acquire and hold property as if the couple had married, the community property laws of the state would apply by analogy.[89] The Mississippi Supreme Court, as recently as 1984, held that policy decisions regarding unmarried cohabitants are best left to the legislative process.[90] But two years later, the Mississippi high court held that courts may order equitable distribution of property jointly accumulated by two parties during cohabitation and that courts may consider domestic services provided by one partner.[91] The Minnesota Supreme Court, following the reasoning of *Marvin*, found an implied contract between an unmarried couple to divide accumulated property on an equal basis.[92]

A few states have continued to follow the traditional reasoning and have refused to recognize contracts between unmarried cohabitants on the ground that such agreements are based on an illegal consideration. The Georgia Supreme Court noted in 1977 that a woman could not recover part of her deceased cohabitant's estate because sexual relations formed part of the consideration for the agreement. She had lived with the decedent for eighteen years, cooked, cleaned, and cared for him, and had contributed money for the purchase of their home.[93] The Illinois Supreme Court in 1979 explicitly rejected the *Marvin* approach and declined to treat the issue of property rights of unmarried cohabitants as one that could be resolved by relying on the law of contracts. Instead, the court asserted, the legal status of unmarried cohabitation raises major public policy questions that should be resolved by the legislature. The Illinois court held that the enforcement of a contract between unmarried cohabitants would contravene public policy.[94] Yet in 1983, an Illinois appellate court allowed a woman to recover a portion of the property that she and her cohabitant had acquired during their relationship on the basis of a constructive trust.[95]

The legal enforcement of contracts between unmarried cohabitants is clearly an improvement over the traditional rule against enforcing such agreements. Nevertheless, the treatment of property disputes between unmarried couples as contract cases raises several problems. Courts that require an express contract as a prerequisite for a division of property create obstacles that may be insurmountable for the people who most need help.[96] Couples who live together usually do not have written contracts; it is more common for the agreement to consist of oral statements such as, "Everything I have is yours," or "I'll always take care of you."[97] Moreover, when the existence of an oral contract is alleged by one party, the other party often denies that such a promise has been made. Thus, actions to divide property at the end of a cohabiting relationship have been characterized as "very difficult contract actions with one person's word against another."[98]

Property division suits are expensive. Few attorneys will accept the cases on a pure contingency basis. Los Angeles attorney Marvin M. Mitchelson, whose services have been in great demand since he represented Michelle Marvin, reportedly charges $250 per hour, a 25 percent contingency, with retainers of $10,000 to $15,000 or more.[99] The cases are extremely time-consuming since the search for evidence of sharing or of an intent to share property requires an extensive examination of the couple's financial records.

The law of contracts treats people who are in unequal positions as though they are equal.[100] Indeed, contract theory has often intensified the exploitation by the wealthy and powerful of the poor and weak.[101] One commentator has argued that freedom of contract is not likely to achieve substantive equality between the sexes, although it is a significant expression of equality of legal capacity. It has been asserted that contract law cannot completely solve the problems of women who perform traditional roles in marriage-like arrangements without the legal protections that marriage offers. The law should take into account gender-related differences in wealth and power.[102]

There is an alternative to the application of contract theory that would facilitate the efforts of dependent cohabitants to obtain a portion of the property accumulated during the relationship and, if needed, to secure continuing support. Instead of requiring a plaintiff to demonstrate the existence of an express or implied contract, courts could examine the behavior of the parties during the relationship. Thus, a long-term, stable relationship—one that functioned like a marriage—during which the participants established a home, created a family environment, raised children, and presented themselves to the community as a couple could be treated as a marriage for the purposes of a division of property.

Grace Blumberg suggested that courts utilize such an approach. She proposed that judges treat cohabitants as married persons for purposes of maintenance, property division, and intestacy. When cohabitation ends in separation rather than death, cohabitation of two or more years' duration or a cohabitation of any duration in which there is a child born to the parties would be treated as comparable to marriage. Where death ends the relationship, a stable cohabitation of any duration ending in the death of one of the parties would be treated as though it were a lawful marriage. According to the scheme, cohabitants could elect to make other arrangements, but these would have to be fair and reasonable or be made with full disclosure of the economic facts. Thus, couples who do not make contracts would not be disadvantaged.[103]

The Washington courts have adopted such an approach to cohabitation. In 1984, an appeals court held that the state law regarding the disposition of property upon dissolution of a marriage should apply where a man and woman have lived together and have established a relationship tantamount to a marital family.[104] The Washington Supreme Court in 1984 overruled the *Creasman* presumption and replaced it with the rule that courts examine the relationship and the property accumulation as the basis for a just and equitable disposition of the property.[105] Washington law provides that one of the factors that courts will take into account in the disposition of marital property is the economic circumstances of each spouse.[106] When such statutory provisions are applied to the disposition of property of unmarried cohabitants in the absence of a written contract, the dependent partner will not have to assume the burden of convincing the court that there was an implied contract to share the property.[107]

No court has relied on either state or federal constitutional provisions in considering the property rights of unmarried cohabitants. Although laws that treat unmarried cohabitants differently from married couples have the effect of disadvantaging women, they actually classify on the basis of marital status rather than sex. Thus, if such laws are challenged on the basis of either state equal rights amendments or state or federal equal protection clauses, courts are likely to use only a rational basis test and to find no constitutional violation. Marvin Mitchelson reputedly hopes to raise the constitutional issues in the U.S. Supreme Court by challenging the Illinois law. He argues that couples have a constitutional equal protection right to contract for services.[108]

The case law strongly suggests that courts are becoming increasingly aware of the problems of the dependent terminated partner—usually the woman. The courts that have held agreements between cohabitants to be enforceable have expressed their concern that the parties be treated fairly and that property be divided equitably.[109] The Washington courts have gone further, holding that relationships approximating marriage will be treated in the same way as a formal marriage. They have demonstrated even greater sensitivity to the problems that arise at the end of such relationships. Legal recognition of unmarried cohabitation not only protects the dependent partner in a conventional relationship that approximates marriage; it also offers to couples who have less traditional relationships more choices in working out their private arrangements. Consequently, a professional couple may agree to live together and keep their respective property entirely separate. In short, legal recognition of unmarried cohabitation will offer couples increased freedom in structuring their relationships.

Conclusion

The marital rape exemption, based on seventeenth-century views of women and marriage, permits women to be brutalized by their husbands. Judicial refusal to enforce agreements between unmarried cohabitants, based on notions of protecting the institution of marriage and discouraging immoral behavior, commonly leaves women destitute.

That some states have abolished the marital rape exemption and that some have begun to recognize property agreements between unmarried cohabitants suggest that legislators and judges are becoming increasingly aware that the traditional rules both reflect and perpetuate unacceptable inequality between men and women. In the future, more judges may be willing to use federal or state constitutional provisions to justify abandoning the traditional rules. Both the marital rape exemption and the laws that treat unmarried cohabitants differently from married couples arguably violate the equal protection clause of the Fourteenth Amendment.

It may be more prudent, however, for courts to rely on equal protection provisions in their own constitutions and thereby move beyond federal equal protection.[110] If state courts cite state rather than federal constitutional provisions, they will have the opportunity to develop doctrines that will reflect greater sensitivity to equality issues than the doctrines formulated by the U.S. Supreme Court.[111] Moreover, if state courts rely on their own constitutions, they can avoid review and possible reversal by the U.S. Supreme Court.[112]

Judges in states that have adopted equal rights amendments may find that the traditional rules regarding both marital rape and the rights of unmarried cohabitants violate such state constitutional provisions.[113] Relying on state equal rights amendments to invalidate the traditional rules would give courts an opportunity to develop their own constitutional doctrines independently of any federal rules. On the other hand, courts that base their decisions on equal protection grounds may find it difficult to justify departures from federal equal protection.[114] Thus, where possible, courts may find it preferable to refer to state equal rights amendments rather than state or federal equal protection clauses.

Legal developments regarding marital rape and the property rights of unmarried cohabitants suggest that courts in a number of states are beginning to realize the necessity of extending the law to the private sphere.[115] The two spheres, public and private, do not really exist separately. In order for authentic gender equality to become a reality, women must gain control over their private lives. This will be possible only when legislators and judges fully recognize the extent of the inequalities that currently exist.

Notes

1. Bradwell v. Illinois, 16 Wall. 130 (1873); Minor v. Happersett, 21 Wall. 162 (1875); Hoyt v. Florida, 368 U.S. 57 (1961).

2. See, for example, Nadine Taub and Elizabeth M. Schneider, "Perspectives on Women's Subordination and the Role of Law," in David Kairys, ed., *The Politics of Law: A Progressive Critique* (New York: Pantheon Books, 1982); and Catharine A. MacKinnon, "Feminism, Marxism, Method, and the State: Toward Feminist Jurisprudence," *Signs*, 8 (1983): 656–57.

3. Comment, "To Have and to Hold: The Marital Rape Exemption and the Fourteenth Amendment," *Harvard Law Review* 99 (1986): 1258.

4. The courts, in a sense, did become involved in the private sphere when they purported to encourage and protect marriage and to punish immoral behavior by refusing to enforce property agreements between unmarried cohabitants.

5. This subtitle was adapted from the question, "When a woman says I do, does she give up her right to say I won't?" Griffin, "In 44 States, It's Legal to Rape Your Wife,"21 *Student Lawyer*, as quoted in Warren v. State, 336 S.E.2d 221, 222, note 1 (Ga. 1985).

6. The term *sanitary stereotype* and the scene from *Gone with the Wind* were found in David Finkelhor and Kersti Yllo, *License to Rape* (New York: Holt, Rinehart, and Winston, 1985).

7. Diana E. H. Russell, *Rape in Marriage* (New York: Collier Books, 1982).

8. Id., p. 7. See also Irene Hanson Frieze, "Investigating the Causes and Consequences of Marital Rape," *Signs* 8 (1983): 532–53.

9. David Finkelhor, "Marital Rape: The Misunderstood Crime" (address to the New York County Lawyer's Association, May 3, 1984), quoted in Comment, "To Have and to Hold," p. 1262.

10. Illinois Annotated Statutes. Ch. 38, sec. 11–1 (1977).

11. 1 Hale, *History of Pleas of the Crown* 290, quoted in People v. Liberta, 474 N.E.2d 567 (N.Y. 1984). Hale also stated, "But of all the difficulties in evidence, there are two sorts of crimes that give the greatest difficulty, namely rapes and witchcraft." Smith v. State, 77 Ga. 705, 712 (1886), quoting Lord Hale, *Pleas of the Crown* 290, quoted in Warren v. State, 336 S.E.2d 221, 223 note 6 (Ga. 1985). Hale reputedly "made a name for himself by presiding over 'witch' trials and leading juries to convictions over enormous odds." He has been characterized as a misogynist. Gilbert Geis, "Rape in Marriage: Law and Law Reform in England, the United States, and Sweden," *Adelaide Law Review* 6 (1978): 285.

12. There was actually some basis for such a statement in early English law. An alleged rapist could avoid punishment if the victim consented to marry him; thus, the marriage relationship excluded the possibility of rape. On the other hand, it has been noted that Hale cited no authority to support his statement and that there was some authority that pointed in the other direction. In a case in 1631, a man was convicted of raping his wife, and the court stated that "she may have the peace against her husband." Michael D. A. Freeman, " 'But If You Can't Rape Your Wife, Who[m] Can You Rape?': The Marital Rape Exemption Re-examined," *Family Law Quarterly* 15 (1982): 10.

13. Blackstone stated in 1765: "The very being or legal existence of the woman is suspended during marriage, or at least is incorporated and consolidated into that of the husband." 1 W. Blackstone, *Commentaries* 442, quoted in Comment, "The Marital Rape Exemption: Legal Sanction of Spouse Abuse," *Journal of Family Law* 18 (1979–1980): 569, note 21.

14. Married women's property acts, which were passed in every state in the nineteenth century, gave married women separate legal identities and enabled them to make contracts, acquire, hold, and convey property, and sue and be sued with full legal capacity, and effectively demolished the unity of person theory. The appropriateness of contract law and the theory of implied consent in the context of marital rape has also been seriously undermined. There have been no holdings outside the context of the rape laws that indicate that unlimited sexual intercourse is an implied element of marriage. Commentators have noted that excessive sexual demands have been the bases for divorces granted on grounds of cruelty or indignities to the person. See Note, "The Marital Rape Exemption," *New York University Law Review* 52 (1977): 306–23.

15. Geis, "Rape in Marriage," p. 292.

16. The case law is replete with references to Hale. The modern cases are cited infra. Nearly all of these cases refer to Hale as the originator of the common law rule.

17. 86 S.W. 754 (Tex. 1905).

18. Eight state legislatures have rejected the marital rape exemption: Florida, Kansas, Massachusetts, Nebraska, New Jersey, Oregon, Vermont, and Wisconsin. New York removed its marital rape exemption through judicial action, People v. Liberta, 474 N.E.2d 567 (N.Y. 1984). The Georgia Supreme Court has held

that its rape statute, which is silent on marital rape, does not implicitly incorporate the common law exemption, Warren v. State, 336 S.E.2d 221 (Ga. 1985).

19. For example, California, Connecticut, Delaware, Hawaii, Iowa, Ohio, Minnesota, New Hampshire, Pennsylvania, Washington, West Virginia, and Wyoming.

20. Alabama, Alaska, Arizona, Colorado, Idaho, Illinois, Indiana, Kentucky, Louisiana, Maine, Maryland, Michigan, Missouri, Montana, Nevada, New Mexico, North Carolina, North Dakota, Ohio, Oklahoma, Rhode Island, South Carolina, South Dakota, Tennessee, Texas, Utah, Vermont, and Virginia.

21. Alabama, Connecticut, Delaware, Hawaii, Iowa, Kentucky, Maine, Minnesota, Montana, North Dakota, Pennsylvania, and West Virginia.

22. Delaware, Hawaii, and Maine.

23. Arizona, Colorado, Maine, Mississippi, and Montana.

24. Kentucky, Louisiana, Maryland, Missouri, North Carolina, North Dakota, Rhode Island, South Carolina, and Utah.

25. Indiana, Nevada, Ohio, Tennessee, Idaho, New Mexico, Oklahoma, and Texas.

26. "Until ... [the *Rideout* case] there was little discussion of marital rape by the general public or by researchers and counselors skilled in dealing with other types of rape cases." Frieze, "Investigating," p. 532. This case is noteworthy for that reason only since it did not involve any new legal developments.

27. State v. Rideout, No. 108,866 (Marion County Cir. Ct., Or., Dec. 27, 1978).

28. Diana E. H. Russell reported that, as of 1981, at least forty-seven husbands had been charged with raping their wives, and of the twenty-three cases that had come to trial, nineteen resulted in convictions. *Rape in Marriage*, p. 22.

29. State v. Smith, 372 A.2d 386 (N.J. 1977).

30. In 1977 New Jersey's rape statute contained no express immunity for husbands but had been construed to include the common law exemption.

31. 372 A.2d 386, 393.

32. 404 A.2d 331 (N.J. 1979).

33. State v. Smith, 426 A. 2d 38 (N.J. 1981). See also State v. Morrison, 426 A.2d 47 (N.J. 1981). The legislature abolished the marital rape exemption in 1979, but in these two cases the court construed the law as it was prior to the revision.

34. "Unlawful" sexual intercourse meant intercourse with a woman not the man's wife; thus, the deletion of the word amounted to an elimination of the common law exemption. Commonwealth v. Chretien, 417 N.E.2d 1203 (Mass. 1981).

35. People v. Liberta, 474 N.E.2d 587 (N.Y. 1984). Earlier in People v. DeStefano, 467 N.Y.S.2d 506 (Co. Ct. 1983), the Suffolk County Court held the New York rape statute unconstitutional on state and federal equal protection grounds.

36. Warren v. State, 336 S.E.2d 221, 224–25 (Ga. 1985), emphasis in original. See also State v. Rider, 449 So.2d 903 (Fla. 1984). The Florida appellate court held that a spouse may be prosecuted for sexual battery on the other spouse and that there has never been a common law exemption to marital rape in Florida. See also State v. Smith, 401 So.2d 1126 (Fla. 1981).

37. 315 S.E.2d 847, 855 (Va. 1984).

38. Kizer v. Commonwealth, 321 S.E.2d 291 (Va. 1984).

39. Id. at 294.

40. In March 1986, the Virginia General Assembly passed a bill that criminalizes forcible rape between spouses, disregards the sex of the offender, and appears to eliminate the "de facto end to the marriage" test used in *Kizer.* The bill, however, provides for less punishment in cases where the spouses were living together and were there was no serious physical injury. See Comment, "Sexism and the Common Law: Spousal Rape in Virginia," *George Mason Law Review* 8 (1986): 385–86.

41. See, for example, Thomas K. Clancy, "Equal Protection Considerations of the Spousal Sexual Assault Exclusion," *New England Law Review* 16 (1980): 1–31. See also Comment, "Abolishing the Marital Exemption for Rape: A Statutory Proposal," *University of Illinois Law Review* (1983): 201–28; Comment, "To Have and to Hold."

42. See Comment, "To Have and to Hold."

43. The states with equal rights amendments are: Alaska (1972), Colorado (1972), Connecticut (1974), Hawaii (1972), Illinois (1971), Maryland (1972), Massachusetts (1976), Montana (1973), New Hampshire (1975), New Mexico (1973), Pennsylvania (1971), Texas (1972), Utah (1896), Virginia (1971), Washington (1972), and Wyoming (1980). Louisiana's constitution provides that "no law shall arbitrarily, capriciously, or unreasonably discriminate" on the basis of sex (1974).

44. The label *unmarried cohabitants* is used here to refer to couples who live together, have a sexual relationship, and who may or may not present themselves as husband and wife. It does not include common law marriage, which is still recognized in a few states. Additionally, unmarried cohabitation does not include putative marriage, a relationship in which one cohabits with another in the good-faith belief that he or she is married to that person. Various other terms have been used to refer to unmarried cohabitation: *meretricious marriage, companionate marriage, new marriage,* and *de facto marriage.* Recently the Washington Supreme Court used the term *CUPOS* ("cohabiting unmarried people of the opposite sex"). A prominent constitutional scholar referred to a partner in a nonmarital relationship as a "spice." *Unmarried cohabitants* is the term used throughout this chapter.

45. Cohabitation was previously common among the lower class, but when large numbers of middle-class couples began to live together without marriage, the practice became more socially acceptable. Mary Ann Glendon noted in 1976: "Most informal marriages in the recent past in the United States have been confined to intellectual elites and to . . . the 'neglected groups' of the law—those subcultures of the poor, racial and ethnic minorities for whom the structures of traditional marriage and divorce law sometimes have been irrelevant and with whom the framers of such laws were rarely concerned." "The Withering Away of Marriage," *Virginia Law Review* (1976): 685–86. See also "Living Together," *Newsweek,* August 1, 1977, p. 46.

46. It was estimated in 1976 that 6 million to 8 million people were involved in unmarried cohabitation arrangements. *Boston Globe,* May 27, 1976, p. 2. The actual number of cohabitants may be higher than the statistics reveal because a large number of people may not want anyone to know of their living arrange-

ments. Andrew J. Cherlin noted, "We have only the barest national statistics on its prevalence." *Marriage, Divorce, Remarriage* (Cambridge: Harvard University Press, 1981), p. 15.

47. See Grace Ganz Blumberg, "Cohabitation without Marriage: A Different Perspective," *UCLA Law Review* 28 (1981): 1125–80, for an examination of the rights of cohabitants in the areas of workers' compensation, social security, an ex-spouse's duty to pay spousal support when the recipient is cohabitating with another, public assistance, and income taxation.

48. Although support payments to terminated cohabitants have been commonly referred to as *palimony*, that term is not used here.

49. It has been noted, however, that "although a contract may be illegal, it does not follow that it is illegal or immoral for the parties to it, after its completion, to fairly settle and adjust the profits and losses which have resulted from it. The vice of the contract does not enter into such settlement." *Mitchell v. Fish*, 97 Ark. 444, 448 134 S.W. 940, 941–2 (1911), quoting *DeLeon v. Trevino Bro.*, 49 Tex. 88, 30 Am Rep. 101 (1878)." Quoted in Carol S. Bruch, "Property Rights of De Facto Spouses Including Thoughts on the Value of Homemakers' Services," *Family Law Quarterly* 10 (1976): 107 note 1.

50. For example, the Arizona Supreme Court in 1953 held that a woman who had lived with a man for more than thirty years was not entitled to a share of his property upon his death: "We cannot establish the precedent of assisting those who deliberately chose to substitute illegal cohabitation for lawful wedlock, especially when the only basis for such assistance is the mere fact that they have chosen such a status. To do so would be the equivalent of giving legal sanction to illegal practice." Stevens v. Anderson, 256 P.2d 712, 715 (Ariz. 1953). See also Creasman v. Boyle, 196 P.2d 835, 839 (Wash. 1948): the court "will leave the parties where it finds them with respect to their property rights."

51. "An increasing number of unmarried cohabitation relationships functionally resemble a marriage." J. Thomas Oldham and David S. Caudill, "A Reconnaissance of Public Policy: Restrictions upon Enforcement of Contracts between Cohabitants," *Family Law Quarterly* 18 (1984): 94.

52. Blumberg, "Cohabitation," p. 1168, asserted: "In most reported cases, the woman wanted to marry and was economically powerless. The man was domineering and economically powerful. The relationship was long and traditional in terms of sex stereotyped role assumption. The woman took the man's name and often bore his children." The cases to which Blumberg referred, those decided prior to 1981, do not differ from those decided since. I found that the same patterns continue to prevail.

53. People choose cohabitation for a variety of reasons, including the desire to try the relationship before making a more serious commitment, to avoid permanent commitments, or because they are unable to dissolve a prior marriage legally. In addition, couples may decide not to marry in order to prevent the application of the community property system or the loss of currently held economic benefits.

54. For example, in Crowe v. DeGioia, 447 A.2d 173 (1982), the woman had kept house for a man for over twenty years. The court noted that when they separated, she was in her sixties and in poor health; he had married a younger woman. He claimed that he had never actually lived with her, although the house

where she lived and raised her seven children belonged to him, a claim the trial court rejected.

55. Marvin v. Marvin, 2d Civil No. 44359 (Cal. Ct. App. July 23, 1975).

56. Marvin v. Marvin, 134 Cal. Rptr. 815 (1976). The court firmly rejected the traditional view that if any part of the consideration for an agreement is based on sexual relations, the entire agreement must fail. Indeed it implied that only agreements for prostitution would be unenforceable: "Of course, they cannot lawfully contract to pay for the performance of sexual services, for such a contract is, in essence, an agreement for prostitution and unlawful for that reason." 134 Cal. Rptr. 815, 825.

57. Id. 134 Cal. Rptr. 815, 825.

58. In addition to express and implied contract, the California Supreme Court noted the existence of remedies based on partnership or joint venture, constructive trust, resulting trust, and quantum meruit for reasonable value of household services rendered less the support received where it is shown that services were rendered with the exception of monetary award. Id., 134 Cal. Rptr. 815, 832.

59. Marvin v. Marvin, 5 F.L.R. 3077, Superior Court, Los Angeles, Memorandum Opinion, April 18, 1979.

60. $104,000 was equivalent to the highest scale that she had ever earned as a singer, $1,000 per week, for two years. The award was subsequently overturned by an intermediate appellate court, which found that the award was not within the issues framed by the pleadings. Marvin v. Marvin, 176 Cal. Rptr. 555 (Cal. 1981).

61. The decision may have been understood by many as establishing the rule that unmarried couples living together had the right to share property if and when they separated.

62. Trutalli v. Meraviglia, 12 P.2d 430 (Cal. 1932). But see Hill v. Estate of Westbrook, 247 P.2d 19 (Cal. 1952), in which a woman who alleged that she had provided services that included keeping house and living with a man "as man and wife" lost her case when on remand from the supreme court the trial court held that her services had been made in consideration of the "meretricious relationship."

63. In re Marriage of Cary, 109 Cal. Rptr. 862, 867 (Cal. 1973). The other states that use community property as the basis for distribution of marital property, in addition to California, are Arizona, Idaho, Louisiana, Nevada, New Mexico, Texas, and Washington. The problem with the court's reasoning in Cary was that it could be used only in those states. Arguably, a broader principle—that a stable relationship be treated as a marriage—could be drawn from the reasoning.

64. Estate of Atherley, 119 Cal. Rptr. 41 (Cal. 1975).

65. Beckman v. Mayhew, 122 Cal. Rptr. 604 (Cal. 1975).

66. See Note, "In Re Cary: A Judicial Recognition of Illicit Cohabitation," *Hastings Law Journal* 25 (1974): 1226–1247; and Herma Hill Kay and Carol Amyx, "*Marvin v Marvin*: Preserving the Options," *California Law Review* 65 (1977): 937–77, for a review of the case law in California prior to *Marvin*.

67 Traver v. Naylor, 268 P. 75 (Or. 1928).

68. Latham v. Latham, 547 P.2d 144 (Or. 1976).

69. Id.

70. Creasman v. Boyle, 196 P.2d 835 (Wash. 1948).

71. Estate of Thornton, 499 P.2d 864 (Wash. 1972).

72. Humphries v. Riveland, 407 P.2d 967 (Wash. 1965); Omer v. Omer, 523 P.2d 957 (Wash. 1974).

73. Walberg v. Mattson, 232 P.2d 827 (Wash. 1951).

74. West v. Knowles, 311 P.2d 689 (Wash. 1957).

75. Tyranski v. Piggins, 205 N.W.2d 595 (Mich. 1973)

76. Green v. Richmond, 337 N.E.2d 691 (Mass. 1975).

77. N.H. Rev. Stat. Ann., Section 457:39 (1968).

78. It was reported that in 1986, thirty-eight states recognized the validity of contracts between cohabitants and in varying degrees had begun to become involved in securing the equitable distribution of property accumulated during live-in relationships. Mary Ann Galante, "Courts Not Wed to 'Palimony,' " *National Law Journal*, July 14, 1986, p. 18. Division of the property of unmarried cohabitants has also been ordered by courts in several states based on resulting, constructive, or express trust. See, for example, Albae v. Harbin, 30 So.2d 459 (Ala. 1947), Ross v. Sampson, 166 S.E.2d 499 (N.C. 1969), and Cluck v. Sheets, 171 S.W.2d 860 (Tex. 1943).

79. Courts in the following states enforced express oral agreements: Florida (Poe v. Estate of Levy, 411 So.2d 253 [Fla. 1982]), Maryland (Donovan v. Scuderi, 443 A.2d 121 [Md. 1982]), but see Baxter v. Wilburn, 190 A. 773 [Md. 1937], and Boyles v. Boyles, 6 F.L.R. 2378 [Md. 1979], Michigan (Carnes v. Sheldon, 311 N.W.2d 747 [Mich. 1981]), Nebraska (Kinkenon v. Hue, 310 N.W.2d 77 [Neb. 1981]), New Jersey (Kozlowski v. Kozlowski, 403 A.2d 902 [N.J. 1979]), and New York (Morone v. Morone, 413 N.E.2d 1154 [N.Y. 1980]).

80. Kozlowski v. Kozlowski, 403 A.2d 902 (N.J. 1979).

81. Crowe v. De Gioia, 447 A.2d 173 (N.J. 1982).

82. Crowe v. De Gioia, 505 A.2d 591 (N.J. 1986).

83. Florida (Poe v. Estate of Levy, 411 So. 253 [Fla. 1982]), Donovan v. Scuderi, 443 A.2d 121 [Md. 1982]), Nebraska (Kinkenon v. Hue, 301 N.W.2d 77 [Neb. 1981]), New Mexico (Dominguez v. Cruz, 617 P.2d 1322 [N.M. 1980]), Pennsylvania (Mullen v. Suchko, 421 A.2d 310 [Pa. 1980]; Knauer v. Knauer, 470 A.2d 553 [Pa. 1983]), Wyoming (Kinnison v. Kinnison, 627 P.2d 594 [Wyo. 1981]), New Hampshire (Joan S. v. John S., 427 A.2d 498 [N.H. 1981]) and Alaska (Levar v. Elkins, 604 P.2d 602 ([Alas. 1980]).

84. Morone v. Morone, 413 N.E.2d 1154 (N.Y. 1980).

85. Carnes v. Sheldon, 311 N.W.2d 747 (Mich. 1981).

86. Tapley v. Tapley, 449 A.2d 1218 (N.H. 1982).

87. Slocum v. Hammond, 346 N.W.2d 485 (Iowa 1984).

88. Beal v. Beal, 577 P.2d 507 (Or. 1978).

89. Hay v. Hay, 678 P.2d 672 (Nev. 1984).

90. In re Estate of Alexander, 445 So.2d 836 (Miss. 1984).

91. Pickens v. Pickens, 12 F.L.R. 1145 (Miss. 1986). Other states that have recognized implied contracts are Indiana (Glasgo v. Glasgo, 410 N.E.2d 1325 [Ind. 1980]), Wisconsin (Matter of estate of Steffes, 290 N.W.2d 697 [Wis. 1980]), Arizona (Cook v. Cook, 691 P.2d 664 [Ariz. 1984]), and Carroll v. Lee, 712 P.2d 923 [Ariz. 1986], holding that implied agreement between unmarried cohabitants with an agreement that consisted of homemaking services for monetary support

during the relationship was limited to where the property was titled jointly),
Hawaii (Artiss v. Artiss, 8 F.L.R. 2313 [Hawaii 1982]), and Kansas (Eaton v.
Johnston, 672 P.2d 10 [Kan. 1983]). A California appeals court found an implied
agreement between an unmarried couple to own and divide property equally
where the couple had purchased the home and landscaped and decorated it,
although the woman had not actually lived there (Milian v. Sanchez, 226 Cal.
Rptr. 831 [Cal. 1986]).

92. Carlson v. Olson, 256 N.W.2d 249 (Minn. 1977). In 1980 the Minnesota
legislature passed a statute providing that such contracts are enforceable only if
they are written and signed by the parties. Minn. Stat. Sec. 513.075, 513.076.
See Tourville v. Kowarsch, 365 N.W.2d 198 (Minn. 1985), Hollom v. Carey, 343
N.W.2d 701 (Minn. 1984) for a decision subsequent to the enactment of the
legislation. But see In re estate of Eriksen, 337 N.W.2d 671 (Minn.1983) holding
that the law does not apply in a case in which a woman was seeking half-interest
in a house on which she had shared mortgage payments.

93. Rehak v. Mathis, 238 S.E.2d 81 (Ga. 1977).

94. Hewitt v. Hewitt, 394 N.E.2d 1204 (Ill. 1979). The Illinois court construed the Illinois Marriage and Dissolution of Marriage Act to disfavor the
rights of unmarried cohabitants and cited the legislature's rejection of no-fault
divorce as further evidence of public policy in favor of traditional marriage.

95. Spafford v. Coats, 455 N.E.2d 241 (Ill. 1983). A Louisiana appellate
court held that the fact that the parties had a financial arrangement whereby
the man had paid certain household expenses and the woman had paid others
was insufficient to imply the existence of a contract between the parties concerning home ownership. Lacour v. Theard, 439 So.2d 1127 (La. 1983).

96. A family law expert in a Newark, New Jersey, firm stated that his office
rejects 90 percent of the twenty or more inquiries that it receives each year:
"Most live together about three years. She makes $20,000 and he makes $50,000.
... We tell them they don't stand a chance.... It's got to be a great disparity and
a long time ... like 20 years, he's got 3 million bucks and she's been left without
a penny." Quoted in Galante, "Courts Not Wed," p. 18.

97. Blumberg, "Cohabitation," p. 1164, noted that American case law did
not reveal one formally executed contract.

98. Quoted in Galante, "Courts Not Wed," p. 18.

99. Id.

100. See, for example, Lochner v. New York, 198 U.S. 45 (1905).

101. But, as Blumberg, "Cohabitation," p. 1161, pointed out, in domestic
relations contract is heralded as a harbinger of freedom of choice, mobility, and
economic well-being: "This is because domestic relations is a developmentally
retarded field. The status disabilities of married women were abandoned centuries after those of serfs. Formal legal economic equality between the sexes has
been attained only in the last two decades. (Actual economic and social equality
is a distant and perhaps unrealizable goal.)"

102. Id. Blumberg went on to explain:

In general, the essence of a cohabitation or marriage contract between heterosexual cohabitants is that the man gives up wealth that would otherwise accrue to him in order to
insure the woman some semblance of economic dignity. Self-interest would lead the man
to give up as little as possible. The woman has scant leverage with which to persuade him

otherwise. She lacks economic power. She needs a stable relationship more than he does: it is vital to the comfortable exercise of her reproductive potential, and it is a means of enhancing her wealth and standard of living. For a male, on the other hand, marriage or stable cohabitation is likely to diminish both his personal wealth and his standard of living. Even a feminist must agree that there is ample economic and biological basis of Midge Decter's assertion that "marriage is something asked by women and agreed to by men." Thus, the cohabitants' unequal bargaining power leads to unjust results under contract theory. (P. 1163)

103. Id., pp. 1166–67.

104. Warden v. Warden, 10 F.L.R. 1259 (Wash. 1984).

105. Marriage of Lindsey, 678 P.2d 328 (Wash. 1984).

106. 26.09.080, Revised Code of Washington Annotated.

107. A California appeals court adopted the same approach when it held that an unmarried cohabitant may bring an action for loss of consortium by showing that the relationship is stable and significant. Stability and significance could be established by duration of the relationship, mutual contract, degree of economic cooperation and entanglement, exclusivity of sexual relationships, and family relationship with children. Butcher v. Superior Court of Orange County, 188 Cal. Rptr. 503 (Cal. 1983). Another appeals court in California rejected that approach, however, objecting that the definition of stable and significant invites "michief and inconsistent results." Ledger v. Tippitt, 210 Cal. Rptr. 814 (Cal. 1985).

108. Galante, "Courts Not Wed," p. 180.

109. The Nevada Supreme Court, for example, stated, "We recognize that the state has a strong public policy interest in encouraging legal marriage. We do not, however, believe that policy is well served by allowing one participant in a meretricious relationship to abscond with the bulk of the couple's acquisitions." Hay v. Hay, 678 P.2d 672, 674 (Nev. 1984).

110. See, for example, William J. Brennan, "State Constitutions and the Protection of Individual Rights," Harvard Law Review 90 (1977): 503; Hans A. Linde, "First Things First: Rediscovering the States' Bills of Rights," University of Baltimore Law Review 9 (1980): 379–96; "Developments in the Law: The Interpretation of State Constitutional Rights," Harvard Law Review 95 (1982): 1359.

111. See, for example, Michael M. v. Superior Court, 450 U.S. 464 (1984), and Rostker v. Goldberg, 453 U.S. 57 (1981).

112. Under the independent and adequate state grounds doctrine, the Supreme Court will not review state court decisions based clearly on state constitutional provisions—see Herb v. Pitcairn, 324 U.S. 117, 125 (1945)—but courts must make it clear that they are relying on their own constitutions. Michigan v. Long, 463 U.S. 1032 (1983).

113. But see G. Alan Tarr and Mary Cornelia Porter, "Gender Equality and Judicial Federalism: The Role of State Appellate Courts," Hastings Constitutional Law Quarterly 9 (1982): 919–73. The authors reviewed cases involving gender discrimination in interscholastic athletics, recovery for loss of consortium, and child custody. They found that only a few states, notably Pennsylvania, Illinois, Massachusetts, Texas, and Washington, have used their equal rights amendments to provide broad protection against sex discrimination and concluded that ex-

plicit bans against sex discrimination do not in themselves guarantee greater protection.

114. See, for example, Sue Davis and Taunya Lovell Banks, "State Constitutions, Freedom of Expression and Search and Seizure: Prospects for State Court Reincarnation," *Publius: The Journal of Federalism* 17, no. 1 (Winter 1987): 13–32. A survey of the case law in ten states demonstrated that most state high courts are reluctant to develop their own state constitutional jurisprudence.

115. Illinois has clearly refused to extend the law to the private realm by refusing to enforce agreements between unmarried cohabitants and by retaining the marital rape exemption.

4

Personal Autonomy and the Limits of State Authority

MARY CORNELIA PORTER with ROBYN MARY O'NEILL

The word *autonomy* has a universalistic connotation, but definitions vary. For purposes of this chapter, we draw upon Laurence Tribe's concept of the "rights of privacy and personhood" and employ his categories of "fundamental" rights. "Privacy," according to Professor Tribe, concerns the "values and activities courts have thought worthy of protection under a wide variety of names but with a single aim: preservation of those attributes of an individual which are irreducible in his selfhood." "Personhood' (like 'autonomy,' 'intimacy,' 'identity,' and 'dignity') is a word thrust into a social and political vacuum to define some reasonable limits on the state's power to shape the behavior of individuals and groups, whether by controlling the experiences available to them or by regulating the experiences with which their choices confront others."

Granting the "gravity or difficulty" of "defining substantive" rights of personhood, Professor Tribe holds that the "location" of a "specific regulatory setting," the state's purpose in imposing certain values and restricting certain activities, and "the nature of the right asserted and the way in which it is brought into play" are "crucial." What Tribe calls the "points of intersection between personhood and law" must be examined "not simply on the aspect of self thought to be at stake but on the way in which government appears to be usurping it."[1]

This chapter examines state judicial responses to "governmental invasion of personality" in regard to the applicable issues that Tribe enumerates. Before proceeding, however, it is necessary to review the U.S. Supreme Court's responses to privacy and personhood claims, which have set the tone for state judiciaries and which establish the contexts of state judicial concern with human rights.

Privacy, Personhood, and the U.S. Supreme Court

The U.S. Supreme Court has recognized the notion of personhood as a basic constitutional value. The sources of the resulting complex of rights may be found in the "liberty" protected by the due process clauses of the Fifth and Fourteenth amendments, in the Ninth Amendment, and in the privileges and immunities clauses of Article IV and of the Fourteenth Amendment.[2]

The lineage of what might be called metaconstitutional rights is traceable to the 1920s when the Court carved out, as described and iterated in later cases, "a private realm of family life which the state cannot enter."[3] But it was not until the 1960s and 1970s that the Court declared that the Constitution guarantees a substantive "right to privacy" capacious enough to ensure that an individual's choices concerning marriage, marital relations, and procreation are no business of the state.[4] And while other constitutional provisions have been utilized, as Professor Tribe aptly notes, to "establish the autonomy principle," to determine the "roles" which the Constitution allocates to the private and the public realms,[5] it is the right to privacy that has become something of a catch-all for the rights we consider as "human."

A cluster of the privacy-personhood cases, however the Court might have sought to limit their reach (the right of married couples to make intimate decisions about procreation, the right of a woman to control her own body, the right of the unmarried and minors to have the same access to contraceptives as that afforded the married and adults), pointed to a right to sexual privacy whatever the relationships of the partners and whatever the sexual practices.[6] Apparently confident that the Court would continue to broaden the right to sexual autonomy under one constitutional rubric or another, two state criminal sodomy statutes were challenged by homosexuals either not directly threatened by prosecution or against whom charges were hastily dropped. Their confidence was misplaced. In 1976 in *Doe v. Commonwealth*,[7] the Court summarily affirmed a lower court's determination that Virginia's criminal sodomy statute had passed constitutional muster. Ten years later, speculation that the summary affirmance was of doubious precedential value to the contrary, the Court, in *Bowers v. Hardwick*,[8] narrowly sustained a similar Georgia law. The majority, it seemed, was reluctant to invite the sort of controversy that greeted and continued to rage fourteen years after the abortion rulings.[9] *Hardwick* gives fair warning that the Court's long-standing concern with the metaconstitutional rights of privacy and personhood may well not survive the Reagan judiciary in general and the

Rehnquist Court in particular.[10] As is the case for those constitutional rights, particularly the protections of the accused, deemed to have been eroded by the Burger Court, the rights of privacy and personhood must, in all likelihood, seek whatever haven there may be in state courts.

State Judiciaries: Civil Liberties and the New Judicial Federalism

Historically, state courts have been little concerned with civil liberties. Indeed, the U.S. Supreme Court's "nationalization" of the federal Bill of Rights, which began in the 1930s and accelerated during the Warren Court years, marks what many consider to have been a necessary intervention. On the other hand, in nonconstitutional cases, the types that seldom reach federal courts—workers' compensation and products liability, for example—state courts have become increasingly "concerned with the individual and downtrodden," becoming "more willing to consider rulings that promote social change." Furthermore, a handful of state courts have provided guidance for constitutional rulings of the U.S. Supreme Court, in some instances anticipating and even going beyond some of the activist decisions of the Warren and Burger courts.[11] Put somewhat differently, there are two state judicial traditions: one relates to routine business, the other to a forward-looking activism based on a concern for civil liberties and/or the claims of the less fortunate.

The advent of the Burger Court and the refusal of some state courts, particularly state supreme courts, to follow federal court retrenchments in the area of civil rights and liberties gave rise to the phenomenon known as the new judicial federalism. This means that state courts, relying on state constitutions, have granted broader protections than those guaranteed by federal courts interpreting the federal Constitution. A growing literature not only follows the course of the new judicial federalism but provides critiques of rulings and offers suggestions for ways that state courts more effectively may perform their new responsibilities. The U.S. Supreme Court's response to the new judicial federalism, initially enthusiastic according to various commentators, has either become less emphatic, thus betraying a policy preference, or has, with effects that will ultimately be considered salutary, firmly (and sternly) insisted that state courts develop state law apart from and independent of federal court interpretation of the federal Constitution. The outcome might have been predicted. State supreme courts, which have traditionally been activist and which have more or less consistently been concerned with individual rights, have begun to address themselves to the task of carefully constraining state constitutions or have stood firm when the U.S. Supreme Court finds the state court ruling insufficiently clear and/or independent. Less confident courts have retreated.[12]

State Judiciaries, Autonomy, and Professor Tribe's Categories: An Overview

State courts have resisted governmental efforts to invade "personality." The cases, however, compared with those at the federal level, are scarce. There is a lack of uniformity, indeed an imbalance. For every ruling declaring a right, many more uphold the state restriction; the sources of resistance are confined to a few courts, with even fewer providing any consistent leadership; and, ominously considering the U.S. Supreme Court's emerging attitude toward state constitutional law development and the Court's sodomy holdings, state courts have little experience in state constitutional construction and either look to the federal Constitution or rely on federal precedent even when rulings are predicated on state constitutions.[13]

Nonetheless, there are positive state judicial rulings in almost all of Professor Tribe's categories. Articulation of a right to use nontherapeutic drugs has counteracted governmental efforts to "determine the contents and processes of the mind" by "screening the sources of consciousness." The recognition of a woman's right to terminate her pregnancy, aided if necessary by public funding, and of the right of terminally ill or brain-dead patients to refuse through surrogates life-prolonging medical treatment, have delineated the extent to which government may legitimately "control the body."[14] The invalidation of regulations, practices, penalties, and punishments that touch upon a wide array of activities ranging from freedom of choice concerning the use of motorcycle helmets, sex preferences, and sexual practices, appearance, and nontraditional living and familial arrangements indicates a judicial concern with an individual's decision about "life plan, pattern or style."[15] This chapter focuses on aspects of governmental efforts to control the body and life-plan pattern or style, focusing specifically on homosexual rights and the "right to die," issues that Tribe would hold as representing a "moral consensus in flux" and are therefore particularly appropriate for judicial intervention.[16] First a brief discussion of other issues is in order.

The Right to Use Drugs: Construction of State Constitutions

Most challenges to laws punishing the use of marijuana have been based at least in part on state constitutional grounds and provide examples of claims "never squarely faced by the Supreme Court."[17] Thus state courts have a prime opportunity to develop systematically a "privacy jurisprudence" based on state law, particularly if the state constitution explicitly guarantees such a right. So far, the Alaska Supreme Court in *Ravin v. State* appears to be the only court that has made an effort to do so.[18]

In 1972, following a ruling that sustained, on state constitutional grounds, the "liberty" of students to wear their hair at any desired length, the Alaska constitution was amended to include a right to privacy.[19] A few years later, an arrest for marijuana possession was challenged on the ground that the pertinent statute violated both the state and federal constitutions. On appeal, the *Ravin* court rejected the federal claim, suggesting that federal case law did not indicate a separate right to privacy distinct from the penumbras of specific federal guarantees and that, under federal law, it would consequently have to hold that there is no fundamental right to use marijuana in the home. However, the state constitution clearly indicated to the court that if "there is any area of human activity to which a right to privacy pertains more than any other it is the home." Echoing John Stuart Mill, the court held that

the authority of the state to exert control over the individual extends only to activities of the individual as it relates to matters of public health or safety, or to provide for the general welfare. We believe this tenet to be basic to a free society. The state cannot impose its own notions of morality, propriety, or fashion on individuals when the public has no legitimate interest in the affairs of those individuals.[20]

While the privacy amendment provided the court with an appropriate constitutional basis for the ruling in *Ravin*, it may be argued that, as demonstrated by the hair-length case, the court was already disposed toward guaranteeing and/or expanding rights either not found in the federal Constitution or federal rights narrowly construed by the U.S. Supreme Court. An earlier case, for example, firmly made the point that the Alaska court did not consider itself limited by decisions of the U.S. Supreme Court ("when we expound our state constitution, the Alaska constitution may have broader safeguards than the minimum federal standards"). Additionally, not only was the Alaska high court among the handful of state courts that had previously relied on state constitutional guarantees to step into the breach left by Burger Court curtailment of Warren Court defendants' rights rulings, but it also made a point of referring to the state's diversity and its libertarian ideals in these terms:

We are free, and we are under a duty to develop additional constitutional rights and privileges under our Alaska constitution if we find such fundamental rights and privileges to be within the intention and spirit of our local constitutional language and to be necessary for the kind of civilized life and heritage which is at the core of our constitutional heritage.[21]

Subsequent privacy rulings, as noted in the commentaries, have slowly and not without difficulty sought to establish principles for the development of a jurisprudence of privacy based on the state constitution. The Alaska court has been influenced by U.S. Supreme Court holdings, but from those holdings a methodology for resolving privacy issues has emerged.[22]

Nontraditional Living Arrangements: Rejection of U.S. Supreme Court Precedent and Expansion of U.S. Supreme Court Purpose

In *Belle Terre v. Boraas*, the U.S. Supreme Court sustained a zoning regulation that restricted the occupancy of single-family homes to those related by blood or by marriage. Here the Court rejected the claim of a group of students that their community was as worthy of constitutional protection as that accorded the traditional family. While the transient nature[23] of the relationships in this particular case indicates that they did not, nor were they intended to, "provide [the familial] intimacy, support and protection" that the Court has long recognized[24] as constitutionally guaranteed, Tribe argues that there is good reason for courts to take so-called communal living arrangements seriously.[25]

A few state high courts have gone far to provide an "answer," and for the most part they have done so on state constitutional grounds.[26] The courts of New York and New Jersey, for example, have "seemed most solicitous of those institutions that serve the essential childbearing functions of the traditional family by providing their members with emotional and economic support."[27] The California and New Jersey supreme courts were sharply critical of both the *Belle Terre* outcome and reasoning, a response not unusual for activist courts that construe state constitutions more generously than the U.S. Supreme Court interprets the federal Constitution.[28]

Two state high court rulings illustrate the manner in which what may be termed the spirit of the U.S. Supreme Court "family protection" rulings has been expanded. *White Plains v. Ferraiolo* pointed out the self-defeating results of zoning when it restricts the use of single-family dwellings; that is, the means employed contradict the goals sought to be achieved:

The fatal flaw in attempting to maintain a stable residential neighborhood through the use of criteria based upon biological or legal relationships is that such classifications operate to prohibit a plethora of uses which pose no threat to the accomplishment of the end sought to be achieved. Moreover, such a classification system legitimizes many uses which defeat that goal.... As long as a group bears the "generic character of a family unit as a relatively permanent household," it should be equally as entitled to occupy a single family dwelling as its biologically related neighbors.[29]

Second, *Santa Barbara v. Adamson* comes close to heeding Tribe's plea to solve "the persistent problem of autonomy and community." The *Adamson* court noted that

> appellants . . . explain they have become a close group with social, economic and psychological commitments to each other. They share expenses, rotate chores, and eat evening meals together. Some have children who regularly visit. Two . . . have contributed over $2,000 each to improving the house. . . . Emotional support and stability are provided by the members to each other . . . ; they have chosen to live together mainly because of their compatibility. They say that they regard their group as a "family" and that they seek to share several values of conventionally composed families. A living arrangement like theirs concededly does achieve many of the personal and practical needs served by traditional family living. It could be termed an alternate family.[30]

The Expression of Gay Personhood: A Test for the New Judicial Federalism?

The gay rights movement and the large and impressive legal advocacy that it spawned raised the hope that the U.S. Supreme Court would set aside the sodomy statutes of twenty-three states and the District of Columbia.[31] However, *Bowers v. Hardwick*, following the enigmatic summary affirmance of *Doe v. Commonwealth*,[32] effectively removed the question of the sexual privacy of gays from the federal judiciary's agenda, placing it within state jurisdictions. "We will struggle in state courts," vowed the president of the American Civil Liberties Union, which had filed a losing brief, "under state constitutions and with state legislatures."[33] The difficulty, as noted by an academic lawyer concerned with gay rights, is that the "advances" won by "gay advocates" in "progressive state courts" could well be "chill[ed]" by a "really adverse" Supreme Court decision.[34] Further, there is no denying that the AIDS epidemic has exacerbated homophobia.[35] At this point, legislators and judges may be little inclined to place their careers in jeopardy to advance the sexual privacy rights of gay men.[36] Legislative efforts to abolish consensual sodomy laws have been conspicuously wanting.[37]

State high courts that have invalidated sodomy statutes have relied primarily on federal grounds, an avenue now foreclosed by *Hardwick*, and challenges to sodomy laws based on state grounds have not fared well.[38] Furthermore, appellate courts in "nonabolitionist" states, with the exception of those of Michigan and Minnesota, are not recognized as espousing either civil libertarian activism or a reliance on state constitutional provisions.[39] Nonetheless, a few pertinent rulings are instructive and may provide stepping-stones for future litigation.

State court rulings grounded in the federal Constitution have contained the type of reasoning and rhetoric that could provide the basis for an implicit right to privacy even when the state constitution does not provide a categorical guarantee. In the New Jersey case of *State v. Saunders*, which invalidated a fornication statute, the court went well beyond federal precedent and sustained claims for a right to privacy viewed as "the freedom of personal development." Dismissing the state's defenses of the statute in question (the prevention of venereal disease, the propagation of illegitimate children, the protection of the marital relationship, and the promotion of morality), the court asserted that private personal acts between consenting adults are "not to be lightly meddled with by the state" and that a so-called remedy for supposed immoral conduct should not come from "legislative fiat." Finally, the court, in defense of judicial integrity, noted that "the dignity of the law is undermined when an intimate personal activity between consenting adults can be dragged into court and 'exposed.'" A subsequent New Jersey holding, relying on the *Saunders* rationale, invalidated consensual sodomy statutes.[40]

Despite the fact that the Pennsylvania Supreme Court held the state's voluntary deviated sexual intercourse statute (which applied only to unmarried people) a violation of state and federal equal protection guarantees, equally forceful privacy-autonomy language pervades *Commonwealth v. Bonadio*:

With respect to regulation of morals, the police power should properly be exercised to protect each individual's right to be free from interference in defining and pursuing his own morality but not to enforce a majority morality on persons whose conduct does not harm others. Many issues that are considered to be matters of morals are subject to debate, and no sufficient state interest justifies legislation of norms simply because a particular belief is followed by a number of people, or even a majority. Indeed, what is considered to be "moral" changes with the times and is dependent upon societal background. Spiritual leadership, not the government, has the responsibility for striving to improve the morality of individuals. Enactment of the Voluntary Deviate Sexual Intercourse Statute, despite the fact that it provides punishment for what many believe to be abhorrent crimes against nature and perceived sins against God, is not properly in the realm of the temporal police power.

Continuing, the court quoted at length from John Stuart Mill's *On Liberty*, concluding that Mill's "philosophy, as applied to the regulation of sexual morality presently before the court, or employed to delimit the police power generally, properly circumscribes state power over the individual."[41]

In *People v. Onofre*, New York's highest court, relying on a virtual laundry list of federal privacy and equal protection rulings, struck down a sodomy statue that applied to unmarried but not to married people. At the same time, in an exhaustive footnote, it condemned, as had the New Jersey and Pennsylvania courts, the state's claim to regulate morality:

We express no view as to any theological, moral or psychological evaluation of consensual sodomy. These are aspects of the issue on which informed, competent authorities and individuals may and do differ. Contrary to the view expressed by the dissent, although on occasion it does serve such ends, it is not the function of the Penal Law in our governmental policy to provide either a medium for the articulation or the apparatus for the intended enforcement of moral or theological values. Thus, it has been deemed irrelevant by the United States Supreme Court that the purchase and use of contraceptives by unmarried persons would arouse moral indignation among broad segments of our community or that the viewing of pornographic materials even within the privacy of one's home would not evoke general approbation. We are not unmindful of the sensibilities of many persons who are deeply persuaded that consensual sodomy is evil and should be prohibited. That is not the issue before us. The issue before us is whether, assuming that at least at present it is the will of the community (as expressed in legislative enactment) to prohibit consensual sodomy, the Federal Constitution permits recourse to the sanctions of the criminal law for the achievement of that objective. The community and its members are entirely free to employ theological teaching, moral suasion, parental advice, psychological and psychiatric counseling and other noncoercive means to condemn the practice of consensual sodomy. The narrow question before us is whether the Federal Constitution permits the use of the criminal law for that purpose.[42]

However unprescient these sentiments, as they pertain to the federal Constitution, may have been, transposed to a state due process "right of privacy" they could be of service for state constitutional protection of the expression of gay personhood.

The Right to Choose Death: New Jersey, California, and the Frontiers of the Law

In 1978, when Tribe's influential treatise was published, only the New Jersey Supreme Court, in the famous *Quinlan* case, had ruled that the federal constitutional "right to privacy" guaranteed the right of a patient (or as in *Quinlan*, her surrogates) to refuse heroic measures to prolong life.[43] Since then, other state courts have addressed the sorts of difficult issues presented by *Quinlan*,[44] and twenty states and the District of Columbia have enacted living will and natural death statutes.[45] There was consideration of the possibilities of responsible legislative action, a point forcefully raised by *Quinlan*'s critics.[46] *Quinlan* by no means enunciated an absolute right to die.[47]

Just one year later in *Superintendent of Belchertown State School v. Saikewicz*, the Massachusetts Supreme Judicial Court was asked to decide if the guardian of a sapient although severely retarded leukemia patient could refuse chemotherapy treatments for his ward.[48] In agreeing to the request, the *Saikewicz* (as did the *Quinlan*) court enunciated a set of carefully drawn guidelines weighing and balancing the various interests of the state and of the individual.[49]

Both *Quinlan* and *Saikewicz* attracted national media attention. What is overlooked is that most decisions to terminate life-support systems from patients unable, for whatever reasons, to make such determinations themselves are made quietly and privately between family members or guardians and attending physicians.[50] State court intervention in such situations is the exception rather than the rule. Nonetheless, since thirty states continue to place the burden for decisions to withdraw life-prolonging equipment on the courts (if and when private arrangements cannot be made), *Quinlan* and *Saikewicz* not only provide guidance but also demonstrate that state courts, in this most difficult arena, are competent to enunciate public policy that is as sensitive as it is workable.

Another aspect of the right-to-die controversy entails patients or surrogates for incompetent patients who request that nourishment as well as medical treatment be withheld. In this respect and in retrospect, *Quinlan* and *Saikewicz* seem relatively noncontroversial, and living wills barely address the problem of the continuation of a hopeless existence. Recalling Tribe's definition of privacy—"the values and activities courts have thought worthy of protection under a wide variety of names but with a single aim: preservation of those attributes of an individual which are irreducible in his selfhood"—[51] perhaps liberties are not taken by claiming that Tribe would indeed defend a court order permitting patients to refuse not heroic but far simpler ministrations to prolong life. Two cases are illustrative.

In *Brophy v. New England Sinai Hospital, Inc.*, Massachusetts's highest court authorized the withholding of nourishment for a forty-nine-year-old comatose patient whose survival did not (unlike Karen Quinlan's) depend on a respirator or other mechanical means. The court held that the feedings through a stomach tube constituted a form of medical treatment that the patient (or his wife speaking for him and iterating his earlier and often-expressed wishes) had a right to refuse. The case, as the *New York Times* put it, "tested the legal limits of a patient's right to death with dignity."[52]

In a case that has received national attention, a California appellate court sustained the right of a quadriplegic to starve herself to death while otherwise receiving care at a county hospital.[53] The patient, Elizabeth Bouvia, was in her late twenties, mentally competent, alert, intelligent, and held a bachelor's degree in social work. Neither she nor her family could afford a private hospital, and, under law, a public hospital was obliged to care for her. Her doctors' refusal to honor her request for the discontinuation of nasogastric feedings was upheld at trial on the grounds that Bouvia was "neither comatose, nor incurably, nor terminally ill, nor in a vegatative state," all conditions that have justified the termination of life support systems in other instances; she could not ask for medical treatment and cut "off that part of it that would be effective"; and she was asking the state to be "party to a suicide."

The appellate court, addressing the case as though it were engaged in more or less routine right to refuse treatment litigation, held that the trial court had "mistakenly attached undue importance to the amount of time possibly available to petitioner, and failed to give equal weight and consideration for the quality of that life; an equal, if not more significant consideration." Put differently, the appellate court equated the quality of Elizabeth Bouvia's life with the quality of Karen Quinlan's life:

All decisions permitting cessation of medical treatment or life-support procedures to some degree hastened the arrival of death. In part, this was permitted because the quality of life during the time remaining in those cases had been terribly diminished. In Elizabeth Bouvia's view, the quality of her life has been diminished to the point of hopelessness, uselessness, unenjoyability and frustration. She . . . may consider her existence meaningless. . . . If her right to choose may not be exercised because there remains to her, in the opinion of a court, a physician or some committee, a certain arbitrary number of years, months or days, her right will have lost its meaning.

Who shall say what the minimum amount of available life must be? Does it matter if it be 15 to 20 years, 15 to 20 months, or 15 to 20 days, if such a life has been physically destroyed and its quality, dignity and purpose gone? As in all matters lines must be drawn at some point, somewhere, but that decision must ultimately belong to the one whose life is in issue.[54]

Despite the court's effort to minimize the novelty of its holding and to treat the case as though it involved no more than the right of a mentally competent patient to accept or refuse treatment or of a comatose or terminally ill patient to refuse (if need be through a guardian) to be kept alive through mechanical means, the implications of *Bouvia*, as the concurring judges made plain, are revolutionary.

Elizabeth apparently has made a conscious and informed choice that she prefers death to continued existence in her helpless and to her intolerable condition. I believe she has an absolute right to effectuate that decision. This state and the medical profession, instead of frustrating her desire, should be attempting to relieve her suffering by permitting and in fact assisting her to die with ease and dignity. The fact that she is forced to suffer the ordeal of self-starvation to achieve her objective is in itself inhumane.

The right to die is an integral part of our right to control our own destinies so long as the rights of others are not affected. That right should, in my opinion, include the ability to enlist assistance from others, including the medical profession, in making death as painless and quick as possible. . . .

If there is ever a time when we ought to be able to get the "government off our backs" it is when we face death—either by choice or otherwise.[55]

Conclusion

The cases reviewed in this chapter indicate that, on controversial lifestyle issues, only a minority of state appellate courts have been willing to go against the grain, and these are the same courts whose rulings repeatedly are cited as examples of the new judicial federalism. It would be a mistake, however, to dismiss courts and cases as aberrational and irrelevant. First, some of the courts in question have made no secret of their disagreements with U.S. Supreme Court rulings, which they regard as overly restrictive of individual liberties.[56] In this sense they may provide inspiration for courts in other states to do likewise. Indeed, the California high court has virtually pioneered in building "tolerance" for "evolving lifestyles" and "adapting" the law to "social change" whatever the inclinations of its federal counterpart.[57]

Second, activist courts provide a stimulus for others to pursue a similar course. In the sodomy cases, for example, the *Onofre* court made a point, citing *Bonadio* and *Saunders*, that it did not "plow new grounds."[58] Third, while state courts still have not fully developed a privacy jurisprudence based on state constitutions, some, particularly after *Hardwick*, may begin to address themselves to the task.

Finally, as the *Quinlan*, *Saikewicz*, *Brophy*, and *Bouvia* line of cases demonstrates, creative courts are in a position to expand the frontiers of the law. *Quinlan* established the right of a comatose patient to be removed from life-sustaining equipment, *Saikewicz* affirmed the right of a patient's guardian to refuse treatment for his ward, *Brophy* sustained the right of a comatose patient to have feeding discontinued, and *Bouvia* upheld the right of a fully competent patient to refuse nourishment while under medical care. What is extraordinary is that, in this most sensitive area— one that will take on increasing significance (and poignance) as the very ill, often against their will, linger on—decisions about the ultimate exercise of personal autonomy are being made as a matter of course in state, not federal, courts.

Notes

The assistance and helpful comments of Harley G. Diamond, Esq., are gratefully acknowledged.

1. Laurence H. Tribe, *The Constitutional Protection of Individual Rights* (Mineola, N.Y.: Foundation Press, 1987), pp. 889–95 passim. For the view that sub-

stantive due process properly understood and illuminated is equal to much the same task, see Michael J. Perry, "Substantive Due Process Revisited: Reflections on and beyond Recent Cases," *Northwestern University Law Review* 71 (1976): 417–69.

2. Tribe, *Constitutional Protection*, pp. 893, 894. Citations omitted.

3. Prince v. Massachusetts, 321 U.S. 158, 166 (1944); quoted by Justice Powell, concurring, Moore v. East Cleveland, 431 U.S. 494, 499 (1977), referring to the *Meyers, Griswold, Roe* line of cases. Meyers v. Nebraska, 262 U.S. 390 (1923), (right of parents to direct the education of their children); Griswold v. Connecticut, 381 U.S. 479 (1965) (right of marital privacy); Roe v. Wade, 410 U.S. 113 (1973) (woman's right over her body for purposes of deciding to terminate a pregnancy).

4. Marriage: Loving v. Virginia, 388 U.S. 1 (1967); Zablocki v. Redhail, 434 U.S. 374 (1978); marital relations and procreation: Griswold v. Connecticut; note 3 supra; procreation: Eisenstadt v. Baird, 405 U.S. 438 (1972) and Carey v. Population Services International, 431 U.S. 678 (1977) held that contraceptives should be made available to the unmarried and minors as well as the married and adults; Roe v. Wade, note 3 supra.

5. Tribe, *Constitutional Protection*, and "Foreword: Toward a Model of Roles in the Due Process of Life and Law," *Harvard Law Review* 87 (1973): 10–15.

6. "Commentators and litigators seeking constitutional protection for gay rights most frequently rely on the right to privacy." "The Constitutional Status of Sexual Orientation: Homosexuality as a Suspect Classification," *Harvard Law Review* 98 (1985): 1288. For the view that the equal protection clause, properly interpreted, provides the remedy for discrimination against gays, see Judith A. Baer, *Equality under the Constitution* (Ithaca, N.Y.: Cornell University Press, 1983), chap. 9. For an overview of the commentary and a bibliography, see Thomas C. Grey, "Eros, Civilization and the Burger Court," *Law and Contemporary Problems* 43 (1980): 83–100. See also "The Right of Privacy and Other Constitutional Challenges to Sodomy Statutes," *Toledo Law Review* (1984): 811–75, David A. J. Richards, "Homosexuality and the Constitutional Right to Privacy," *Review of Law and Social Change* (1978–1979): 311–23. The American Bar Association and the American Law Institute recommend the repeal of such laws. For an overview of gay rights in general and a bibliography, see E. Carrington Boggan, Marilyn G. Haft, Charles Lister, John P. Rupp, and Thomas B. Stoddard, *American Civil Liberties Union Handbook: The Rights of Gay People* (New York: Bantam Books, 1983).

7. Doe v. Commonwealth, 425 U.S. 901 (1976) (Justices William Brennan, Thurgood Marshall, and John Paul Stevens dissenting). For a discussion of the significance of summary affirmances generally and in respect to *Doe* particularly, see "The Right of Privacy and Other Constitutional Challenges," pp. 838–40; Steven O. Ludd, "The Aftermath of Doe v. Commonwealth's Attorney: In Search of the Right to Be Let Alone," *University of Dayton Law Review* 10 (1985): 705–43. For a comparison of state criminal sodomy statutes, see Boggan et al., *ACLU Handbook*, pp. 131–66, "The Right to Privacy and Other Constitutional Challenges," pp. 868–75.

8. Bowers v. Hardwick, 106 S. Ct. 2841 (1986) (Justices William Brennan, Thurgood Marshall, and Harry Blackmun dissenting).

9. Justice Byron White noted that by expanding the list of fundamental

rights, "the judiciary necessarily takes to itself further authority to govern the country without express constitutional authority." Id. at 2846.

A newspaper account included the following comments and analysis:

This portion of the opinion was an unusually explicit discussion of a factor that is always present when the Court finds itself at the frontiers of constitutional law: the Court's sense of where its judgment fits within the broader social consensus. Historically, many Justices have believed that to place the Court too far ahead of the consensus too often is to hurt the institution, to make it "vulnerable," to use Justice White's word, to attack from the political branches.

In this context, Justice Byron White did not mention the Court's landmark privacy decision, *Roe v. Wade*, which established abortion as a constitutional right. But he and William Rehnquist, the Chief Justice designate, who also joined today's opinion, were the two dissenters in the 1973 abortion case. They have dissented from all the subsequent decisions expanding on the principles of Roe v. Wade.

The Court is keenly aware that the political furor over Roe v. Wade has yet to die down. The fact that Justices White and Rehnquist garnered a majority for the decision today may indicate that the Court simply has no appetite for venturing once again into uncharted territory. The expected arrival of Antonin Scalia will not change that mood; it is virtually certain, based on his judicial and scholarly writing, that he would have voted with the majority. Chief Justice Warren Burger, who is retiring next month, voted in the majority.

Linda Greenhouse, "Privacy, Law and History," *New York Times*, July 1, 1986, pp. 1, 11.

10. Greenhouse, "Privacy, Law and History."

11. Robert A. Kagan et al., "The Business of State Supreme Courts, 1870–1970," *Stanford Law Review* 30 (1977): 155. For the role that one state high court played in influencing the U.S. Supreme Court, see Daniel C. Kramer and Robert Riga, "The New York Court of Appeals and the U.S. Supreme Court," in Mary Cornelia Porter and G. Alan Tarr, eds., *State Supreme Courts: Policymakers in the Federal System.* (Westport, Conn.: Greenwood Press, 1982). The California Supreme Court has on several occasions gone beyond the U.S. Supreme Court. Despite San Antonio Independent School District v. Rodriguez, 411 U.S. 1 (1973), and Frontiero v. Richardson, 411 U.S. 677 (1973), the California Supreme Court held education to be a "fundamental" right and poverty and sex to be "suspect classifications." Serrano v. Priest, 487 P.2d 1241 (Cal. 1971) and Sail'er Inn v. Kirby, 485 P.2d 529 (Cal. 1971). Almost twenty years prior to U.S. Supreme Court action, the California high court invalidated antimiscegenation laws: Loving v. Virginia, 388 U.S. 1 (1967); Perez v. Lippold, 198 P.2d 17 (Cal. 1948). California invalidated the death penalty and criminal abortion statutes prior to the U.S. Supreme Court's holdings. Furman v. Georgia, 408 U.S. 238 (1973); People v. Anderson, 483 P.2d 880 (Cal. 1972), cert. denied, 405 U.S. 958 (1972); Roe v. Wade, supra n. 3; People v. Barksdale, 503 P.2d 275 (Cal. 1972).

12. There is a growing literature on the new judicial federalism. Stanley H. Friedelbaum, "Independent State Grounds: Contemporary Invitations to Judicial Activism," and Mary Cornelia Porter, "State Supreme Courts and the Legacy of the Warren Court: Some Old Inquiries for a New Situation," both in Porter and Tarr, *State Supreme Courts*, chaps. 2, 1, and G. Alan Tarr, "Bibliographical Essay," in id., pp. 201–11, 206–8; G. Alan Tarr and Mary Cornelia

Porter, "Gender Equality and Judicial Federalism: The Role of State Appellate Courts," *Hastings Constitutional Law Quarterly* 9 (1982): 910–27; for a listing of activist courts, see pp. 953–54; G. Alan Tarr and Mary Cornelia Porter, eds., "New Developments in State Constitutional Law," *Publius: The Journal of Federalism* 17 (1987); "Developments in the Law—The Interpretation of State Constitutional Rights," *Harvard Law Review* 95 (1982): 1326–1502; Ronald K. L. Collins and Peter J. Galie, "State High Courts, State Constitutions and Individual Rights Litigation since 1980: A Survey," *Publius: The Journal of Federalism* 16 (1986): 141–61. In Florida v. Casal, 103 S. Ct. 3100 (1983), Chief Justice Warren Burger, concurring, made a point of reminding state electorates that "when state courts interpret state law to require more than the federal constitution requires, the citizens of the state . . . have the power to amend state law to ensure rational law enforcement," at 3102; Robert Welsh and Ronald K. L. Collins maintain that the U.S. Supreme Court lost interest in the new judicial federalism when it became apparent that state courts were serious about establishing guarantees above the federal floor. Robert C. Welsh, "Whose Federalism?—The Burger Court's Treatment of State Civil Liberties Judgments," *Hastings Constitutional Law Quarterly* 10 (1983): 819–75. "Today the Supreme Court is anxious to review—and in many instances to reverse—state court decisions, particularly those vindicating civil rights. What is noteworthy about this change is that the Court has even been willing to intrude into decisions based on state law." Ronald K. L. Collins, "Plain Statements: The Supreme Court's New Requirement," *American Bar Association Journal* 70 (1984): 92–94, citing inter alia Michigan v. Long, 463 U.S. 1032 (1983). On the other hand, *Long* may force state courts to be careful to "pin their decisions on specific portions of state law and constitutions, focusing their attention on the state's basic law." Charles A. Sheldon, "A Century of Judging: Judicial Review with a State Supreme Court" (paper delivered at the 1986 Annual Meeting of the American Political Science Association, Washington, D.C., August 28–31, 1986), n. 91. A revised version of the paper, "Judicial Review and the Supreme Court of Washington," is published in Tarr and Porter, eds. *New Developments in State Constitutional Law*, pp. 69–90. The New York Court of Appeals reiterated that despite a U.S. Supreme Court reversal based on *Long*, it had indeed based a search and seizure ruling on the state constitution. "Where, as here, we have already held that the state constitution has been violated, we should not reach a different result following reversal on federal constitutional grounds unless appellant demonstrates that there are extraordinary and compelling circumstances." People v. Class, May 29, 1986, New York Court of Appeals, No. 209, reported in "Criminal Law: N.Y. Stands Firm on State Constitutional Protections," *American Bar Association Journal*, September 1, 1986, p. 84. For an account of a court far less willing to hold the line, see Mary Cornelia Porter and G. Alan Tarr, "The New Judicial Federalism and the Ohio Supreme Court: Anatomy of a Failure," *Ohio State Law Journal* 45 (1984): 143–59.

13. For some listings and discussion, see Tribe, *Constitutional Protection*, chap. 15; "Developments in the Law—The Interpretation of State Constitutions."

14. Drug use: See notes 18 infra and accompanying text. Abortion and abortion funding: People v. Barksdale, note 11 supra; Committee to Defend Reproductive Rights v. Meyers, 624 P.2d 779 (Cal. 1981); Dodge v. Department of Social Services, 657 P.2d 969 (Col. App. 1982); Doe v. Maher, Conn. Super. Ct.,

Oct. 9 (1981), *Family Law Reporter* (BNA) 2006; Moe v. Secretary of Administration and Finance, 417 N.E.2d 387 (Mass. 1981); Planned Parenthood Association, Inc. v. Department of Human Services, 663 P.2d 1245 (Or. App. 1983). Right to Choose v. Byrne, 440 A. 2d 925 (N.J. 1982). The U.S. Supreme Court, by contrast, had held that public funding for abortion may be denied. Beal v. Doe, 432 U.S. 438 (1977); Harris v. McRae, 448 U.S. 297 (1980). Right to die: see notes 43–53 and accompanying text.

15. Tribe, *Constitutional Protection*, p. 939. Nonetheless, "The vast majority of state courts have rejected...challenges to helmet laws." A. E. Dick Howard, "State Courts and Constitutional Rights in the Day of the Burger Court, *Virginia Law Review* 62 (1976): 874–944, 929. Two state courts (temporarily) adopted John Stuart Mill's argument that government may not legitimately prohibit conduct that does not harm others; People v. Fries, 240 N.E.2d. 49, (Ill. 1969), overruled; People v. Kohrig, 498 N.E.2d 1158 (Ill. 1986) American Motorcycle Association v. Department of State Police, 158 N.W.2d 72, 75–76 (Mich. 1968), overruled; People v. Poucher, 247 N.W.2d 798 (Mich. 1976). Sex preferences and sexual practices: see notes 32–42 infra and accompanying text. Appearance: courts in Alaska, Connecticut, Idaho, Illinois, and Ohio have invalidated grooming rules for students. Courts in Arizona, California, and Florida have sustained similar impositions. "Developments in the Law—The Interpretation of State Constitutional Rights," p. 1431. The U.S. Supreme Court has sustained hair length standards for police. Kelly v. Johnson, 425 U.S. 238 (1976). The Alaska case, Breese v. Smith, 501 P.2d 159 (Alas. 1972), provides an early Burger Court era example of reliance on a state constitution, as well as judicial recognition of a state's unique political culture. (Alaska's traditions place high value on "the preservation of maximum individual choice, protection of minority sentiments and appreciation for divergent lifestyles," at 169). For nontraditional living and familial arrangements, see notes 23–30 infra and accompanying text.

16. Laurence H. Tribe, "Structural Due Process," *Harvard Civil Rights-Civil Liberties Law Review* 10 (1975): 269–321.

17. Tribe, *Constitutional Protection*, p. 908; "Developments in the Law—The Interpretation of State Constitutional Rights," p. 1431, and cases listed, note 8, id.

18. "Developments," p. 1431; "Alaska's Right to Privacy Ten Years after Ravin v. State: Developing a Jurisprudence of Privacy," *Alaska Law Review* 2 (1968): 159–83; Ravin v. State, 537 P.2d 494 (Alas. 1975). Eleven states have right-of-privacy provisions in their constitutions. For the most part, such provisions are little used. Robert A. Sedler, "The State Constitutions and the Supplemental Protection of Individual Rights," *Toledo Law Review* 16 (1985): 491. In People v. Sinclair, 194 N.W.2d 878 (Mich. 1972), it was held that marijuana was not harmful and to classify it with hard drugs violated the equal protection clauses of the state and federal constitutions. In People v. Woody, 394 P.2d 813 (Col. 1964), the right to use peyote in Indian religious ceremonies was sustained on First Amendment grounds. For a similar holding, see Arizona v. Whittingham, 504 P.2d 940 (Ariz. 1973), cert. denied 417 U.S. 946 (1974).

19. Breese v. State, 501 P.2d 159 (Alas. 1972), was based on Article I, Sec. 1 of the Alaska Constitution: "This constitution is dedicated to the principles that all persons have a natural right to life, liberty, the pursuit of happiness, and the

enjoyment of the reward of their own industry; that all persons are equal and entitled to equal rights, opportunities, and protection under the law; and that all persons have corresponding obligations to the people and the State. The right of the people to privacy is recognized and shall not be infringed. "Article I, Sec. 22, approved August 1972.

20. The following provide a basis for the discussion: Gerald Solk, "Privacy in Alaska, Milestone or Malaise?" *Texas Southern Law Review* 4 (1976): 50–65; Ravis v. State, 537 P.2d 494, 509 (Alas. 1975).

21. Roberts v. State, 458 P.2d 386 (Alas. 1970). For a comparison of the Alaska high court's jurisprudence compared with others (California, Michigan, and New Jersey) that have circumvented the U.S. Supreme Court to afford greater guarantees of personal liberty, see Porter, "State Supreme Courts and the Legacy of the Warren Court."

22. "Alaska's Right to Privacy," pp. 167–83.

23. Tribe, *Constitutional Protection*, p. 989. Belle Terre, 416 U.S. 1 (1974). Tribe notes that the "Court should have ... demanded at least a substantial justification for the [ordinance challenged] in *Belle Terre*.... [possibly] *the associational rights of the villagers themselves*" (emphasis in original). Id., p. 977. In White Plains v. Ferraioli, the New York high court distinguished *Belle Terre* on the ground of transiency ("every year or so, different college students would come to take the place of those before them"). 313 N.E.2d 756, 758 (N.Y. 1974).

24. "Developments in the Law—The Constitution and the Family," p. 1218. Commentary drew inter alia upon Moore v. East Cleveland, 431 U.S. 494 (1977), U.S. Department of Agriculture v. Moreno, 413 U.S. 528 (1973), and Smith v. Organization of Foster Families for Equality and Reform, 431 U.S. 816 (1977), as well as the venerable precedents of Pierce v. Society of Sisters, 268 U.S. 510 (1925) and Meyer v. Nebraska, 262 U.S. 390 (1923) to support the contention.

25. Tribe, *Constitutional Protection*, p. 988.

26. The Michigan and New Jersey high courts have relied on the due process clauses of their state constitutions, Delta v. Dinolfo, 351 N.W. 2d 831 (Mich. 1984) and State v. Baker, 405 A.2d 368 (N.J. 1979), and the California Supreme Court on the right to privacy guarantee, Santa Barbara v. Adamson, 610 P.2d 436 (Cal. 1980). Discussed in Sedler, "State Constitutions," p. 489.

27. "Developments in the Law—The Constitution and the Family," p. 1217 n. 126, citing Berger v. State, 362 N.E.2d 993 (N.Y. 1976), and White Plains v. Ferraioli, 313 N.E.2d 756 (N.Y. 1974).

28. The New Jersey justices found "the reasoning of *Belle Terre* to be ... unpersuasive," State v. Baker, 405 A.2d 368, 374 (N.J. 1979), and the California majority directly quoted from Justice Thurgood Marshall's *Belle Terre* dissent ("The choice of household companions—of whether a person's 'intellectual and emotional needs' are best met by living with family, friends, professional associates, or others—involves deeply personal considerations as to the kind and quality of intimate relationships within the home. That decision surely falls within the right to privacy protected by the Constitution" (416 U.S. 16) and from a law review article ("The New Jersey Supreme Court is beginning to deal realistically with the problems of the mid–1970's; the United States Supreme Court, rather surprisingly is still merely repeating what were the liberal shibboleths of the mid–1930s") (citation omitted here), Santa Barbara v. Adamson, 610 P.2d 436,

440, n. 3 (Cal. 1980). State courts that have invalidated restrictions on public funding for abortion have been equally disparaging about U.S. Supreme Court holdings to the contrary. For cases, see note 14 supra. For commentary, see "Developments in the Law—State Constitutions," p. 1443.

29. 313 N.E.2d 756. Citations omitted.

30. 610 P.2d 436, 438 (Colo. 1980).

31. "Constitutional Status of Sexual Orientation," p. 1292.

32. Bowers v. Hardwick, 106 S. Ct. 2841 (1986), Doe v. Commonwealth, 425 U.S. 901 (1976). The majority of sodomy laws apply to heterosexual as well as homosexual acts, including those sustained in *Doe* and *Hardwick*. Justice Harry Blackmun's *Hardwick* dissent focused on the majority's eagerness to narrow the statute's reach: "The sex of status of the persons who engage in the act is irrelevant as a matter of state law. In fact, to the extent that I can discern a legislative purpose for Georgia's ... enactment ..., that purpose seems to have been to broaden the coverage of the law to reach heterosexual as well as homosexual activity.... Michael Hardwick's standing may rest in significant part on Georgia's willingness to enforce against homosexuals a law it seems not to have any desire to enforce against heterosexuals." 106 S. Ct. 2845. Five states—Arkansas, Kansas, Montana, Nevada, and Texas—criminalize homosexual sodomy only. The following states have no sodomy laws: all of the New England states and the eastern states of Delaware, New Jersey, and Pennsylvania; the border state of West Virginia; the midwestern states of Illinois (the first state in the nation to decriminalize sodomy), Indiana, Iowa, Nebraska, North Dakota, Ohio, and Wisconsin; and the western states of California, Colorado, New Mexico, Oregon, Washington and Wyoming. *New York Times* July 1, 1986, p. 11. New Mexico, New York, and Pennsylvania statutes were invalidated by judicial action. State v. Elliot, 539 P.2d 207 (N. Mex. 1975), People v. Onofre, 415 N.E. 2d 936 (N.Y. 1980), Commonwealth v. Bonadio, 415 A.2d 47 (Pa. 1980). The Massachusetts high court ruled that a statute prohibiting "unnatural and lascivious acts" does not apply to sexual conduct between consenting adults. Commonwealth v. Balthazar, 318 N.E.2d 478 (Mass. 1974). State v. Pilcher, 242 N.W.2d 348 (Iowa 1976) held that a sodomy statute could not provide the basis for the prosecution of unmarried heterosexuals but avoided the issue of homosexual sodomy.

33. Larry Rohter, "Friend and Foe See Homosexual Defeat," *New York Times*, July 1, 1986, p. 11.

34. Rhonda R, Rivera, "Queer Law: Sexual Orientation Law in the Mid-Eighties," *University of Dayton Law Review* (1985): 473, and note 85.

35. For an account of the effects of AIDS on the San Francisco gay community and efforts of public authorities to balance the rights of the gay community and their responsibilities to protect public health, see Frances FitzGerald, "A Reporter at Large (San Francisco—Part II), *New Yorker*, July 28, 1986, pp. 44–63. For the legal and constitutional dimensions of the disease, its victims and public fears, see "The Constitutional Rights of AIDS Carriers," *Harvard Law Review* 99 (1986): 1272–92; "Preventing the Spread of AIDS by Restricting Sexual Conduct in Gay Bathhouses: A Constitutional Analysis," *Golden Gate University Law Review* (1985): 301–30; David Freedman, "Wrong without Remedy," *American Bar Association Journal*, June 1, 1986, pp. 36–40. Arthur S. Leonard, "Employment Discrimi-

nation against Persons with AIDS," *University of Dayton Law Review* 10 (1985): 681–703. An ABA poll revealed that "lawyers oppose most AIDS-related discrimination," Laurie Rubenstein Reskin, *American Bar Association Journal* 72 (1986): 34.

36. "Depending on the courage of state judges, American citizens may or may not be protected from governmental intrusion into their intimate decisions concerning sexual relations." Ludd, "Aftermath of Doe v. Commonwealth Attorney," p. 742. In State v. Walsh, July 15, 1986, No. 67465, the Missouri Supreme Court, relying on *Hardwick*, held that a man who "suggestively touched an undercover policeman must be tried for misconduct." "The Missouri case represents the first defeat since *Hardwick* of challenges to state sodomy laws. According to [the American Civil Liberties Union], such challenges are pending before three federal courts but [are expected to be dismissed]." The Missouri court held that the state's sodomy statute "bore a rational relation to the enforcement of a permissible state goal [the enforcement of morality]" and that it protected the public against the threat of AIDS. According to a St. Louis attorney, the law is employed for purposes of entrapment: "The police regularly solicit gay men for sex. The officer asks a man to go home with him and then arrests him. There doesn't even have to be any physical contact." Paul Reidinger, "Missouri Vice," *American Bar Association Journal*, November 1, 1986, p. 78.

37. A brief for abolition appears in Tribe, *Constitutional Protection*, pp. 943–44.

38. Neville v. State, 430 A.2d 841 (Md. 1981), the court holding that it would not consider the state claim in the absence of proper briefing by counsel; State v. Santos, 413 A.2d 58 (R.I. 1980), holding that the federal Constitution was inapplicable, and there was no explicit right to privacy in the state constitution.

39. While at least twenty-five state courts have in about 350 published opinions gone beyond the federal floor in guaranteeing rights based on state constitutions, few state high courts are considered to be concerned with civil liberties and/or with the practice of the new judicial federalism. Robert Pear, "State Courts Move beyond U.S. Reach in Rights Rulings," *New York Times*, May 4, 1986, p. 1; Tarr and Porter, "Gender Equality and Judicial Federalism," p. 953. The courts are those of Alaska, California, Maine, Massachusetts, Michigan, New York, Oregon, Washington, and Wyoming. Justices most prominently associated with the development of the new judicial federalism are Hans Linde (Oregon), Stewart Pollock (New Jersey), Ellen Peters (Connecticut), Stanley Mosk (California), Robert Utter (Washington), and Shirley Abrahamson (Wisconsin). For a positive report on state court civil libertarian activism, see Paul Marcotte, "Federalism and the Rise of State Courts," *American Bar Association Journal*, April 1, 1987, pp. 601–64. State courts that have responded favorably to the claims of gay litigants in such diverse areas as discrimination in employment, occupational licensing, associational rights, and child custody determinations are, on the whole, among the nation's more activist and located along the northeastern seaboard and western states. See generally Boggan et al., *Rights of Gay People*, and the exhaustive research conducted by Professor Rhonda Rivera: "Our Straight-Laced Judges: The Legal Position of Homosexual Persons in the United States," *Hastings Law Journal* 30 (1979): 799–955; "Recent Developments in Sexual Preference Law," *Drake Law Review* (1980–1981): 311–46; "Queer Law I,"

"Queer Law II: Sexual Orientation Law in the Mid-Eighties," *University of Dayton Law Review* 11 (1986: 275–398. Deferring to legislative judgment and ignoring federal precedent, the Arkansas Supreme Court's validation of the state's sodomy statute is instructive: "If social changes have rendered our sodomy statues un-suitable to the society in which we now live, we need not be concerned about the matter because there is a branch of our government within whose purview the making of appropriate adjustment and changes peculiarly lies." Carter v. State, 500 S.W.2d 368, 371 (Ark. 1973). The challenged statute provided pun-ishments of a maximum of twenty-one years for consenting adults for sodomy and a disorderly conduct citation for married couples. In an appeal of a sodomy conviction, the Alabama court of criminal appeals noted that the constitutional question had been improperly raised. State v. Woodruff, 460 So.2d 325 (Ala. 1984).

40. State v. Saunders, 381 A.2d 333, 341–43 (N.J. 1977). State v. Ciuffina, 395 A.2d 904 (N.J. 1978). Earlier, the New jersey court had determined that the state sodomy statute discriminated against homosexuals. Concurring, Justice Joseph Weintraub said: "I have reservations as to the constitutionality of the application of a sodomy statute to a consensual act between adults committed in private. As to the homosexual act . . . I doubt the existence of a public interest sufficient to justify an edict that the homosexual shall behave as a heterosexual or not at all." New Jersey v. Lair, 301 A.2d 748, 754 (N.J. 1973).

41. 415 A.2d 50–51. The court did not consider Doe v. Commonwealth, 425 U.S. 901 (1976), as controlling.

42. People v. Onofre, 415 N.E. 2d 936, 940, note 3 (1980). "Constitutional Status of Sexual Orientation," note 6 supra. In reference to the Alaska high court's privacy rulings and on the applicability of John Stuart Mill to constitu-tional construction, Michael J. Perry writes: "Whether the Alaska constitution enacts Mill's *On Liberty*, surely the United States Constitution no more enacts *On Liberty* than it enacts Mr. Herbert Spencer's *Social Statics*. [However] we may be nearing the point where Mill's philosophy of government and conventional American attitudes about the proper role of government in regulating *personal* matters, sexual and otherwise, are converging." "Substantive Due Process Re-vised," p. 434.

43. In re Quinlan, 355 A.2d 647 (N.J. 1976), cert. denied, 429 U.S. 922 (1976). The "right to die" also arises out of the long-standing personal right to make decisions concerning one's body. In Schloendorff v. Society of New York Hos-pital, 105 N.E.2d 92 (N.Y. 1914), it was held that a physician commits a criminal assault when surgery is performed and the surgeon knows that the patient neither wants nor has expressly consented to surgery. More recently, the Kansas Supreme Court has expanded *Schloendorff*. In Natanson v. Kline, 305 P.2d 1093, 1097 (Kans. 1960), the court stated, "Each man is considered to be the master of his own body, and he may if he be of sound mind, expressly prohibit life saving surgery or other medical treatment."

44. A growing literature addresses the right-to-die issue. For a representative sampling and discussion of cases, see "The Right to Die: An Extension of the Right to Privacy," *John Marshall Law Review* 18 (1985): 895–914; "Voluntary Active Euthanasia for the Terminally Ill and the Constitutional Right to Privacy," *Cornell Law Review* 69 (1984): 363–83.

45. Living will or natural death legislation has been enacted in Alabama, Arkansas, California, Delaware, Florida, Idaho, Illinois, Kansas, Louisiana, Mississippi, Nevada, New Mexico, North Carolina, Oregon, Texas, Vermont, Virginia, Washington, West Virginia, and Wyoming. The New York legislature, under pressure from some Catholic organizations and right-to-life groups, defeated a living will bill. "Its sponsor... charged that lobbyists had 'misinformed some members' of the Assembly by presenting the bill as one that would have legalized euthanasia or assisted suicide." *New York Times*, May 5, 1977, p. 46, quoted in Tribe, *Constitutional Protection*, p. 937 n. 15.

46. The *Quinlan* decision "... was roundly condemned by the state's attorney general who accused the court of usurping the legislature's authority to decide if brain death constitutes legal death. The court's confident claim to the contrary, it is the legislature, he contended, that is in the best position to speak for the 'moral judgement' of the community." Mary Cornelia Porter, "State Supreme Courts and the Legacy of the Warren Court: Some Old Questions for a New Situation," in Porter and Tarr, *State Supreme Courts*, p. 16. William F. Hyland and David S. Baume, "In Re Quinlan: A Synthesis of Law and Medical Technology," *Rutgers-Camden Law Journal* 8 (1976): 37–64.

47. The court articulated two general sets of principles that must be considered when the issue is the termination of life-supporting equipment. First, the court held that a person does have the right to terminate life support under the constitutionally guaranteed right to privacy and that this right may be exercised through a guardian or family member through the doctrine of substituted judgment if the patient is incompetent (as was Karen Quinlan) to make the decision.

In addition, the court established three criteria that must be met before life-sustaining equipment can be discontinued. First, the family and the guardian must approve removal of the equipment. Second, the attending physician must find that there is no reasonable possibility of recovery. And third, the hospital ethics committee must agree that there is no reasonable possibility of the patient's returning to a cognitive, sapient state. The *Quinlan* court found that the particular facts of this case met these requirements.

In allowing Joseph Quinlan to make the decision to terminate life-supporting medical equipment for his daughter, the court stated: "We have no doubt, in these unhappy circumstances, that if Karen were miraculously lucid for an interval (not altering the existing prognosis of the condition to which she would soon return) and perceptive of her irreversible condition, she would effectively decide upon discontinuance of the life support apparatus, even if it meant the prospect of natural death." The *Quinlan* court further stated, "Our affirmation of Karen's independent right of choice, however, would be based upon her competence to assert it.... It should not be discarded solely on the basis that her condition prevents her conscious exercise of the choice. The only practical way is to permit her guardian and the family to render their best judgement, subject to the qualifications." 355 A.2d at 662, 664. *Quinlan* provided the catalyst for the enactment of living will and natural death statutes and precedent for their construction, e.g., Severns v. Wilmington Medical Center, 421 A.2d. 1334 (Del. 1980).

48. Superintendent of Belchertown State School v. Saikewicz, 370 N.E.2d 417 (Mass. 1977). Chemotherapy involves a series of intravenous injections of drugs,

some of which may be experimental. Although side effects vary from person to person, many patients suffer from loss of appetite, nausea, vomiting, skin problems, and loss of hair. Saikewicz's guardian argued that because of the pain involved, the invasive nature of the procedure, the patient's fear, and his inability to understand the need for the therapy, his ward's best interests would be served by supportive care only. The guardian pointed out that even with chemotherapy, the preservation of the sixty-seven-year-old patient's life was uncertain at best.

49. The court established four state interests that must be considered. The preservation of life was the most important. If a life could be saved by medical procedures, the state's interest outweighed the individual's right to privacy. On the other hand, if the treatment would extend life for only a short period of time and at great cost to the individual, the individual's interest would prevail. Second, the court addressed the question of the protection of innocent third parties, holding that under the doctrine of parens patriae, this particular case did not present the issue. Next, the court ruled that the state's interest in the prevention of suicide was not undermined by the desire of a terminally ill patient to refuse treatment. Suicide, the court noted, requires a specific and express intent to die, and the act of suicide requires that the individual take an active part in bringing about his or her death. In refusing medical treatment, Saikewicz neither expressed intent nor would take an active part in bringing about his demise. Finally, the court held that the maintenance of the ethical integrity of the medical profession does not demand that in all cases every effort to maintain life must be employed. For the *Quinlan* guidelines, see note 47 supra.

50. George Annas, "Competence to Refuse Medical Treatment: Autonomy v. Paternalism," *Toledo Law Review* 15 (1984): 568.

51. Tribe, *Constitutional Protection*, pp. 889–95.

52. Brophy v. New England Sinai Hospital, Inc., 376 N.E. 1232 (Mass. 1978); 487 N.E.2d 626 (Mass. 1986). Paul Brophy was kept alive on feeding tubes for three and one-half years and died eight days after they were removed. *New York Times*, October 24, 1986, p. 17. For an extended discussion of the issues similar to those presented in *Brophy*, see Joanne Lynn, ed., *By No Extraordinary Means: The Choice to Forgo Life-Sustaining Food and Water* (Bloomington: Indiana University Press, 1986).

53. Bouvia v. The Superior Court (Glenchur), 225 Cal. Reptr. 279 (Cal. 1986). Bouvia lost in two earlier rulings.

54. The matter of patient competence is crucial. One of Bouvia's physicians testified that he considered Bouvia's decision to discontinue the tube feeding as "impaired." Another testified: "Doctors like patients to agree with them. When a patient agrees with me that is rational. When an eighty-year-old-lady refuses to have a massive bowel resection for wide-spread cancer, then I send her to a psychiatrist because she is not agreeing with me." See Annas, "Competence to Refuse Medical Treatment," at p. 571, n. 3.

55. *Bouvia*, cite note 53, at 305–8. For the California, Michigan, and New Jersey courts, see Porter, "State Supreme Courts." For New York, see People v. Class, reported in *American Bar Association Journal*, September 1, 1986, p. 84.

56. For a discussion of the California high court's leadership in breaking new legal paths in areas such as marital and nonmarital relationships, adult sexual behavior, sex-oriented expression, and marijuana use, see Michael A. Willemsen,

"Justice Tobriner and the Tolerance of Evolving Lifestyles: Adapting the Law to Social Change," *Hastings Law Journal* 29 (1977): 73–79.

57. People v. Onofre, 415 N.E.2d 936, 943 (N.Y. 1980). Commonwealth v. Bonadio, 415 A.2d 47 (Pa. 1980), State v. Saunders, 381 A.2d 333 (N.J. 1977).

58. In the Netherlands, active euthanasia (terminating life by lethal injection) as opposed to passive euthanasia (removal of artificial life-support systems) is relatively common despite strictures of the nation's criminal code. Relatives or surrogates cannot make decisions for patients who must be competent to choose death. In one instance a quadriplegic woman elected to die, and her request was honored. Francis X. Clines, "Dutch Quietly Lead in Euthanasia Requests," *New York Times*, October 31, 1986, p. 6. While some federal courts have been presented with the right-to-die issue, state courts are providing the significant rulings and, thereby, leadership. For federal cases, see "The Right to Die: An Extension of the Right to Privacy" and "Voluntary Active Euthanasia for the Terminally Ill."

5

Social Services and Egalitarian Activism

PETER J. GALIE

The Warren Court, it is now generally acknowledged, made its signal contribution to an "egalitarian ethos," which many commentators saw as becoming dominant in American society.[1] The impact of the Warren Court in this area is attested to by the attention accorded equality concerns in recent casebooks on constitutional law.[2] While the Burger Court did not attempt a wholesale reversal of these decisions, neither did it continue the move toward an egalitarian society. Professor Gerald Gunther describes this phenomenon as a "thus far and no further" approach.[3]

One of the unintended consequences of this startling burst of judicial energy and innovation by the Warren Court was to place the rest of the judiciary, federal and state, in eclipse. Constitutional law had become federal constitutional law, and the focus of casebooks, law courses, and appellate briefing was on the national Constitution and the Supreme Court.

In response to the Burger Court's "thus far and no further" approach, a number of state courts began to resort to their own constitutions to extend greater protection in the area of individual rights than was forthcoming from the Burger Court in applying the national Bill of Rights. This resurgence of state court activism has been well studied.[4]

This chapter investigates one aspect of this resurgence, that of social services and egalitarian activism among state courts. Specific areas selected are educational financing, welfare, and exclusionary zoning. These choices have been directed by the state judiciaries themselves since it is in these areas that state courts have been most active.

Education

Education has been accorded a preeminent legal status in the United States from the Northwest Ordinance's recognition of the essential role of education to the presence in every state constitution of provisions establishing a system of public schools. Thirty-two constitutions require that these schools be "free." For most of the nation's history and even today, providing for the education of children has been the responsibility of the states and their localities. This responsibility rests primarily on the state legislatures, the state education bureaucracies, and local school boards.

Beginning in the early 1970s, a number of challenges to the educational systems of the states arose. Suits challenging the methods of financing education have been heard in twenty-seven states. Such suits were not isolated phenomena. Efforts to reform the nation's educational systems by equalizing the financial resources of the school districts were also undertaken by reform groups before state legislatures and state educational departments throughout the country. That these reforms were not exclusively or even primarily the result of successful court decisions may be seen when it is noted that by 1981, twenty-eight states had reworked their aid formulas, not only by increasing the amount allocated to each district but also by adding to the funds set aside for poorer districts.[5] In 1972, about 39 percent of school funding came from states and more than 50 percent from localities. By 1982 those figures were reversed.[6]

State supreme courts have played a vital role in the movement toward equal educational opportunity for all. In responding to state constitutionally based challenges to school financing programs, these courts have based their rulings on three grounds: cases resting on educational clauses of the constitution, cases using the federal test for equal protection (strict scrutiny triggered by the presence of fundamental rights), and cases resting on other constitutional provisions.

Cases Resting on Educational Clauses of the Constitution

New Jersey. Robinson v. Cahill[7] was the first state case following the Supreme Court decision on the same question[8] to strike down a financing system on state constitutional grounds. The decision precipitated a major political and fiscal crisis in New Jersey that continues to excite interest in that state;[9] it illustrates the limitations of, as well as the prospects for, achieving social reform through the judiciary.

Robinson struck down the state's system of financing public school education. Chief Justice Joseph Weintraub, writing for the court, rejected the notion of education as a fundamental right as too vague and potentially too inclusive. Wealth, the chief justice continued, may or may not be "an invidious basis" for the imposition of a burden or enjoyment of a benefit.[10] To allow local areas to decide how much they will raise for social services means that expenditures per resident will vary from district to district. "If this is held to constitute classification according to 'wealth' and [is] therefore 'suspect,' " the political structure will be fundamentally changed.[11] Chief Justice Weintraub was not willing to accept the consequences of embracing such a position. Even more surprising was the court's refusal to rely on equal protection.[12] Instead, Weintraub turned to language that provides for a "thorough and efficient" system of free public schools.[13]

Although rejecting reliance on the equal protection provisions, the court's decision rested on considerations of equality and equal opportunity. The court was reluctant to mandate a specific course of action and left it to the legislative and executive branches to develop a program consistent with its decision. Given the potential impact of the ruling, that course of action may have been politic, but it made it likely that the issue would eventually be back in the courts. Seven decisions (*Robinson I* through *VII*),[14] spanning almost seven years, precipitated bitter controversy in the state. A direct result of the decision was the Public School Education Act of 1975, which the court declared "in all respects constitutional on its face."[15]

A study commissioned by the Joint Legislative Committee on Public Schools concluded that the new financing system had achieved property tax relief but that it had failed to assist poor school districts to raise per-pupil expenditures to levels equal to those in wealthier districts.[16] Spurred by such disparities, another challenge was raised to the 1975 legislation. It reached the New Jersey Supreme Court in *Abbott v. Burke*.[17] The education act was upheld, and the issue was placed in the hands of the state department of education and the legislature. More important, Justice Alan Handler rejected the warnings and counsels of restraint offered by Justice Weintraub regarding the use of the equal protection clause. Referring to New Jersey's rejection of federal equal protection analysis in earlier cases, he called for a balancing test when equal protection claims are raised under the state constitution.

With both the education and equal protection provisions implicated, Handler developed a relationship between them. Under the education provision, the crux of the matter was "whether it appears that the disadvantaged children will not be able to compete in and contribute to the society entered by the relatively advantaged children."[18] The equal protection provision, on the other hand, called for proof that "even if all children receive a minimally thorough and efficient education, the financing scheme engenders no more inequality than is required by any other state interest."[19] One such legitimate state interest, according to Handler, might be local governmental autonomy.

While Weintraub's decision in *Robinson I* was viewed at the time as a prime example of judicial activism, his argument did not provide any precedent for a resort to the equal protection clause as a basis for achieving equality in the more general area of social welfare. Handler's decision in *Abbott*, on the other hand, while seeming to be an example of judicial restraint, may well have laid the groundwork for greater use of the equal protection clause to achieve an egalitarian society. Whatever is the future of the equal protection clause in New Jersey as a vehicle for social reform, the question of equalizing educational financing is still before the courts, and the much-noted goal has yet to be attained.

What has been the impact of this experiment in judicial activism in the educational policy arena? If impact is measured in terms of the judiciary's ability to act as an agenda setter, the court's intervention has been a resounding success. A new public school education act was the direct result of the court's decisions; indirectly, the court can claim some credit for increasing the aid coming from the state, as well as a corresponding reduction in the reliance on property taxes. Richard Lehne, after taking account of increases in state aid previously added by the state legislature, estimates that "in the years after 1976–1977 credit for a modest increase of about seven percent in state assistance to local school districts can be attributed to *Robinson*."[20] If, however, the measure relates to the levels of disparities that exist among school districts, judicial activism in New Jersey has had a negligible impact on the policy process. Substantial evidence exists that inequities have not been reduced, and in some cases new ones have been created.[21]

An assistant commissioner of education noted the difficulty of determining the precise impact of the fiscal changes wrought by *Robinson* on educational achievement: "Despite the fact that urban districts have made progress on the Minimum Basic Skills Test, passage of which has been required for graduation from high school, the major urban centers in New Jersey still have the highest failure rate."[22] Fundamental reform is needed, unfortunately more than any court, however aggressive, is capable of achieving.

Washington. In Washington, the state supreme court, in *Seattle School District No. 1, Kings County v. State,*[23] ruled that the education clause of the state constitution gives the state's schoolchildren the right to an "ample education" through a "general and uniform system of public schools." Because Seattle's claim was that state financing did not provide sufficient funds to enable districts to carry out basic educational programs required by the constitution, the question of equal funding was not involved, and the equal protection clause played no part in the decision. However, the court did transform what seemed to be a mandate to and an obligation of the legislature into a personal right or guarantee.[24] The Washington Assembly passed legislation providing for such funding, but subsequent budget cuts by the governor occasioned further litigation. In a subsequent case, *Seattle School District No. 1, Kings County v. State (Seattle II)*,[25] the Washington court refused to enjoin the governor while the state was in the throes of a fiscal crisis. In *Seattle II*, the court held that the right to an "ample education" did not ensure an entitlement, without a clear demonstration, to a specific dollar amount. The court reserved comment on the merits until such time as the issue came before it.[26] Like the outcome in New Jersey, the Washington result remained inconclusive, the issue moving from the judiciary, to the legislature, to the executive, and back to the judiciary.

State Courts Using the Federal Test: Strict Scrutiny Triggered by Fundamental Right

California. California's supreme court first declared its school financing scheme unconstitutional exclusively on independent state grounds in *Serrano v. Priest (Serrano II)*.[27] The court stated that discrimination in educational opportunity on the basis of wealth involved a suspect classification violative of state equal protection and that education was a "fundamental interest" under California law.[28] However, the court rejected the notion that education was fundamental merely because it was mentioned in the constitution. Education was a fundamental right, the court argued, because it was one of those interests that "lies at the core of our free and representative form of government."[29]

Education in contemporary America, like voting, is a right indispensable to effective representative government, and, as such, it is fundamental. The effect of this line of reasoning has been twofold. First, it freed the court from having to consider every interest noted in the California Constitution as fundamental. The court took official notice of the size and character of the state constitution, agreeing with the description of that document as a "prolix and formidable Charter."[30] Second, the court was not restricted to describing as fundamental only those rights or interests mentioned explicitly in the constitution.

California has made significant strides since *Serrano*, and much of the credit must be given to the court. According to figures from the California State Department of Education, in 1985–1986, 94.8 percent of all school districts showed average daily attendance within the *Serrano* closure. That compares with a 50 percent figure in 1974–1975.[31] Not all of this progress can be directly attributable to the court's decision, but there is no doubt that the California reform acts were the direct result of *Serrano*. On this issue, both compliance and implementation were achieved.

Connecticut. Unlike the decision in California, the Connecticut case of *Horton v. Meskill*[32] relied on the presence of an education clause in the state constitution to confer on education a fundamental right status. The

supreme court found no compelling state interest to justify the disparities. *Horton*, like the rulings in New Jersey and Washington, left it to
the legislature to fashion acts consistent with its mandate. Remedial legislation, adopted in 1977, provided a new financing equalization formula
to be phased in over a five-year period.[33]

The original plaintiffs did not challenge the constitutionality of the
act, but in 1980, the general assembly twice amended the law, and these
amendments precipitated suit. After an interim decision concerning
which localities could be intervenors,[34] the challenge once again reached
the Connecticut Supreme Court in *Horton v. Meskill* (*Horton III*).[35] The
court upheld the constitutionality of the 1979 legislation; in doing so, it
rejected the first part of the fundamental interest–strict scrutiny–compelling state interest formula used in *Horton I*. The majority drew a
distinction between racial discrimination and discrimination based upon
wealth: "The former is absolute, the latter is relative."[36] From this starting
point, the court went on to argue that the sui generis nature of litigation
involving school financing militates against formalistic reliance on the
usual standards of equal protection analysis. Instead the court turned
to the test suggested by the Supreme Court in deciding apportionment
cases. Applying this approach to the educational financing legislation,
Justice Allen Peters concluded:

Like legislative apportionment plans, educational financing legislation must be
strictly scrutinized using a three-step process. First, the plaintiffs must make a
prima facie showing that disparities in educational expenditures are more than *de
minimis* in that the disparities continue to jeopardize the plaintiffs' fundamental
right to education. If they make that showing, the burden then shifts to the state
to justify these disparities as incident to the advancement of a legitimate state policy. If the state's justification is acceptable, the state must further demonstrate that
the continuing disparities are nevertheless not so great as to be unconstitutional.[37]

The case was remanded to the trial court for consideration "in accordance with the new standard articulated by the court," taking into
account "the possibility of embarrassment to the operations of government."[38]

The court had obviously retreated; it was willing to adopt a less stringent standard and to allow factors beyond state control to shape its determination. Has the series of court decisions had any impact on achieving
"the policy of providing significant equalizing state support to local education"?[39] If the percentage interval between the wealthiest and poorest
districts is taken as the measure, the gap has been reduced from 86.9 percent in 1972 to 70.1 percent in 1983–1984. Even here it is difficult to
characterize *Horton*'s impact; the trend toward equalization had begun
much before the *Horton* decision had its real impact in the 1979 legisla-

ture. The trial court noted that, from 1978 to 1984, the state share of local education had increased from 28.2 percent to 42.9 percent, while the local communities' share decreased from 63.3 percent to 49.8 percent.[40] Should budget surpluses continue to be available, the Connecticut legislature may be expected to meet the requirements of *Horton III*.

West Virginia. In *Pauley v. Kelley*,[41] the West Virginia Supreme Court struck down the state's educational financing scheme. According to the court, the constitutional mandate of "a thorough and efficient system of free schools" meant that education was "a fundamental constitutional right" in West Virginia.[42] Thus "under our equal protection guarantees, any discriminatory classification found in the educational system cannot stand unless the state can demonstrate some compelling state interest to justify the unequal classification."[43] So far the *Pauley* court had merely repeated a formula that appeared in most of the other school finance cases. But Justice Sam Harshbarger noted that the standard enunciated by the court might require more than "merely equality of educational financing to the counties."[44] Perhaps the court had in mind a focus on educational outcomes rather than financial inputs.

In remanding the case to the circuit court, the West Virginia Supreme Court gave instructions for an inquiry into the causes of the lack of a high-quality educational system in the state. This was, in effect, a commission to examine the entire public school system of West Virginia. In the interim, the court was faced with the first serious challenge to its goal of making West Virginia meet its constitutional responsibility to provide quality education to all residents of the state. Petitioners in *State ex rel. Board of Education v. Rockefeller*[45] had sought a writ of mandamus to compel the governor to restore a 2 percent reduction in expenditures authorized by the legislature for public education in 1981. The court declared the reductions unconstitutional and issued the writ. Since education had been declared a fundamental interest, there was a "constitutionally preferred status" for public education expenditures, and these "expenditures cannot be reduced in the absence of a compelling factual record to demonstrate the necessity thereof."[46] The *Rockefeller* decision had gone further than that of any other court in the country in giving education the status of a fundamental right.[47]

Three years after *Pauley*, the circuit court submitted an opinion[48] that amounted to an indictment of not only the state's method for financing education but also of the West Virginia Board of Education. The court appointed a special master to oversee the development of a master plan for the "constitutional composition, operation and financing of the educational system in West Virginia."[49] A plan was drawn up, presented to, and approved by the circuit court. Suit was filed challenging the plan. This challenge reached the West Virginia Supreme Court in *Pauley v. Bailey (Pauley III)*.[50] The court found that a specific timetable "would not be efficacious at this time," that the plan did provide specific enforcement, but that the board of education was not in compliance with the plan. It then remanded the case to the circuit court for further monitoring.[51] *Pauley III* went further than any other court decision in requiring not just a minimally adequate education but also mandating that the state must ensure "the development of every child to his or her capacity."[52] The *Rockefeller* decision indicated that the West Virginia court was willing to enforce that constitutional standard.

The results of the *Pauley* trilogy and the *Rockefeller* decision were dramatic. A major overhaul of the West Virginia school system was undertaken. Everything from the quality of the physical facilities to the character of the curriculum was evaluated. Included were a variety of monitoring and assessment measures to determine the extent to which schools were meeting the twin goals of "equality of substantive educational offerings" and of producing students "who are competent in functional skills, and prepared for the next academic or occupational level."[53] While major progress has been made in the fifty-five county school districts in the areas of noncost endeavors, the funding remains unequal. The court as of late 1987 had not yet forced a resolution of the funding issue, but it had not retreated in two cases that came to the court subsequent to *Pauley III*.[54]

Wisconsin. In *Buse v. Smith*,[55] the school financing program was based on a constitutional requirement that "the rule of taxation shall be uniform." This is the only decision premised upon a uniform or equal tax provision. Yet it has been one of the most successful in terms of implementation. This success is ironical, however, since the law struck down was one that required wealthier districts to contribute locally raised monies to a state fund, which was then distributed to the poorer districts of the state.

Educational Malpractice

In 1983 the National Commission on Excellence in Education issued a report entitled *A Nation at Risk*. In one of its most-quoted passages, the commission noted: "The educational foundations of our society are presently being threatened by a rising tide of mediocrity that threatens our future as a nation and a people."[56]

One prominent student of American education concluded that for many years, urban public schools have "failed to educate millions of their students adequately."[57] In such an atmosphere and in an age when individuals and groups have been turning to the courts for redress of grievances in areas heretofore thought to be outside judicial scrutiny, it is not surprising that suits arose claiming that the failure to educate constitutes educational malpractice. Because tort law is a matter of state concern and constitutional provisions dealing with education are found in all state constitutions, success would appear most likely in state courts. Success, however, has not been forthcoming. As of 1985, no high court has recognized a cause of action in educational malpractice on any grounds, constitutional or otherwise. In view of the willingness of some state courts to take active roles in other areas of controversy and complexity, such restraint is remarkable. An examination of one case, *Torres v. Little Flower Children's Services*,[58] will help to explain this reluctance.

Torres, a former student who was functionally illiterate despite having received public schooling, brought action against the social services department and the child agency alleging malpractice. The New York Court of Appeals rejected both the statutory and constitutional claims. Justice Judith Kaye described state-created entitlements to an education as "nebulous." She went on to state that they "do not lend themselves to protection" through procedural due process requirements.[59] Thus the state's highest court, in a 4–3 decision, voted to continue its hands-off policy. More generally, despite the willingness of state courts to extend tort law in other areas and the presence of educational provisions in their state constitutions, the prospects for judicial activism and innovative court policymaking in this area are not auspicious.

The Handicapped and Education

In a few states, the rights of the handicapped to an education have been litigated under state constitutional provisions dealing with education. In *In the Interest of G.H.*,[60] the North Dakota Supreme Court, calling education a fundamental right under the state constitution,[61] ruled that failure to provide educational opportunity for handicapped children violated the privileges and immunities clause and the education article of the state constitution.[62] On the other hand, in *Levine v. State*,[63] the New Jersey Supreme Court held that parents of handicapped children who could afford to provide adequate care and educational services to those children were not entitled to reimbursements by the state under a constitutional provision that guarantees a free education to all school-age children or under the state's equal protection clause.[64] The court, going beyond Justice Weintraub in *Robinson I*, conceded that education was a "fundamental right" under the New Jersey Constitution; but the majority argued that the classification here, though based on "persons afflicted with mental impairments," was not "suspect."[65]

It is best to view the activities of the courts as a part of a broader movement toward reform of the educational systems. In the 1970s, that movement focused on financial inequities; in the 1980s, it has centered on matters of curriculum, pupil achievement, and teacher competency. The courts have not been the only or even the primary actors in the move toward educational reform. By the mid–1980s, approximately thirty states had revised their aid formulas, generally providing additional aid to poor districts.[66] By 1986, every state had a full-time panel on education; six years earlier, there were only a handful. Forty-five states have revised their school curricula related to training in basic skills; forty-seven have altered their laws regarding teacher certification; and a growing number have required proficiency tests for students as a condition of graduation.[67] In the summer of 1986, the nation's governors issued a report calling for authority for the state to take over the operation of any school district that fails to meet basic standards.[68]

To the extent that courts have been successful in producing fiscally neutral financial systems and to the extent that their decisions have focused attention on the condition of their respective educational establishments, they have contributed to the goal of equal educational opportunity. But as a number of commentators have pointed out, a fiscally neutral standard is of "limited future usefulness" and is not likely to "sustain further progress in school finance reform."[69] For these reasons, educational reform groups have tried to have courts adopt standards that would define equal educational opportunity in terms of substance and quality as measured by outcomes. Such a course would involve the courts even more deeply in the complexities and subtleties of the educational process. With the possible exception of the West Virginia Supreme Court, no state court has been willing to accept this challenge, and, it appears, they are not likely to do so in the near future as concerns for equity continue to be superseded by other issues.

Welfare Benefits

The U.S. Constitution and the Bill of Rights are designed to protect individual political rights. Social and economic rights are not a part of either document. In contrast, twentieth-century constitutions have addressed such issues. The United Nations Declaration of Human Rights is typical in this respect.[70] Unlike many contemporary constitutions, the U.S. Constitution is silent with respect to affirmative rights.[71] To the contrary, a number of state constitutions include explicit provisions guaranteeing the right to the care and support of the needy,[72] the right to bargain collectively,[73] the right to work,[74] environmental rights,[75] provisions for free education,[76] and protection of the handicapped.[77]

Despite this range, constitutionally based state court decisions treating welfare benefits or rights are not copious. Three cases illustrate the possibilities as well as the limitations on state court activity in this area.

In *Tucker v. Toia*,[78] the New York Court of Appeals struck down a provision of the social service law that determined eligibility for home relief. The section provided that home relief was not to be provided to persons under the age of twenty-one who do not live with their parents or legally appointed guardians unless the applicant instituted support proceedings against any such parent or guardian. The court noted that assistance was not a matter of legislative grace.[79] After reviewing the legislative history of the provision, the court concluded that the constitution "imposes on the state an affirmative duty to aid the needy."[80] The judiciary, the judges declared, has an obligation to see that this "responsibility which is as fundamental as any responsibility of government" is not shirked.[81]

In *Butte Community Union v. Lewis,*[82] the Montana Supreme Court was faced with a challenge to a statute that denied general assistance benefits to able-bodied individuals under 50 with no minor children. The trial court judge had ruled that the Montana Constitution established a fundamental right to welfare "for those who by reason of age, infirmities, or misfortune may have need for aid of society."[83] The supreme court rejected this analysis, concluding that the state constitution does not establish a fundamental right to welfare for the aged, infirm, or unfortunate. However, because the constitutional convention delegates had declared welfare to be sufficiently important to warrant a reference in the constitution, the court held that "a classification which abridges welfare benefits is subject to heightened scrutiny under equal protection analysis, and [the act] must fall under such scrutiny."[84] Justice Frank Morrison, Jr., explicitly based the decision on the Montana equal protection clause and the notion that "we will not be bound by decisions of the U.S. Supreme Court where independent state grounds exist for developing heightened and expanded scrutiny rights under our state constitution."[85] Interestingly, Morrison argued that, because the welfare clause was not in the declaration of rights, it was not in the category of fundamental rights but "as a benefit lodged in our state constitution is an interest whose abridgement requires something more than a rational relationship to a government objective."[86] This was an attempt to incorporate the various interests mentioned in the constitution within a rights-expanding scheme while avoiding the problem of extending heightened scrutiny to all the interests mentioned, no matter how incidentally or casually. The Montana Supreme Court addressed the unique character of its constitution and incorporated that document's feature into an intelligible rights-expanding framework. Thus *Tucker* and *Butte* stand as signal examples of judicial activism in the area of equality of treatment.

Bonnett v. State[87] was a bold attempt to extend the *Robinson* principle to the system of financing welfare in New Jersey. That system, as well as the judicial and administrative functions, were challenged on equal-protection grounds and the principle of uniformity of taxation. The limiting consequences of Chief Justice Weintraub's decision to rest *Robinson* on the education clause rather than equal protection, because of the "convulsive implications" of doing so, provided a receptive court in

Bonnett with the precedent and rationale for its rejection of the challenge.[88]

Perhaps the court was prompted by the bitter experience with the *Robinson* decisions and the complexities that unfolded in the wake of forays into the zoning area.[89] For whatever reasons, it was unwilling to move any further into an area that potentially struck at the heart of the state's welfare financing system.

Although little state court activity has taken place, there is, by virtue of the numerous provisions dealing with the welfare of individuals, potential for the continuing development of social and economic rights, a potential not readily available at the federal level. *Butte* demonstrated that potential; to the contrary, *Bonnett* made clear that there are ample grounds open to courts unwilling to play a more prominent role in constitutional policymaking in this area.

Exclusionary Zoning and Economic Inequality

Zoning was first used extensively in the 1920s. Initially, a few courts held that the separation of single and multifamily dwellings was a form of unconstitutional economic segregation.[90] The Supreme Court decision in *Euclid v. Ambler*[91] changed all of that. "State courts fell in line and the segregation of multiple family dwellings became an accepted fact."[92] The effect of *Euclid* and subsequent decisions was to make zoning law a part of real estate law. The Supreme Court reinforced this position by ruling in *Lindsey v. Normet* that "absent a constitutional mandate the assurance of adequate housing is a legislative not a judicial function."[93] This hands-off policy was colorfully and cogently summed up by one judge: "As long as the communities don't impinge on race or religion I say let them do as they please."[94]

Local governments and legislatures were even less likely to take the initiative in this area by placing limits on the economic segregation and divisiveness that were the most obvious but by no means the only consequences of widespread exclusionary zoning.

Four state judiciaries have taken noteworthy steps in applying constitutional standards to exclusionary zoning practices. Pennsylvania adopted a fair-share approach to the question of apportioning low- and moderate-income housing to relevant communities. In *Surrick v. Zoning Hearing Board*,[95] applications of the principle were to be based on actual effect;[96] questions of intent were peripheral. The bold doctrines expressed in *Surrick* were questioned in subsequent cases,[97] but they were reaffirmed in *Fernley v. Board of Supervisors*.[98] Writing for a unanimous court, Justice William Hutchinson set forth the governing principle that any zoning ordinance that totally excludes a legitimate use will be regarded with "circumspection, and therefore, must bear a substantial relationship to a stated public purpose."[99]

In reaching its conclusion in *Fernley*, the court ruled that the ordinance violated the due process clause of the Pennsylvania Constitution. A "substantial relationship" standard appeared to be the equivalent of a strict scrutiny test. Consequently, the court required zoning regulations with exclusionary aspects to meet a standard not required by the U.S. Supreme Court or, for that matter, by the overwhelming majority of state supreme courts.

There was a lack of consensus in the Pennsylvania court with regard to such crucial issues as to when exclusions are total or partial, the definition of particular uses, and the degree of deference to be accorded local zoning board decisions.[100] Yet it has ensured that lower- and middle-income families are not wholly at the mercy of local communities and their zoning boards. The goals set by the judiciary in Pennsylvania may not be as lofty as those established by the New Jersey Supreme Court, but its decisions do provide a constitutional basis for limiting or reversing the economic and social segregation brought on or maintained by exclusionary zoning practices.

If the Pennsylvania courts were the first to apply constitutional standards to zoning practices that prohibited the construction of low- or moderate-income housing, the New Jersey Supreme Court has made the most dramatic and expansive decisions in this area. In 1975, that court announced its decision in *Southern Burlington County NAACP v. Township of Mt. Laurel (Mt. Laurel I).*[101] It was the most far-reaching exclusionary zoning decision in the state's history and indeed in the rest of the country. *Mt. Laurel I* held a zoning ordinance in violation of the general welfare clause of the New Jersey Constitution.[102] Specifically, the court declared that a developing municipality violated the state constitution by excluding housing for low-income people; for a municipality to satisfy its constitutional obligation under the general welfare clause, it had to provide a realistic opportunity to meet its fair share of the present and prospective regional need for a particular type of housing. Despite the sweeping character of this decision and the controversy that it engendered, it was not clear exactly what response was being required of localities.[103] Moreover, the court, perhaps hoping to gain the support of municipalities, gave them "full opportunity . . . to act without judicial supervision."[104] By explicitly adopting the role of agenda setter, the court left the details of implementation to local governments.

In view of its experience with *Robinson v. Cahill*, the New Jersey court should not have been surprised by the nonresponse. In the eight years between *Mt. Laurel I* and *Mt. Laurel II*, not one unit of lower-income housing had been built as a result of the decision.[105] The court went on to reaffirm *Mt. Laurel I* in *Southern Burlington County NAACP v. Township of Mt. Laurel (Mt. Laurel II).*[106] But, abandoning the relatively passive stance of *Mt. Laurel I*, the court, in a 246-page unanimous decision, bristled with anger at the inaction of the state and localities.[107] The court proceeded to adopt a system imposing numerical fair shares on the regional requirements. It defined the need for low- and moderate-income housing strictly, adopting standards used in the federal housing subsidy programs. It also reversed its earlier ruling to limit the decision to developing areas; and it provided remedies. In addition, the court established a three-judge panel to hear all *Mt. Laurel II* cases throughout the state. In adopting these specific directives, the court had moved emphatically into uncharted areas.

The most significant result of *Mt. Laurel II* was the passage by the New Jersey legislature of the Fair Housing Act of 1985.[108] This legislation essentially incorporated into statutory form the remedies fashioned by *Mt. Laurel II*. Zoning, once almost entirely within the purview of local governments, was now brought under the direct control of the state judiciary and legislature. At this point, all three branches of the state government were committed to guaranteeing that the housing needs of low- and moderate-income persons would be met and to eliminating exclusive enclaves of wealth and privilege. The supreme court also extended *Mt. Laurel II* to areas that had been under the jurisdiction of other state administrative agencies.

By 1986, the *Mt. Laurel II* decision had generated nearly 150 lawsuits. In *Hills Development Co. v. Bernards Twp. in Somerset County (Mt. Laurel III)*,[109] the court sustained the constitutionality of the fair housing act. In upholding the law, the court explicitly applauded the state government and the lower court judges for their efforts; it then addressed the criticisms directed at its activism.[110] The fair housing act, the court concluded, is the "kind of response that would permit us to withdraw from their field, [which] is what this court has always wanted and sought."[111]

Hills Development may signal the end of judicial involvement with exclusionary zoning in New Jersey, and it marks what appears to be a major shift in the locus of decisionmaking. The crucial question, in terms of policymaking, is what has changed as a result of ten years of activism by the court and legislature. The court, in *Hills Development*, noted the settlement of twenty-two Mt. Laurel cases[112] and, by one estimate, zoning to accommodate 25,000 lower- and middle-income units had resulted.[113] Whether the court will accomplish its stated goal of ensuring a "realistic opportunity for lower income housing in all parts of the state where sensible planning calls for such housing"[114] remains problematic.

A second consequence of the *Mt. Laurel* series is less conjectural: the result of the ten-year controversy was to centralize what was once an essentially local matter. The pursuit of equal opportunity in the zoning area, as in the financing of education, has had the effect of moving power and decisionmaking away from local governments and toward the state.

Standards for judging whether zoning ordinances would pass constitutional muster in New York were first announced in *Berenson v. New Castle*,[115] a decision handed down the same year as *Mt. Laurel I*. The court established a two-pronged test for determining the reasonableness of zoning ordinances: whether the town provided for present and future housing needs of the town's residents and whether regional needs were considered.[116] Five years later, the court returned to the question of exclusionary zoning in *Kurzius v. Upper Brookville*.[117] Applying the two-pronged test of *Berenson*, it found that the large-lot zoning ordinance had met the test. The court, throughout its decision, made clear its unwillingness to take on the active role assumed by the New Jersey Supreme Court. It presumed the constitutionality of zoning ordinances and referred approvingly to the *Berenson* court's view that "zoning is essentially a legislative act...and until the day comes when regional rather than local governmental units can make such determinations, the courts must assess the reasonableness of what the locality has done."[118] The New York courts generally have been more cautious and have been unwilling to go beyond the *Berenson* test.

California's first steps in dealing with exclusionary zoning practices came from the state legislature rather than from the courts. The purpose of the law was to prohibit exclusionary zoning practices by localities.[119] Prior to the act's passage in 1980, the California courts had already determined that zoning decisions were essentially matters for localities and the state legislature.[120] Indeed, passage of the housing legislation could have been taken as a signal for a more activist role for the courts. One section of the act seemed to provide some encouragement since it placed the burden of proof on the locality when an exclusionary action was challenged in the courts.[121] But the California courts so far have focused on another part of the law, which defines the standard of review as "whether the housing element *substantially* [my emphasis]...complies with the requirements of this article."[122]

No California court has yet required a municipality to adopt a particular type of housing program.[123] In spite of the unwillingness of the California courts to take a more active role, over twenty municipalities had adopted some form of inclusionary housing programs by 1985.[124]

Aside from a few scattered cases, generally dealing with mobile home exclusions, only in California, New York, New Jersey, and Pennsylvania have the courts taken active steps to deal with the question of exclusionary zoning. Among these, only New Jersey has gone so far as to mandate affirmative action under fair share plans that direct specific results for the various communities.[125]

An overall assessment of the role of the state judiciaries in promoting equality of access and social diversity is difficult. The majority of state courts have played no role in applying constitutional principles of equality to issues of zoning. In some states like New York, the judiciary has placed some limitations on exclusionary zoning practices, but no low-income housing has been constructed as a result of the *Berenson* line of cases.[126] This is likely due to the New York Court of Appeals' refusal to mandate fair share goals for specific communities and its unwillingness to imitate the more aggressive stance adopted by the New Jersey judiciary.[127] The Pennsylvania judiciary has played a role somewhere between these two positions.[128] Where the courts have been most aggressive, the impact has been greatest; where they have been content merely to lay down general guidelines and to place the burden on the plaintiffs, little change has taken place.

It is doubtful whether the judiciary, even one as determined as that of New Jersey, is capable of creating a balanced distribution of population by social and economic class. Surely the courts have no illusions concerning their ability to provide significant help to the urban poor. But the record of the states does show that, once a constitutional basis is established, courts can limit or reverse some of the egregious manifestations of social and economic segregation brought about or maintained by exclusionary zoning practices. In New York and California, the doctrines and mechanisms now in place will enable courts to consider fair share allocations of lower-income housing. To that extent, at least, state judiciaries can and have played an important role in protecting and fostering egalitarian values.

Conclusion

The degree to which state courts have had an impact on the policy process in terms of promoting equality is limited; the results have been mixed, but the courts can point to a measure of success. All the same, the pursuit of equality has caused a centralization of authority and decisionmaking. Control moved initially to the judiciary and subsequently lodged in the bureaucracy. The courts did not cause this centralization, which was well underway for a number of decades, but it is fair to say that they have contributed to it. The result may be an unintended one, and even a necessary one, but it has placed the state judiciaries in the position of contributing to the bureaucratization of society in the name of equality.

Traditionally, state courts have not played a major role in defining and protecting individual rights, though they have served as active policymakers in other areas. The change began to occur in the 1970s as state courts, with increasing frequency, resorted to their state constitutions to provide greater protection for individual rights than was available from the Supreme Court. In 1986 alone, in over sixty cases state supreme courts relied exclusively on their own charters to grant protections to their citizens more extensive than those found at the federal level. Moreover, at least some of these courts have been willing to fashion remedies and to develop structures to ensure that their decisions are implemented. The decisions have provided ample and vivid evidence of tension between the traditional role of courts and the new model of public law litigation.[129]

The courts have entertained suits that are multipolar, involving numerous parties and points of view, as opposed to the traditional bipolar private suit. The West Virginia Supreme Court, in its education decisions, mandated the creation of a body that would include all of the relevant parties concerned with education in the state. The courts have been forward looking with the use of broad remedial decrees such as those mandated by the New Jersey Supreme Court in *Mt. Laurel II* and *Robinson IV*. Finally, they have been willing to resort to special masters and special courts to ensure that implementation is carried out in an informed and intelligent fashion.

Almost all state constitutions contain provisions dealing with education, and all have equal protection clauses or language that has been interpreted to be the functional equivalent of such a clause. Despite these facts, of the twenty-seven challenges to school financing schemes, only a third have been successful. The difference between the results reached by the Supreme Court in the *Rodriguez* case and the nine courts that have overturned their respective methods for financing education cannot be explained simply in terms of the presence of provisions explicitly relating to education. These courts have relied upon their equal protection clauses, usually in conjunction with provisions dealing with education, to justify treating education as a fundamental right. Other state courts have turned innocuous clauses like "a thorough and efficient system of free public education" or the vague "ample provision for education" into powerful tools for effecting significant policy changes.

By moving to the center of the policymaking process, state courts have occasioned turmoil, disrupted the political process, and precipitated sharp confrontations with other branches of government and powerful interest groups. Yet the observer is struck not so much by the failures as by the successes of courts like those in New Jersey and West Virginia, which persevered when their initial decisions created opposition and confusion. Admittedly, the cost of accomplishing these results must be factored into any final evaluation. That courts may ignore certain important variables, distort priorities, and act on assumptions not supported by the relevant data serves to demonstrate that when courts move beyond declaring policies invalid and into the fashioning of remedies, they, like their counterparts in the legislative and executive branches, sometimes make mistakes. That is not surprising. It is remarkable that they have not erred more often.

Numerous areas have been left undeveloped by the Supreme Court because of the absence of federal constitutional provisions, judicial disinclination as in economic due process, considerations of federalism, national perspective, or ideological bent. It would seem appropriate for state supreme courts to play a more active role to fill the lacunae. Such areas include a variety of state economic regulations not reviewed by the Supreme Court, education, zoning, employment, the right to shelter for the homeless, environmental issues, and social services traditionally provided by state and local governments.

State courts can contribute to the growth of a free and humane society. They have already added a new dimension to equal protection, one that would not otherwise have been available had reliance been placed solely on federal courts.

State courts, in effect, have made two decisions: to interpret relevant constitutional clauses so that they bear directly on pressing questions and to read these provisions as primary rights rather than as grants to the legislature, thus retaining responsibility for enforcement in the courts. The combination of these creative readings, along with the activism involved in assuming the responsibility for decisionmaking, are first steps in the creation of a body of state-based constitutional law unprecedented in American history. State courts, it appears, are finally emerging from the shadow of the Warren Court.

Notes

I would like to acknowledge the financial support of the Canisius College Research and Publications Committee. I also extend special thanks to William Kubik for his assistance with the research and to Paulette Kirsch and Ann Reinhold for their assistance in preparing the manuscript.

1. Philip Kurland, *Politics and the Warren Court* (Chicago: University of Chicago Press, 1970), pp. xx, 98ff; Alexander Bickel, *The Supreme Court and the Idea of Progress* (New York: Harper Torchbooks, 1970), p. 13.

2. Gerald Gunther, *Constitutional Law*, 11th ed. (Mineola, N.Y.: Foundation Press, 1985).

3. Id., p. 589.

4. Ronald Collins and Peter Galie, Special Supplement, "State Constitutional Law: Cases and Selected Secondary Materials," *National Law Journal*, September 26, 1986. This listing, by no means exhaustive, contains over 250 articles or monographs.

5. Jonathan Friendly, "The Disparity of Resources," *New York Times*, February 19, 1985, p. C1. For example, subsequent to San Antonio Independent School District v. Rodriquez, 411 U.S. 1 (1973), in which the Supreme Court ruled that unequal funding of school districts did not violate the national Con-

stitution, the Texas state legislature enacted a comprehensive education reform that included a more fully equalized financing scheme. House Bill No. 72, Act of July 13, 1984, ch. 28, 1984 Tex. Sess. law. Serv. 269 (Vernon). While the legislation provided for equalization of funds from the state, it allowed each district to supplement the state funds with local tax resources. A district court judge in Texas has ruled that the resulting inequalities are a violation of the Texas Constitution, "Texas Plan for School Financing Is Found Discriminatory by Judge" *New York Times*, April 29, 1987, p. A20.

6. Faye A. Silas, "Schools v. States: Suits Challenge Fund Equality," *American Bar Association Journal* 70 (March 1984): 40.

7. Robinson v. Cahill, 303 A.2d 273 (N.J. 1973).

8. In San Antonio Independent School District v. Rodriguez, 411 U.S. 1 (1973), the Supreme Court, by a 5–4 decision, ruled that existing state school financial programs did not violate the equal protection clause of the Fourteenth Amendment.

9. See Richard Lehne, *The Quest for Justice: The Politics of School Finance Reform* (New York: Longmans, 1978), for an excellent account of this crisis. Lehne takes the story to 1977.

10. 303 A.2d at 282.

11. Id., at 283.

12. There is no equal protection clause in the New Jersey Constitution. The New Jersey Supreme Court has read into a "natural and inalienable rights" provision a due process and equal protection clause. See State v. Baker, 405 A.2d 368, 375 (N.J. 1979); Greenberg v. Kimmelman, 494 A.2d 294, 302 (N.J. 1985).

13. Id., at 291.

14. Robinson v. Cahill (Robinson I), 303 A.2d 273 (1973); cert. denied, 414 U.S. 978; aff'd on rehearing, jurisdiction retained (Robinson II), 306 A.2d 65 (1972), order entered (Robinson III), 335 A.2d 6 (1975), order entered 339 A.2d 193, republished (Robinson IV), 351 A.2d 713 (1975), order vacated (Robinson V), 335 A.2d 129 (1976), injunction issued (Robinson VI), 358 A.2d 457 (1976), injunction dissolved (Robinson VII), 360 A.2d 400 (1976.)

15. Robinson v. Cahill (V), 355 A.2d 129, 139 (1976).

16. *New York Times*, June 10, 1980, II, p. 8. Lehne, *Quest for Justice*, p. 173, found substantial disparities in funds available in 1977.

17. Abbott v. Burke, 495 A.2d 376 (1985).

18. Id., at 390.

19. Id.

20. Lehne, *Quest for Justice* p. 170.

21. See Friendly, "Disparity of Resources," p. C1; New Jersey State Board of Education, *The Four-Year Assessment of the Public School Education Act of 1975* (Trenton, N.J.: N.J. Dept. of Education, 1980); Paul Itzak, "Disparity Found in Schools' Use of Computers,' *New York Times*, April 8, 1984, II, p. 1.

22. Personal correspondence, August 19, 1986.

23. Seattle School District No. 1, Kings County v. State, 585 P.2d 71 (Wash. 1978).

24. 585 P.2d at 86.

25. Seattle School District No. 1, Kings County v. State, 647 P.2d 25 (Wash. 1982).

26. Id., at 26.

27. Serrano v. Priest, 557 P.2d 929 (Cal. 1977). In Serrano v. Priest, 482 P.2d 1241 (Cal. 1971), the court had struck down the financing scheme, but the grounds of that decision were ambiguous. In the interim, the Supreme Court had decided the federal question in San Antonio School District v. Rodriguez.

28. Id., at 950.

29. Serrano v. Priest II at 952.

30. Id., n. 47.

31. Table II–22 "Revenue Limit Closure," mimeo., California State Department of Education, 1986.

32. Horton v. Meskill, 376 A.2d 359 (Conn. 1977).

33. Public Acts 1979 No. 79–128.

34. Horton v. Meskill (Horton II), 445 A.2d 579 (Conn. 1982).

35. Horton v. Meskill, 486 A.2d 1099 (Conn. 1985).

36. Id., at 1105.

37. 486 A.2d at 1006.

38. Id., at 1111.

39. Id., at 1007.

40. Id., at 1108 n. 16, 17.

41. Pauley v. Kelley, 225 S.E.2d 859 (W. Va. 1979).

42. Id., at 878.

43. Id. There is no equal protection clause in the West Virginia Constitution; Article III, sec. 10, which reads in part, "No person shall be deprived of life, liberty or property without due process of law," has been interpreted to contain an equal protection component.

44. Id., at 882.

45. State ex rel. Board of Education v. Rockefeller, 281 S.E.2d 131 (W. Va. 1981).

46. Id., at 136.

47. Compare *Rockefeller* with *Seattle School District II*, supra, p. 7. In Seattle I, the court, following the wording of the constitution, called education a "paramount duty" of the state and required the state to give specific content to the clause and provide sufficient funding for education. In Seattle II, the court refused to enjoin the governor from implementing an across-the-board reduction in expenditures that made no exception for education.

48. Unreported Circuit Court Opinion (1982), as cited in Pauley v. Bailey (Pauley II), 301 S.E.2d 608 (W. Va. 1983) and Pauley v. Bailey (Pauley III), 324 S.E.2d 128 (W. Va. 1984).

49. 324 S.E.2d at 132.

50. Pauley v. Bailey, 324 S.E.2d 128 (W. Va. 1984).

51. Id., at 137.

52. Pauley I, at 877.

53. *Educational Policies Related to Improving Learning in West Virginia Public Schools.* 1985 West Virginia Conference for Learning (West Virginia Department of Education), p. 1.

54. Cf. Pauley v. Gainer (Pauley IV), 353 S.E.2d 318 (W. Va. 1986). The court was asked to declare unconstitutional the exercise of the governor's line-item veto of an appropriation for financing salary equity adjustments for teach-

ers. The court reversed the judgment, ruling that the governor as an "indispensable party" must be included in the suit. In Collins v. Ritchie, 351 S.E.2d 416 (W. Va. 1986), the court held the West Virginia Highway Department responsible for providing roads that will enable school boards to provide adequate transportation.

55. Buse v. Smith, 247 N.W.2d 141 (Wisc. 1976).

56. National Commission on Excellence in Education, *A Nation at Risk* (Washington, D.C.: Government Printing Office, 1983), p. 5.

57. Gershon Ratner, "A New Duty for Urban Public Schools: Effective Education in Basic Skills," *Texas Law Review* 63 (1985): 777, 787.

58. Torres v. Little Flower Children's Services, 474 N.E.2d 223 (N.Y. 1984).

59. Id., at 227.

60. In the Interest of G.H., 218 N.W.2d 441 (N.D. 1974).

61. Id., at 445.

62. Id., North Dakota Constitution, secs. 11, 30, 147, 148.

63. Levine v. State, 418 A.2d 229 (1980).

64. Id., at 231.

65. Id., at 242. Cf. Cleburne v. Cleburne Living Center, 473 U.S. 432 (1985)(mental retardation is not a suspect classification). The Mississippi court, in Clinton Municipal Separate School District v. Byrd, 477 So.2d 237 (Miss. 1985), recognized that "while there may be no federally created fundamental right to education . . . the right to a minimally adequate public education . . . is one we can label fundamental." At 240. Mississippi has yet to sustain a challenge based on this clause.

66. Friendly, "Disparity on Resources," p. 1.

67. T. H. Bell, "Renaissance in American Education: The New Role of the Federal Government," *St. Mary's Law Journal* 16 (1985): 771, 772.

68. John Herbers, "Governors Asking Greater Control over Schools" *New York Times*, August 24, 1986, p. 1.

69. Robert Lindquist and Arthur Wise, "Developments in Education Litigation," *Journal of Law and Education*, 5(1976): 27–29. For a discussion of the limits of the fiscally neutral standard as well as the setback experienced in the 1980s, see John Elson, "Suing to Make Schools Effective or How to Make a Bad Situation Worse: A Response to Ratner," *Texas Law Review* 63 (1985): 889; Eric Hanushek, "Throwing Money at Schools," *Journal of Policy Analysis and Management* 1 (Fall, 1981): 19; and the quotations from educators and experts in Thomas Tomasson, "New Round in School Funds Debate," *New York Times*, August 10, 1980, p. 8.

70. United Nations Declaration of Human Rights, 1948 Arts. 22–28.

71. Cf. Indian Const. 1949, Art. 38–46; Irish Const. 1937, Art. 45, sec. I. For further analysis, see Ivo Duchacek, *Rights and Liberties in the World Today* (Santa Barbara: ABC-Clio, 1973), esp. chap. 3.

72. New York Const., Art. XVII, sec. 1.

73. Florida Const., Art. I, sec. 61; Montant Const., Art. I, Sec. 29; New Jersey Const., Art. I, Sec. 19; New York Const., Art. I, sec. 17.

74. Georgia Const., Art. I, sec. 6; North Dakota Const., Art. I, sec. 7; South Dakota Const., Art. IV, sec. 2.

75. Montana Const., Art. II, sec. 3; Rhode Island Const., Art. I, sec. 17.

76. For a listing, see Hullihen Moore, "In Aid of Public Education: An

Analysis of the Educational Article of the Virginia Constitution of 1971," *University of Richmond Law Review* 5 (1971): 271 n. 40.

77. Massachusetts Const., Art. 114; Illinois Const., Art. I, sec. 19; Idaho Const., Art. X, sec. 1; Louisiana Const., Art. I, sec. 12; Florida Const., Art. I, sec. 2; Mississippi Const., Art. 4, sec. 86; Montana Const., Art. XII, sec. 3; Ohio Const., Art. VII, Sec. 1, Utah Const., Art. XIX, Sec. 3; Washington Const., Art. XIII, sec. 1; Arkansas Const., Art. XIX, sec. 109; South Carolina Const., Art. 8, sec. 8.

78. Tucker v. Toia, 43 N.Y.2d 1, 371 N.E.2d 449 (1977).

79. Id., 7, 451.

80. Id., 8, 452.

81. Id.

82. Butte Community Union v. Lewis, 712 P.2d 1309 (Mont. 1986).

83. Quoting Montana Const., Art. XII, sec. 3(3).

84. Id., at 1311.

85. Id., at 1313.

86. Id. Such reasoning would apply to a number of school finance decisions, but none of the courts has resorted to this middle-tier analysis. Board of Education v. Nyquist, 83 A.D.2d 217, 241 (N.Y. 1982) implicitly adopts this position, applying intermediate scrutiny to the school finance program. The reasoning, as well as the result, was overruled in Board of Education v. Nyquist, 439 N.E.2d 359 (N.Y. 1982).

87. Bonnett v. State, 382 A.2d 1175 (N.J. 1978), aff'd 395 A.2d 194 (N.J. 1985).

88. Id., at 1179.

89. See infra, p. xx.

90. Robert Babcock and Fred Bosselman, "Suburban Zoning and the Apartment Boom," *University of Pennsylvania Law Review* 111 (1963): 1040, 1148.

91. Euclid v. Ambler, 272 U.S. 365 (1926).

92. Babcock and Bosselman, "Suburban Zoning," p. 1048.

93. Lindsey v. Normet, 405 U.S. 56 (1972).

94. As quoted in Babcock and Bosselman, "Suburban Zoning," p. 108 n. 177.

95. Surrick v. Zoning Hearing Board, 382 A.2d 105 (Pa. 1977).

96. Id., at 180.

97. In re Kravitz, 460 A.2d 1095 (Pa. 1983); In re Appeal of Elocin, 461 A.2d 771 (Pa. 1983).

98. Fernley v. Board of Supervisors, 502 A.2d 585 (Pa. 1985).

99. Id., at 587.

100. While the decision was unanimous, not all justices agreed on the text set forth by Hutchinson.

101. Southern Burlington County NAACP v. Twp. of Mt. Laurel, 336 A.2d 713 (N.J. 1975).

102. While the majority rested its decision on the general welfare clause, Art. I, sec. 1, it was clear that equality considerations were directly and indirectly implicated. Justice Hall noted that shelter, along with food, was one of the "most basic needs" and that the provision for adequate housing of all categories of people is essential in the promotion of the general welfare required in all local land use regulation. Id., at 727. Justice Pollock also noted the equality aspects of this

decision when he wrote: "The majority based its decision on the assurance of equal protection of the law." See Pollock, "Land Use and Public Resources," in B. McGraw, ed., *Developments in State Constitutional Law* (St. Paul, Minn.: West Publishing Co., 1985), pp. 145, 151.

103. See, e.g., "Symposium—Mt. Laurel II and Developments in New Jersey," especially G. Alan Tarr and Russell S. Harrison, "Legitimacy and Capacity in State Supreme Court Policy Making: The New Jersey Court and Exclusionary Zoning," *Rutgers Law Journal* 15 (1984): 513, and the sources cited at 518 n. 20.

104. 336 A.2d 713, at 734.

105. "Recent Developments," *Zoning and Planning Law Report* 6 (1983): 145, 146.

106. Southern Burlington County NAACP v. Twp. of Mt. Laurel, 456 A.2d 390 (N.J. 1983).

107. Id., at 410.

108. N.J.S.A. 30:4C–2(m)–30:4C–26.1–92, 40:55D (Suppl. 1986).

109. Hills Development Co. v. Bernards Twp., in Somerset County, 510 A.2d 621 (N.J. 1986).

110. Id., at 654. Some saw affirmation of the Fair Housing Act, which granted some relief to municipalities from the "builder's remedy," as a retreat from the strong stand of *Mt. Laurel II*. In mid–1987, there were bills under discussion in the New Jersey legislature that, if passed, would further relax the requirements of *Mt. Laurel II*. Such legislation could tempt the courts to reenter the picture. On the other hand, the political pressures on the court over its housing decisions might act as a countervailing factor.

111. Id., at 655.

112. 510 A.2d 621, 654 (N.J. 1986).

113. John R. Nolon, "Exclusionary Zoning: New York, New Jersey Cases Compared," *New York Law Journal*, July 3, 1985, p. 15.

114. 510 A.2d 632. See Tarr and Harrison, "Legitimacy and Capacity," pp. 556–66, for a sympathetic but skeptical review of the assumptions and theory underlying the *Mt. Laurel* decisions. See also Daniel Bernstein, "Why Mt. Laurel Won't Work," *New Jersey Law Journal* 112 (1983): 413. Jerome Rose, "The Mt. Laurel II Decision: Is It Based on Wishful Thinking?" *Real Estate Law Journal* 12 (1983): 115, claims that the decision is based on flawed economic assumptions that may ultimately defeat the good intentions of the judiciary.

115. Berenson v. New Castle, 342 N.E.2d 236 (N.Y. 1975).

116. Id., at 243.

117. Kurzius v. Upper Brookville, 414 N.E.2d 680 (N.Y. 1980).

118. Id., at 682–83.

119. Cal. Gov't Code 35302.8, 65580–65589 (West 1983)(Suppl. 1986). See Carolyn Burton, "California Legislature Prohibits Exclusionary Zoning. Mandated Fair Share: Inclusionary Zoning Programs a Likely Response," *San Fernando Law Review* 9 (1981): 19.

120. Adams v. Superior Court, 534 P.2d 375 (Cal. 1974)(housing is not a fundamental right under state constitution); Associated Homebuilders v. City of Livermore, 557 P.2d 473 (Cal. 1976). In Bownds v. City of Glendale, 170 Cal. Rptr. 342 (Cal. 1980), the court noted that "absent a complete failure of local government agencies to adopt a plan which approximates legislative desires,

courts are ill-equipped to determine whether the language used in local plans is 'adequate' to achieve the broad general goal of the legislature." To take any other course would "involve the court in the writing of the plan. That issue is for determination by the political process not by the judicial process." Id., at 347.

121. California Government Code, 65587.6 (West, 1983).

122. California Government Code, 65587(b) (West Suppl. 1986).

123. Michael Banzaf, "Are Mandatory Inclusionary Housing Programs Passé? The Orange County Experience," *Western State University Law Review* 13 (1986): 473, 491.

124. Id., at 481.

125. In addition to the legislation adopted by Massachusetts, California, and New Jersey, Michigan (Mich. Com. Laws 125.586a, 125.216a, 125.271a (Suppl. 1986) and Colorado (Colo. Rev. St. 1973 50–28–115(2) a & b, 31–23–301) have passed legislation prohibiting certain types of exclusion. The Colorado legislation, for example, deals with exclusions based on age or handicap. For a listing of cases, see Township of Chesterfield v. Brooks, 489 A.2d 600 (N.H. 1985)(discriminatory ordinance involving mobile homes is invalid on due process grounds); Robinson Township v. Knoll, 302 N.W.2d 196 (mobile home exclusion is invalid on due process grounds); Negin v. Board of Building and Zoning Appeals, 432 N.E.2d 165 (Ohio 1982) (minimum lot size is invalid on due process grounds); Board of County Supervisors of Fairfax County v. Capper, 107 S.E.3d 390 (Va. 1959)(intentional purpose and exclusionary effect of two-acre minimum lot size was to prevent low-income bracket from living in area, void on due process grounds); Bristow v. City of Woodhaven, 192 N.W.2d 322 (Mich. App. 1971)(exclusion of mobile homes was held invalid on due process grounds).

126. Nolon, "Exclustionary Zoning," p. 15, n. 15.

127. For a comparison, see id. pts. I and II; and Terry Rice, "Exclusionary Zoning: Mt. Laurel in New York?" *Pace Law Review* 6 (1986): 135, 149–79.

128. For a comparison of the Pennsylvania approach with that of New Jersey, see note, "Pennsylvania Supreme Court and Exclusionary Zoning Dilemma," *Villanova Law Review* 20 (1983–1984): 477, 478–79 and n. 86.

129. The categories have been developed by Abram Chayes, "The Role of the Judge in Public Law Litigation," *Harvard Law Review* 89 (1976): 1281, and Owen Fiss, "The Supreme Court, 1978 Term—Foreword: The Forms of Justice," *Harvard Law Review* 93 (1979): 661.

6

Reactions of State Courts to Pro-Prosecution Burger Court Decisions

_____ DANIEL C. KRAMER

Some of the scholars and lawyers who complain that the Burger Court was not sufficiently attentive to the protection of the rights of persons accused or convicted of crime believe that state judiciaries have done an outstanding job of compensating for that conservative trend. Alexander Williams, Carol Peterkort, and Ted M. Benn agree, for example, that a number of state courts have interpreted the criminal procedure clauses of their state constitutions to grant persons enmeshed in the criminal justice process broader rights than the Burger Court conceded to them.[1] However, other commentators assert that, as a whole, state judges have not moved with great vigor against the tide of Burger Court decisions limiting the constitutional guarantees extended to criminal defendants. As one of the first to point out that state high courts were not completely supine in the face of the Burger counterrevolution, Donald Wilkes cautioned, nonetheless, that "by no means all or even a majority of state high courts disagree with the Burger Court's approach to the rights of criminal suspects."[2] And John Gruhl indicates that twenty-one of twenty-seven state supreme courts that were offered the opportunity to adopt the rule of the Burger Court in _Harris v. New York_ (that statements obtained in violation of the _Miranda_ rules could be used to impeach a defendant's credibility) did follow _Harris_.[3]

Both those who argue that state court resistance to the anti–criminal defendant decisions of the Burger Court is extensive and those who contend the opposite convey elements of accuracy. More specifically, a majority of state appellate courts does accept many Burger Court decisions but, for most of these holdings, a minority (in some instances, a minority of significant size) of state tribunals rejects them. To examine prevailing patterns, I shall review the responses of state higher courts to several Burger Court criminal law rulings that were, at least to some extent, victories for the state against a criminal suspect. Some of these decisions are well known; others are mentioned only in minute casebook footnotes.

State Appellate Court Reaction to Anti–Criminal Law Decisions of the Burger Court

Gregg v. Georgia

Perhaps the most spectacular antidefendant decision of the Burger Court was *Gregg v. Georgia*,[4] in which the Court declared that the death penalty was not per se a violation of the Eighth Amendment's cruel and unusual punishment clause. The great majority of state appellate courts in those states (thirty-eight in 1984) with death penalty legislation refuse to hold that this penalty is automatically invalid.[5]

As subsequent sections of this chapter will demonstrate, the Supreme Court of Washington is willing to expand the rights of criminal defendants beyond the minimum required by federal constitutional law. However, in *State v. Campbell*,[6] even the Washington court refused to invalidate the state's capital punishment act. It pointed out that in 1975 the electorate, by way of the initiative process, had authorized executions by a vote of 2–1; and an act passed by the legislature in 1981 allows death to be imposed when aggravating circumstances are present. Thus, the court reasoned, "Clearly the mandate of the people of Washington, as expressed through the legislative and initiative processes, is to impose the death penalty. We, as Justices, are bound to uphold and enforce this law absent a constitutional prohibition. We must not superimpose... strained interpretations of the law to sidestep this difficult issue."[7] The court concluded, accordingly, that the death penalty did not violate the Washington State Constitution.[8]

The California Supreme Court is another tribunal that has often accepted the constitutional claims of criminal defendants. In the much-noted case of *People v. Anderson*,[9] it struck down capital punishment as infringing the state constitutional ban on cruel or unusual punishment. The electorate responded by approving a constitutional initiative declaring that the death penalty did not constitute an infringement of the state's basic charter. In 1977 the state legislature passed a death penalty law, and, subsequently, the state supreme court declared in *People v. Frierson*[10] that the act met the requirements of both the U.S. and the state constitutions.

Most of the executions in the United States since *Gregg* have occurred in the South, and appellate courts there have welcomed the case. In *Ex parte Granviel*,[11] the defendant complained that the Texas law providing for death by intravenous injection of a lethal drug rather than by electrocution was cruel and unusual punishment. The Court of Criminal Appeals of Texas cited *Gregg* to reiterate its view that the imposition of the death penalty was not intrinsically cruel and unusual punishment; it sustained the new technique as valid under both the U.S. and Texas constitutions. The court pointed out, perhaps overoptimistically, that the legislature had "substituted death by lethal injection as a means of execution in lieu of electrocution for the reason it would be a more humane and less spectacular form of execution."[12]

In *State v. Bass*,[13] this Superior Court of New Jersey faced a challenge that the state's death penalty law was invalid. The court did not accept this position, pointing out, first, that *Gregg* had not declared it so under the U.S. Constitution. It went on to assert that the state can provide its citizens with wider-ranging rights than those accorded by the federal charter. Nonetheless, it refused to aver that depriving a convicted murderer of his life necessarily violated the New Jersey Constitution. It emphasized that the state supreme court had upheld the penalty as recently as 1968;[14] and the court added that in 1972 the state supreme court had invalidated it only because of its reading of federal constitutional requirements.[15] The superior court admitted that the capital punishment law before it would have to be reviewed to determine if it met the procedural protections afforded convicted murderers by various U.S. Supreme Court decisions.[16]

Since *Gregg*, only two state appellate courts have declared their states' death penalty statutes unconstitutional: the Supreme Judicial Court of Massachusetts and the Oregon Supreme Court. In *District Attorney for the Suffolk District v. Watson*,[17] the Massachusetts court had held that capital punishment was impermissibly cruel under the state constitution's cruel or unusual punishment clause. However, in 1982, the voters approved an amendment to the constitution declaring that no provision of that charter should be read as outlawing the death penalty and, during the same year, the state legislature approved a new capital punishment law.

Subsequently, in *Commonwealth v. Colon Cruz*,[18] a suspect was arrested with two companions for the murder of a state trooper. On the basis of evidence presented in pretrial motions, the trial judge found that the suspects, if convicted, might be sentenced to death. At the request of the commonwealth, the state supreme court was asked to decide in advance of the trial the constitutionality of the new death penalty act; and, in *Colon Cruz*, it declared that this measure too contravened the Massachusetts Constitution. Under the law, the death penalty could be imposed only by a jury; however, a defendant who pleaded guilty to murder in the first degree could not be put to death. A consequence of this provision was to discourage the accused from asserting rights to trial by jury and to plead not guilty. For this reason, it was held to violate not the state constitution's cruel and unusual punishment clause but the protection against self-incrimination and the right to a jury trial. The court made clear, however, that it was declaring this particular death penalty law invalid and not asserting that capital punishment itself is unconstitutional. Similarly, in *State v. Quinn*,[19] the Oregon Supreme Court overturned that state's death penalty act on the ground that, as framed, it violated the state constitution's guarantee of a right to a jury trial. Under the law, an accused could be executed only if he or she had deliberately taken the victim's life; and the statute made it the prerogative of the judge rather than that of the jury to determine whether the prisoner had acted with the necessary deliberation.

Beckwith v. United States

The Burger Court, in *Beckwith v. United States*,[20] declared that *Miranda* warnings need not be given to one not in custody when interviewed by employees of the Internal Revenue Service on suspicion of income tax fraud. To spare the taxpayer the embarrassment of being interrogated at his place of employment, the IRS agents interviewed him at a private home. Prior to the questioning, the suspect was informed of most but not all of his *Miranda* rights. He was interrogated in a manner that he himself admitted did not place him under excessive pressure. Subsequently Beckwith agreed to let the agents inspect his records at his place of business. Nevertheless, he later contended that all the statements made to the IRS employees at the interview, as well as the evidence derived from these statements, should have been suppressed during his trial for tax evasion because the requirements of *Miranda* had not been met.

The Supreme Court, in an opinion by Chief Justice Burger, affirmed Beckwith's conviction. The chief justice asserted that, on the whole, *Miranda* warnings need be given only to a suspect who is in custody since compulsion to testify is inherent only in a detention situation. Although the investigation had focused on Beckwith at the time of his interview, it did not take place after he had been deprived of his freedom in any significant way. Thus there was no need to advise him of his *Miranda* rights.

Beckwith is one of the two U.S. Supreme Court cases dealt with here that was not expressly rejected by any state appellate court. Several rulings illustrate how it was used by state judiciaries to absolve law enforcement officials of the need to extend to criminal suspects their *Miranda* warnings in certain situations. In the course of a noncustodial investigation for possible tax fraud, a businessman made several incriminating statements and revealed the name of his bank. The state then subpoenaed the bank records, and the merchant subsequently was tried for filing fraudulent retailers' occupational tax returns. However, because no *Miranda* warnings had been forthcoming, the trial court suppressed the introduction in evidence of the statements that he had made during his interview and of all the records obtained from his bank.

The Appellate Court of Illinois reversed the suppression order in *People v. Myers*.[21] The court explicitly rested its judgment on the *Beckwith* decision. Since the suspect was not in custody, the investigators were under no obligation to advise the merchant of his *Miranda* guarantees. Consequently, statements made in the course of the conversation and the resulting revelations could be used against him in a criminal trial.

In *State v. DeConingh*,[22] the defendant was hospitalized after her husband had been shot to death. While in the hospital, she was twice interrogated by a deputy sheriff. Before talking to her there, the officer handed her an "advice of rights" form whose contents were not specified. It was later admitted, however, that the deputy had made no attempt to ascertain if the wife understood the consequences of furnishing a statement. Thus the Florida District Court of Appeal admitted that *Miranda* warnings had not been properly given. Nonetheless, it reversed the ruling of the trial court suppressing the confession that she had made to the deputy sheriff while hospitalized. Citing *Beckwith*, among other cases, the court noted that the *Miranda* warnings need be provided only in custodial situations; questioning by police officers in a hospital room was said not to constitute such a setting. It was irrelevant, according to the opinion, that the person questioned had become the focus of the investigation.

In *State v. Fields*,[23] a deputy sheriff was informed by car radio that there had been an accident on a North Dakota highway and that the driver had been taken to a hospital in a nearby town. The deputy proceeded to the scene of the accident and asked the town's police chief to visit the hospital and to obtain a blood alcohol test from the driver. The chief did so and asked Fields if he had been the driver of the automobile at the time of the accident. Fields answered in the affirmative, and the officer next asked him to submit to a blood-alcohol test. He agreed and was then arrested for drunken driving. It was not until after his arrest that Fields was informed of his *Miranda* rights.

The North Dakota Supreme Court reversed the trial court's decision to exclude as evidence the admission that Fields had made to the police chief. It mentioned *Beckwith* as one of various cases supporting the proposition that *Miranda* warnings do not have to be provided a suspect in a criminal case when he is not under physical restraint. Fields was not in custody when the police officer questioned him at the hospital. A friend, not the police, had taken him there. Moreover, when the sheriff propounded the questions, he did so in the presence of the friend and the nurse on duty—that is, in a basically nonthreatening situation.

In *State v. Swise*,[24] sheriff's officers investigating a murder went to the defendant's place of business. Without reading him his *Miranda* warnings, they interviewed him for seven to ten minutes but placed him under no constraint. After the officers left, the suspect contacted his attorney, who told him not to meet further with them. However, during his brief talk with the officers, Swise had made incriminating statements. The trial court granted his motion to suppress these admissions, but the New Mexico Supreme Court reversed the suppression order. *Beckwith* was invoked to sustain the proposition that a suspect has to receive *Miranda* warnings only when he or she has been deprived of freedom and that the mere fact that the suspect has become the focus of the inquiry does not mean that these warnings must be provided.

Kastigar v. United States

In *Kastigar v. United States*,[25] the U.S. Supreme Court, in an opinion by Justice Lewis Powell, held that the state or federal government may compel testimony from a witness who invokes the Fifth Amendment privilege against compulsory self-incrimination by granting "use" and "derivative use" immunity. That is, the government can require disclosure by conceding that the evidence derived will not be used in a subsequent criminal prosecution. (For purposes of style, *use immunity* will be employed to cover both use and derivative use immunity.) The witnesses contended that, under the self-incrimination clause, they could not be forced to testify unless they were granted "transactional immunity"— that is, total immunity from prosecution for the crime that they had to discuss while on the witness stand. (Under use immunity, witnesses can be prosecuted for the crime if the evidence used is not what was said on the stand or obtained as a result of any statements made there.) Powell reasoned that the self-incrimination clause grants protection only against the use and derivative use of one's statement and that the immunity granted a witness who fears incrimination need not be greater than the scope of the constitutional privilege. Thus the *Kastigar* witnesses could be forced to testify even though they were not granted transactional immunity.

Kastigar is not of interest to the many states that provide transactional immunity by statute. Moreover, a few state higher courts in jurisdictions whose statutes allow only use immunity have held that state constitutions require a grant of transactional immunity. In *State v. Miyasaki*,[26] the defendant had been summoned before a grand jury and asked about his gambling activities. The prosecutor, expecting that Miyasaki would invoke the privilege against self-incrimination, obtained a court order granting him use immunity and compelling him to speak. The witness admitted that he had placed bets on football games, but he refused to identify his bookmaker. He was then indicated for obstruction of justice. The defendant moved to dismiss the indictment on the ground that he should have been accorded transactional immunity. The court denied his contention but allowed him to appeal the decision.

The Hawaii Supreme Court ruled that the extension of use immunity alone violated the self-incrimination clause of the state constitution. Although the wording is identical to the grant appearing in the U.S. Constitution's Fifth Amendment, the court asserted that those who framed the Hawaii Constitution during the 1950s assumed that the privilege against self-incrimination would be coextensive with that embodied in the Fifth Amendment as interpreted by the U.S. Supreme Court. And, at that point in American constitutional history, the Supreme Court was construing the Fifth Amendment to require transactional immunity.

The Oregon Court of Appeals, in *State v. Soriano*,[27] also held that use immunity failed to meet constitutional requirements. Here the defendants had refused to provide information to a grand jury investigating a burglary. The trial court provided use immunity under an Oregon statute, but the defendants still refused to testify. The court then held them in contempt. The court of appeals reversed, emphasizing that Oregon courts should consider state constitutional claims before they analyze the extent of rights granted by the U.S. Constitution. Under the Oregon Constitution's self-incrimination clause, as interpreted by the court of appeals, a witness who is made to testify under the mantle of immunity must be protected from the nonevidentiary as well as the evidentiary use of testimony. Use immunity does not grant total protection from nonevidentiary use; the use-immunized statement still may be utilized by the prosecutor to determine whether to pursue the investigation, to plea bargain, or to employ a contemplated trial strategy. Thus transactional immunity is required under the Oregon Constitution before a reluctant deponent can be coerced into testifying.

More common than cases such as *Soriano* and *Miyasaki* are decisions accepting the principle of *Kastigar* that only use immunity need be accorded to compel one to testify under oath. *Rivera v. City of Douglas*[28] is one such ruling. Here municipal employees of Douglas, Arizona, had been suspected of conducting personal business while at work. The city manager ordered them to take a lie detector test. In his letter, he stated that their answers could not be used against them in any criminal prosecution but that they might be introduced in a dismissal proceeding. The employees sought an injunction preventing the city from forcing them to undergo the test. One of the arguments advanced was that the use immunity that the city manager was willing to grant did not sufficiently preserve their constitutional rights since what they said during the polygraph examination might be made the basis of their dismissal. Thus the only way that the city could validly compel them to undergo the lie detector ordeal was to extend a type of transactional immunity that would protect their jobs no matter how extensive the offenses to which they admitted. The Arizona Court of Appeals, citing *Kastigar*, held that use immunity met the requirements of the U.S. Constitution's Fifth Amendment; the civil servants either had to submit to the inquiry or forfeit their positions.

In *State v. Vinegra*,[29] the defendant was the assistant city engineer of Elizabeth, New Jersey. Suspected of having asked for a political contribution from a corporation that sought to participate in a road and sewer project, he appeared before a grand jury that asked him detailed questions about his role in recommending a contractor for the undertaking. After his testimony, he was indicted for misconduct in office. A New Jersey statute automatically extends use immunity to public employees called upon to testify before a court or grand jury. The New Jersey Superior Court made clear that, despite this statute, Vinegra could still be tried on the misconduct charge. Relying on *Kastigar*, the court maintained that the Fifth Amendment did not require transactional immunity, though the trial court had to ensure that the state did not introduce any evidence against him that was directly or indirectly derived from his admissions before the grand jury.

In Georgia, one Dean Smith was subpoenaed to testify before a grand jury investigating cocaine sales. He refused, on self-incrimination grounds, to state whether he had been arrested on a specified date and whether he had provided information to the state and federal governments about a theft of narcotics. He was then granted use immunity and ordered to talk. When he refused to do so, he was convicted of contempt of court. The Georgia Court of Appeals upheld this judgment in *Smith v. State*,[30] which cited *Kastigar* for the proposition that the shelter of use immunity is all that is necessary to protect a deponent's Fifth Amendment privilege against self-incrimination.

In Colorado, the state sought to enjoin a businessman from making further misrepresentations concerning the quality of his appliances and warranty services. He was subpoenaed to testify at the trial but refused to do so, citing his privilege against self-incrimination. He then received use immunity under the relevant section of the consumer protection act. When the merchant remained obdurate in his refusal to talk, he was held in contempt. This ruling was upheld by the Colorado Court of Appeals in *People ex rel. Smith v. Jordan*.[31] *Kastigar* was noted to demonstrate that under the Fifth Amendment, a grant of immunity may constitutionally be used to compel a defendant to testify if the immunity is coextensive with the privilege and that use immunity suffices for this purpose since it leaves the deponent and the state in substantially the same position as if the privilege had been invoked.[32]

North Carolina v. Pearce

North Carolina v. Pearce & Simpson v. Rice (henceforth referred to as *Pearce*)[33] was decided at the end of Earl Warren's tenure as chief justice. Yet is is relevant for purposes of this chapter as a case (albeit "liberal" in some respects) that does not go as far in protecting defendants' rights as some believe is desirable. Consequently, state appellate court reactions to it are helpful in determining whether these tribunals have gone further than the U.S. Supreme Court in safeguarding the rights of persons who come under the scrutiny of the criminal justice system.

Pearce involved cases from North Carolina and Alabama. In the first, the defendant was initially imprisoned for twelve to fifteen years. A few years later, the state supreme court reversed his conviction on the ground that an involuntary confession had been used. On retrial, he was convicted and sentenced to eight years, which, added to the time already served, amounted to a longer term than the original twelve to fifteen years. In the other, the defendant had pleaded guilty to second-degree burglary and was sentenced to ten years by the trial court in Alabama. Two and a half years later, this judgment was set aside by a state court on the ground that the suspect had been denied his constitutional right to counsel. On retrial, the defendant was sentenced to twenty-five years. The Supreme Court, in an opinion by Justice Potter Stewart, declared that neither the double jeopardy nor the equal protection clause absolutely barred the imposition of a more severe sentence upon retrial when a defendant had had the first conviction set aside. In this respect, the decision limits the rights of criminal defendants.

At the same time, Justice Stewart noted that the due process clause requires that a defendant not be given a longer sentence upon retrial simply because the authorities want to punish him or her for appealing or for collaterally attacking the first conviction. To ensure that vindictiveness is not the motivating force behind the more severe treatment, the trial judge must explicitly indicate the reasons for increasing the sentence, and these reasons need to be based upon reliable information about the defendant's behavior from the time that the first penalty was imposed. Since in neither case before the Court had the state articulated any basis for the additional punishment, Stewart held that it had been unconstitutional to impose it.

Several state appellate court cases took a more emphatically pro-defendant position than did *Pearce* and held that a defendant whose first conviction was attacked on appeal and/or set aside could never be sentenced to a longer term on retrial. In *Shagloak v. State*,[34] the defendant had been arrested for burglary and charged as a habitual criminal. He filed a motion to withdraw his guilty plea to several previous charges, a plea that had led to a twenty-month jail term. This motion was granted, and the habitual criminal charge was dismissed. A few months later, Shagloak was tried on the charges to which he had originally pleaded guilty and was sentenced to five years' imprisonment, over three years more than he had originally been given on these counts. The sentencing judge properly followed the requirements of *Pearce* and justified the harsher penalty on the ground that Shagloak had committed a burglary since the expiration of the incarceration resulting from the guilty plea. Nonetheless, the Supreme Court of Alaska vacated the new sentence, asserting that, notwithstanding *Pearce*, the due process clause of the Alaska Constitution precludes a more severe sentence from being imposed subsequent to a second trial whatever the reason. The possibility of a longer sentence, the court reasoned, might "well deter a defendant from exercising the right to assert his innocence and request a retrial."[35] (The court implicitly deemed a trial after a guilty plea has been withdrawn a retrial.)

In *State v. DeBonis*,[36] the defendant had pleaded guilty in municipal court to various motor vehicle charges and was ordered to pay fines and costs. He appealed to a county court for a de novo determination of the punishment. Much to his chagrin, that court sentenced him to jail. The New Jersey Supreme Court reversed the judgment of the county court. It held that, despite the loophole created by *Pearce*, a defendant who appears before one of these local courts should not have to risk a longer sentence on appeal from its verdict. The supreme court based this holding not on any constitutional provision but simply on considerations of public policy. And in *State v. Sorenson*,[37] the Utah Supreme Court held, notwithstanding *Pearce*, that upon retrial for theft after a first conviction reversed on appeal for trial errors, a defendant could not be given one to fifteen years as compared to six months at the conclusion of the first trial. The court cited the state constitution and a state statute to buttress its view that a successful appeal may never be followed by a more rigorous punishment.

A preponderance of state appellate tribunals, however, has taken advantage of *Pearce* to permit imposition of more severe sentences upon retrial. In *State v. Martin*,[38] the Oklahoma Court of Criminal Appeals allowed a higher penalty to be established by a jury upon retrial after appeal. The need mandated by *Pearce* to justify the stricter sentence by reference to the defendant's conduct after the first verdict was said to apply only to sentences imposed by judges. *Spidle v. State*[39] and *Chaffin v. State*[40] are similar cases that led to a similar result. (In *Chaffin v. Stynchcombe*,[41] the U.S. Supreme Court affirmed the view that a jury could impose a more severe penalty on retrial even without specifying the reasons for the additional strictness.) In *People v. Olary*,[42] the defendant was convicted by a justice of the peace of cruelty to his cows and was fined and placed on two years' probation. He appealed to a circuit court for a trial de novo before a jury and was sentenced to seventy-five days in jail. The Michigan Supreme Court upheld the higher sentence after the retrial. There was need here, the court declared, to follow the requirement of *Pearce* that the second judge justify it; in this situation, the court reasoned, the initial penalty had been imposed by a legally untrained individual, and the circuit court judge was more capable of imposing a suitable penalty. (The doctrine that a judge, apparently without giving reasons, may impose a higher sentence after a trial de novo upon appeal from a justice-of-the-peace-type tribunal was endorsed by the U.S. Supreme Court in *Colten v. Kentucky*.)[43] Finally, in *Beltkowski v. State*,[44] the Minnesota Supreme Court allowed a ten-year term to be meted out to a burglar who had received four years after pleading guilty but then was allowed to withdraw this plea upon a claim that he had been the victim of entrapment.[45]

United States v. Edwards

In *United States v. Edwards*,[46] the defendant had been arrested late at night for attempting to break into a post office. Investigation indicated that entry had been made through a wooden window and that paint chips had been left on the window sill and wire mesh screen. Edwards spent the night in jail in the clothes in which he had been arrested, no suitable prison garb having been available because of the late hour. The next morning, the suspect's clothing was taken from him without a warrant; examination of it revealed paint chips matching those taken from the scene of the crime. This evidence was admitted at his trial, notwithstanding Edwards's contention that the warrantless seizure of the garments and scrapings violated his Fourth Amendment rights. The Supreme Court, in an opinion by Justice Byron White, upheld the conviction. Traditionally, warrantless searches incident to a valid custodial arrest are permissible; White considered this search "incidental" to such an arrest even though the taking of the apparel occurred the morning after the defendant had been detailed.

Apparently no state appellate court has questioned the willingness of the Burger Court to consider a search chronologically removed from the arrest as one "incidental" to the arrest. In fact, a number of courts have taken advantage of *Edwards* to sustain convictions based on evidence obtained by warrantless searches effectuated considerably later than the taking into custody. For example, in *People v. Spencer*,[47] the defendant was arrested for criminal sexual conduct and brought to the police station. The police ordered him to disrobe and seized his undershorts without first obtaining a warrant. The underwear was chemically analyzed, and bloodstains and traces of semen were found on it. The bloodstains came from a person with the blood type of the complaining witness, who testified that she had started to menstruate after the defendant had had intercourse with her. Additionally, the semen came from an individual with the suspect's blood type. The trial court admitted into evidence the results of the tests. The Court of Appeals of Michigan, citing *Edwards*, declared that the lower court had not abused its discretion in taking this step.

Commonwealth v. Hrynkow[48] is another case involving the warrantless seizure of clothing. The defendant had been convicted of the murder of a security guard. Eight days after the murder, a fellow employee of the decedent described the perpetrator. The defendant was arrested and positively identified as the killer. He was brought to the police station where, among other things, the coat he was wearing was taken from him without a warrant. An analysis of the coat and of clothing taken from his residence produced circumstantial evidence that linked him to the murder. (For example, telltale paint chips were discovered, matching some found at the scene of the crime.) The Supreme Court of Pennsylvania, relying on *Edwards*, sustained the seizure of the coat without a warrant. The court emphasized that the police had good reason to believe that it was the one that the defendant had been wearing the night of the homicide.

In *Pickens v. State*[49] the defendant was convicted of felony murder. He and his companions had held up a store, raped the female clerk, and robbed and murdered several of the customers. One piece of evidence against the defendant was the rape victim's diamond wedding band, which had been removed without a warrant from his finger during a search at the jail after his arrest. The Supreme Court of Arkansas looked to *Edwards* to declare the ring admissible. And in *People v. Young*,[50] the defendant had been taken into custody during the weekend for burglary of a store. When arrested, he had with him a backpack with a sleeping bag tied to it. This personal property was brought to the jail along with the defendant and "booked in." On the Monday after the arrest, the sleeping bag was examined by the police without a warrant and found to have been stolen. The California Court of Appeal, on the basis of *Edwards*, declared that the trial court had been within its rights in admitting the sleeping bag as evidence. The court was especially impressed by the fact that the bag had not been concealed within a closed container and, therefore, that the suspect had had no expectation of privacy with respect to it even though it had to be unrolled to discover the identity of its true owner.[51]

United States v. Robinson

In *United States v. Robinson*[52] the U.S. Supreme Court held that a warrantless full search of a person incidental to a valid custodial arrest is legitimate under the Fourth Amendment even though the suspect is detained for a minor offense such as a violation of the traffic laws. This search is necessary, Justice William Rehnquist reasoned, to allow the arresting officer to protect his safety by taking any weapon that the suspect may have on his or her person. If the search turns up evidence of other crimes (in this case, the possession of heroin), the suspect may be tried for those offenses, and the seized objects may be used as evidence.

Several state appellate courts have rejected *Robinson* and refuse to allow the police to effect a full search when arresting someone for a minor offense. The California Supreme Court case of *People v. Brisendine*[53] may be the best known of these.[54] The defendant was arrested by two deputy sheriffs for maintaining an open campfire in a national forest in violation of the local fire code. One of the deputies searched Brisendine's knapsack and, in a side pocket, found envelopes and a frosted plastic bottle with a cap on it. Opening the bottle revealed marijuana, and undoing the envelopes disclosed other illegal drugs. The court held that the police had been justified in "patting down" the sack to determine if it contained weapons and that they could search further if the pat proved inadequate. It also stated that under *Robinson*, the warrantless searches of the bottle and the envelopes had been legitimate under the U.S. Constitution's Fourth Amendment. However, this ferreting, which could not be justified as a search for weapons, was invalidated under the California Constitution's search and seizure clause.

In *Commonwealth v. Toole*,[55] a truck driver was stopped by the police and arrested on an outstanding warrant for assault and battery. He was handcuffed, and a warrantless search of the vehicle's cab revealed a gun. The Supreme Judicial Court of Massachusetts upheld the lower court's refusal to admit the weapon into evidence at his trial on weapons charges. The court relied on a 1974 state statute declaring that a search incidental to a valid arrest may be made only to seize, for example, the fruits or instrumentalities of the crime for which the arrest has been made or weapons that might be used against the arresting officers. The act, which was said to embody the principles of the *Robinson* dissent, provided that property obtained in violation of its provisions would not be admissible in evidence in criminal proceedings. The commonwealth did not claim that the search of the cab was made to discover evidence of assault and battery, nor was it necessary to remove weapons that could have been turned against the police. The defendant already had been handcuffed when the officers foraged through the cab.

The Hawaii Supreme Court case of *State v. Kaluna*[56] is similar to *Brisendine, Toole*, and *Robinson*. In all, a thorough, warrantless search incidental to the arrest uncovered evidence of guilt of a crime other than the one for which the suspect had been taken into custody. After being escorted to the police station following her arrest for robbery, the defendant was told to strip for a search. She then reached into her brassiere and pulled out a piece of folded tissue. Handing it to the matron, she claimed that this was all that she had. The matron unfolded the tissue and found a barbiturate. At a pretrial hearing, the defendant's motion to suppress the drug was granted on the ground that it had been illegally seized. The state supreme court affirmed this suppression order. The tribunal noted that, as a matter of federal constitutional law, the search was lawful under *Robinson*. Nonetheless, the warrantless opening of the tissue paper packet was unlawful under the Hawaii Constitution's search and seizure clause. Though it had been proper for the matron to search Kaluna for weapons, it was unlikely that one was hidden in the tissue. Even if a razor were concealed there, it presented no danger to prison officials, for at the time the packet was opened, it was in the matron's possession.

In *Zehrung v. State*,[57] the defendant had been stopped by a state trooper because his truck was emitting excessive smoke. The trooper discovered that there were two bench warrants outstanding for Zehrung, one for his failure to appear on a misdemeanor charge and another for his failure to pay a fine for possession of marijuana. The officer arrested him and took him to jail. His wallet was searched for money and contraband; a white paper packet was found containing two credit cards. The packet was removed from the wallet, and the credit cards were taken from the packet. The cards were later used to connect Zehrung with the rape for which he was being prosecuted. The Alaska Supreme Court subsequently stated that the order to suppress the cards should have been granted by the lower court. It was admitted that the warrantless taking of these documents was valid under *Robinson*. Nonetheless, a full warrantless search after an arrest violates the Alaska Constitution's search and seizure clause. This offers more protection to the individual than does the U.S. Constitution's Fourth Amendment as interpreted by the U.S. Supreme Court. Therefore, the court concluded, when the police arrest someone without a warrant, officers can search the suspect only for weapons and for evidence concealable on the person that is relevant to the crime for which the suspect has been taken into custody.

More state appellate courts than not have accepted *Robinson*. For example, in *People v. Cannon*,[58] the defendant was a passenger in a vehicle halted by a police officer for failure to have brake lights. The officer discovered that the driver did not have a license. He ordered him out of the car; a warrantless search under the front seat revealed guns. The defendant was prosecuted on weapons charges, and the Illinois Appellate Court denied a motion to suppress the weapons. Citing *Robinson*, among other cases, the court pointed out that the officer had had the right to arrest the motorist for driving without a license, and this right gave him authority to carry out a full search of his person and (using *Robinson* to buttress a point for which the case does not really stand) to effect at least a cursory search of the area around his seat for weapons. In *State v. Mims*,[59] a police officer arrested the defendant for breach of the peace. After Mims was taken into custody, he was "frisked," and controlled substances were found in his pocket. Thereafter, he was prosecuted and convicted for possession of narcotics. The Supreme Court of South Carolina affirmed his conviction. To the defendant's contention that the substances were taken by a warrantless and therefore unconstitutional search, the supreme court cited *Robinson* to hold the search lawful and the narcotics admissible.

A series of additional cases illustrate the state appellate courts' reliance on *Robinson*. In *State v. Lohff*,[60] a policeman arrested the defendant for reckless driving. He was taken to the police station and pat-searched for a weapon. The officer felt a lump in the defendant's jacket pocket, which turned out to contain marijuana. The South Dakota Supreme Court, looking to *Robinson*, upheld the warrantless discovery of the drug as incidental to a proper arrest. It declared the cannabis admissible in evidence and affirmed the conviction for possessing it. In *State v. Beaucage*[61] the defendant shouted obscenities at another person in an apartment house parking lot and was arrested for disorderly conduct. While under arrest, she was ordered to empty her handbag so that its contents could be inventoried. Two cigarettes found during the inventory were discovered to contain marijuana, and she was prosecuted and convicted for possessing it. The Rhode Island Supreme Court, citing *Robinson* among other U.S. Supreme Court holdings, sustained the warrantless search that led to the discovery of the drug and affirmed her conviction. The inspection of the purse, the court reasoned, was incidental to a valid arrest. Finally, in *Hughes v. State*[62] the defendant was taken into custody for reckless driving and driving without a license. He was handcuffed on the spot, and his pockets were examined without a warrant. Codeine was found, and the defendant was convicted of possession of a controlled substance. The Oklahoma Court of Criminal Appeals, the highest court in the state for criminal matters, mentioned *Robinson* to support the view that a full warrantless personal search incidental to a valid custodial arrest violates neither the U.S. Constitution's Fourth Amendment nor the search and seizure provision of the state constitution. The conviction was upheld.[63]

United States v. Ross

United States v. Ross[64] clarified a cluster of confusing precedents and declared that "if probable cause (e.g., that the vehicle contains contraband) justifies the search of a lawfully stopped vehicle, it justifies the search of every part of the vehicle and its contents that may conceal the object of the search."[65] The holding made it clear that the police, under these circumstances and without a warrant, can rummage through not only the passenger compartment but also the trunk and all bags and containers anywhere in the car.

At this point, only one state appellate court system, that of Washington, has rejected *Ross*. In *State v. Ringer*,[66] the defendant had been convicted of possession of various controlled substances. He was arrested on an outstanding felony warrant while driving his van. As the state troopers were taking him into custody, they smelled marijuana coming from the vehicle. They searched the van for weapons and the drug and came upon a clear bag of cannabis and luggage. Opening the latter, they found more cannabis, cocaine, and other narcotics. The Washington State Supreme Court admitted that, under *Ross*, the search of Ringer's van was valid under the U.S. Constitution's Fourth Amendment. Yet the court reversed the conviction on the ground that this warrantless scrutiny violated a section of the Washington State Constitution declaring that "no person shall be disturbed in his private affairs... without authority of law." The opinion went on to state that the search might have been proper had exigent circumstances made it impractical to secure a warrant before it was carried out, but the state made no showing that an emergency of this sort prevailed. (Most of the opinion considered whether the examination could be justified under the Washington Constitution as "incidental to a valid arrest"; the court concluded that it could not. Thus even *Ringer* does not constitute a clear-cut repudiation of *Ross*.)

Every other state appellate tribunal that has considered *Ross* has embraced it. For example, in *State v. Eubanks*,[67] a state patrolman detected the smell of cannabis emanating from the defendant's automobile after he had stopped it for a faulty headlight. The officer looked in the suspect's purse, which she was holding as she was standing outside the vehicle; he found marijuana in a bag in a make-up case. The defendant was then given a summons for possession of this drug. The trial court granted her motion to suppress the marijuana on the ground that no exigent circumstances existed to justify its warrantless taking. The Iowa Supreme Court reversed on the basis of *Ross*. Once the officer had probable cause to search the automobile for contraband, the court held, he could lawfully open all containers within the vehicle. The purse could not be insulated from this warrantless search by its removal from the automobile while the search was in progress. Thus the seizure of the drug did not violate Fourth Amendment rights. (The court mentioned in passing that no state constitutional issue had been raised by either side.)

Ross was held to have positive applications in other circumstances and conditions. In *Commonwealth v. Duell*,[68] an automobile in which Duell was a passenger was stopped for making an illegal turn. When the driver's window was rolled down, police officers smelled marijuana. One reached into the car and pulled out a paper bag on the seat next to Duell. Cannabis was found inside. The Pennsylvania Superior Court, relying upon *Ross*, declared the warrantless search of the bag to be valid; the smell of marijuana provided probable cause to believe that the vehicle contained contraband. In *Estep v. Commonwealth*,[69] the defendant had been convicted of armed robbery. He contended on appeal that a gun should not have been introduced at his trial since it was found by means of a warrantless search of the automobile's glove compartment. However, probable cause to halt Estep's car was said to exist since the police had been given the description and license number of the vehicle used in the robbery, and both matched Estep's car. Therefore, the Kentucky Supreme Court, noting *Ross*, sustained the seizure; where probable cause justifies making a vehicle pull up, every part of the car and its compartments that may conceal the object of the search may be examined without violating the U.S. and Kentucky constitutions.

In *State v. Jackson*,[70] the defendant and an accomplice had entered a department store and behaved suspiciously. The sales staff subsequently discovered that $2,200 worth of clothing was missing and observed the defendant and her friend leave the store and enter an automobile. Police were called, and the pair was arrested emerging from another nearby shop. The vehicle was towed to a police garage, and a warrantless search revealed a purse. This handbag, also opened without a warrant, was found to contain evidence of the identity of the occupant of the vehicle and an instrument used to cut devices attached to the clothing that would have caused an electric alarm to sound had they not been removed. This evidence of identity and the tool were admitted in evidence at defendant's shoplifting trial. Pointing to *Ross*, the Missouri Court of Appeals declared the purse search to be valid and upheld the conviction.[71]

Illinois v. Gates

In *Aguilar v. Texas*[72] and *Spinelli v. United States*,[73] the U.S. Supreme Court developed the rule that the judge must ask two questions in determining whether probable cause exists to issue a search warrant where the officer requesting it relies on an informer's tip. First, does the affidavit supporting the warrant reveal the means by which the informant acquired the information (that is, what is the basis of his knowledge)?

Second, does it set forth facts to establish the veracity of the informant or the reliability of the report in the particular case? For the judge to determine that "probable" cause for the search of person or property prevailed, both halves of this two-pronged test normally had to be satisfied. In *Illinois v. Gates*,[74] the U.S. Supreme Court, in an opinion by Justice Rehnquist, rejected the *Aguilar-Spinelli* test in favor of a "totality of the circumstances" standard. Among the circumstances are "basis of knowledge" and "general veracity" or "reliability in the instant case"; but the weakness of the affidavit in one of these respects does not automatically mean that the magistrate should refuse to issue the warrant. The judge's duty, in short, is to make a common-sense decision whether, given all the facts in the affidavit, "there is a fair probability that contraband or evidence of a crime will be found in a particular place."[75] If this probability exists, the warrant should be granted.

A number of state appellate courts have rejected *Gates* and adhered to the *Aguilar-Spinelli* test. In *State v. Jackson*,[76] the Washington State Supreme Court declared that the latter criterion was mandated by the state constitution. Acting partly on an informant's tip that the defendant was a major distributor for a well-known drug dealer, a federal magistrate had issued a warrant to search Jackson's home for marijuana. The substance was found, and the defendant and his wife were convicted for cannabis possession. The state supreme court relied upon *Aguilar-Spinelli*, but it upheld the conviction. It noted that the affidavit revealed that the informant was highly credible. Though the informant never clearly indicated how he came to know that the defendant was a distributor, independent police observations tended to confirm that he played this role. Thus there was probable cause to issue the warrant. In *State v. Jones*,[77] the Alaska Supreme Court similarly asserted that the search and seizure and right-to-privacy clauses of the Alaska Constitution require a resort to *Aguilar-Spinelli*. Here the court upheld a reversal of a conviction for possession of cocaine. The search warrant was issued on the basis of information provided by a juvenile. Since the affidavit failed to establish the young person's veracity, the *Aguilar-Spinelli* standard was not satisfied, and the warrant allowing the search for the drug should not have been issued.[78]

Apart from such cases, the majority of state appellate courts have been willing to discard *Aguilar-Spinelli* in favor of *Gates*. Thus in *Wolf v. State*,[79] the Court of Appeals of Arkansas found an affidavit sufficient to establish probable cause for a search for marijuana when it stated that a confidential informant had observed green vegetable matter appearing to be cannabis on certain property and that the informer had helped the police in a previous case. The court, quoting the new *Gates* standard, declined to accept the defendant's argument that the affidavit was insufficient to support the issuance of the warrant because it did not establish the informant's reliability. In *Tatman v. State*,[80] the Delaware Supreme Court used *Gates* to find probable cause that the defendant's car contained drugs and to declare the search of the vehicle (uncovering heroin) legitimate. Here a police officer had heard from an informant of unestablished veracity that the defendant was going to New York to buy heroin and would be returning in a white car. The officer knew from his own observation and from information received from reliable sources that the defendant was a heroin dealer. Moreover, he confirmed the informant's tip by telephoning two other informers who had provided solid information in the past. Thus the police had sufficient probable cause to believe that the automobile contained contraband. And in *State v. Abbott*,[81] the police, armed with a search warrant based on informants' assertions, found marijuana in the defendant's bedroom. The Appellate Court of Connecticut affirmed the conviction. Though the warrant had just been issued, some of the informants' statements that drugs were being sold at the house were thirty to ninety days old. Nonetheless, one of the reliable sources had told the police no more than three days before the issuance of the warrant that one of the building's occupants was dealing in drugs and had offered to sell some to him. Relying on *Gates*, the court noted that the totality of the circumstances demonstrated probable cause that drug sales were occurring at the premises in question.[82]

Conclusions

The cases reviewed demonstrate that a majority of state appellate courts throughout the country have accepted Burger Court decisions limiting the constitutional protections accorded criminal defendants. For purposes of style, *North Carolina v. Pearce*[83] is considered a Burger Court decision even though it was one of the last efforts of the Warren Court. Each of the antidefendant U.S. Supreme Court rulings whose effects were analyzed was adopted by a majority of state appellate tribunals. Nonetheless, the state holdings also reveal that a pro-prosecution U.S. Supreme Court decision is likely to be opposed by a substantial minority of state appellate tribunals that offer criminal suspects more extensive rights than the U.S. Supreme Court requires. Six of the eight Burger Court cases selected—all except *United States v. Edwards*[84] and *Beckwith v. United States*[85]—were rejected by at least one state appellate court. In fact, *Illinois v. Gates*,[86] *United States v. Robinson*,[87] and *North Carolina v. Pearce*[88] were spurned by several courts.

States that have had at least one higher court take exception to one or more of these pro-prosecution Burger Court rulings include Alaska, California, Hawaii, Massachusetts, New Jersey, New York, Oregon, Utah, and Washington. The only unexpected entry is Utah, whose supreme court until recent years was so conservative that it refused to admit that the U.S. Constitution's First Amendment was binding on the states.[89] (In *State v. Sorenson*,[90] the Utah court held that a defendant, after a successful appeal, may not be given a longer sentence upon retrial then that received at the conclusion of the original litigation.) Appellate courts in most of the other eight states are noted in other chapters of this work as often more willing to safeguard human rights than was the Burger Court.

In the criminal procedure area, at least, state appellate tribunals that seek to formulate higher standards for rights protection than does the U.S. Supreme Court will normally rely on state constitutions to justify the result. Thus, where a state court has rejected a "conservative" Burger Court decision, all but two rested primarily on the state's fundamental law. (The exceptions are the "no-longer-sentence-after-appeal" holding of *State v. DeBonis*,[91] grounded in public policy considerations; and the "no-unlimited-search-incidental-to-arrest" judgment of *Commonwealth v. Toole*,[92] based on a state statute.) Moreover, these decisions, except in the *Aguilar-Spinelli v. Gates* dispute, relied minimally upon "liberal" pre-Burger U.S. Supreme Court precedents; and even some "conservative" state opinions (albeit a minority) considered seriously whether their acceptance of Burger Court jurisprudence would violate the state's fundamental charter. (See, for example, the death penalty case of *State v. Campbell*[93] and the search-incidental-to-arrest holding of *Hughes v. State*.)[94] Thus it is fair to conclude that, in a number of states, a state constitutional law of defendants' rights relatively independent of federal doctrine will probably flourish in future years. This is especially likely to occur as long as individuals such as Oregon's Justice Hans Linde sit on state courts. He insists that a state court should always consider state before federal constitutional claims.[95]

Though much of state constitutional law may be more considerate of criminal suspects than the products of the Burger and Rehnquist courts, there are limits to the safeguards that will be accorded defendants. State judges are aware that the voters of California in November 1986 ousted California Supreme Court Justice Rose Bird and two of her colleagues because they voted against upholding "the death sentences of scores of convicted murderers."[96] They also know of the simultaneous defeat of Chief Justice Frank Celebrezze of the Ohio Supreme Court by Republican Thomas Moyer. Though Celebrezze probably lost because of a newspaper story revealing that he had accepted contributions from union locals with ties to organized crime,[97] he was a liberal who, his opponent implied, did not accept the principle of judicial restraint.[98] Whether the defeat of Justices Bird and Celebrezze was appropriate is a question outside the scope of this chapter; that it will lead state appellate courts to be more cautious in using the state constitution to protect the rights of suspects is likely.

Notes

1. Alexander Williams, "The New Patrol for the Accused: State Constitutions as a Buffer against Retrenchment," *Howard Law Journal* 26 (1983): 1307, 1323; Carol Peterkort, "The Conflict between State and Federal Constitutionally Guaranteed Rights: A Problem of the Independent Interpretation of State Constitutions," *Case Western Reserve Law Review* 32 (1981): 158, 160–61; Ted M. Benn, "Individual Rights and State Constitutional Interpretations: Putting First Things First," *Baylor Law Review* 37 (1985): 493, 511.

2. Donald Wilkes, "The New Federalism in Criminal Procedure: State Court Evasion of the Burger Court," *Kentucky Law Journal* 62 (1974): 421, 436.

3. John Gruhl, "State Supreme Courts and the U.S. Supreme Court's Post-Miranda Rulings," *Journal of Criminal Law and Criminology* 72 (1981): 886, 894. Harris v. New York may be found at 401 U.S. 222 (1971).

4. Gregg v. Georgia, 428 U.S. 153 (1976).

5. See the list of courts that have upheld the death penalty and of states with this penalty in State v. Campbell, 691 P.2d 929, 947–49 (Wash. 1984).

6. State v. Campbell, 691 P.2d 929 (Wash. 1984).

7. Id. at 948.

8. Id.

282   9. People v. Anderson, 493 P.2d 880 (Cal. 1972).

10. People v. Frierson, 599 P.2d 587 (Cal. 1979).

11. Ex parte Granviel, 561 S.W.2d 503 (Tex. 1978).

12. Id. at 513.

13. State v. Bass, 460 A.2d 214 (N.J. 1983).

14. 245 A.2d 181 (N.J. 1968).

15. In State v. Funicello, 286 A.2d 55 (N.J. 1972).

16. See also Tichnell v. State, 415 A.2d 830 (Md. 1980) (Maryland death penalty law violates neither state nor U.S. Constitution); Smith v. Commonwealth, 248 S.E.2d 135 (Va. 1978) (Virginia death penalty statue is facially valid under U.S. Constitution); Hopkinson v. State, 632 P.2d 79 (Wyo. 1981) (Wyoming death penalty law violates neither state nor U.S. Constitution).

17. District Attorney for the Suffolk District v. Watson, 411 N.E.2d 1274 (Mass. 1980).

18. Commonwealth v. Colon Cruz, 470 N.E.2d 116 (Mass. 1984).

19. State v. Quinn, 623 P.2d 630 (Or. 1981).

20. Beckwith v. United States, 425 U.S. 341 (1976).

21. People v. Myers, 349 N.E.2d 658 (Ill. 1976).

22. State v. DeConingh, 400 So.2d 998 (Fla. 1981).

23. State v. Fields, 294 N.W.2d 404 (N.D.1980).

24. State v. Swise, 669 P.2d 732 (N.M. 1983). See also Commonwealth v. Borodine, 353, N.E.2d 649 (Mass. 1976) (no *Miranda* warnings are necessary when interrogation is carried out in a laundry room in the basement of the victim's home); State v. Hatton, 568 P.2d 1040 (Ariz. 1977) (no *Miranda* warnings are necessary when questioning took place in the defendant's home with his wife and children present); Koah v. State, 604 S.W.2d 156 (Tex. 1980) (incriminating statements were held admissible when made in a letter responding to one by a

state civil servant concerning possible violations of Texas's securities laws by defendant's company; the state's letter contained no *Miranda* warnings).

25. Kastigar v. United States, 406 U.S. 441 (1972).

26. State v. Miyasaki, 614 P.2d 915 (Hawaii 1980).

27. State v. Soriano, 684 P.2d 1220 (Or. 1984).

28. Rivera v. City of Douglas, 644 P.2d 271 (Ariz. 1982).

29. State v. Vinegra, 341 A.2d 673 (N.J. 1975).

30. Smith v. State, 227 S.E.2d 84 (Ga. 1976).

31. People ex rel Smith v. Jordan, 689 P.2d 1172 (Colo. 1984).

32. See also Ex parte Shorthouse, 640 S.E.2d 924 (Tex. 1982)(granting use rather than transactional immunity violates neither the U.S. nor the Texas Constitution); Novo v. Scott, 438 S.2d 477 (Fla. 1983) (Florida statute granting use immunity only is constitutional); Commonwealth v. Webster, 470 A.2d 532 (Pa. 1983) (the granting of use immunity only does not violate the state constitution).

33. North Carolina v. Pearce & Simpson v. Rice, 395 U.S. 711 (1969).

34. Shagloak v. State, 597 P.2d 142 (Alas. 1979).

35. Id. at 145.

36. State v. DeBonis, 276 A.2d 137 (N.J. 1971).

37. State v. Sorenson, 639 P.2d 179 (Utah 1981).

38. State v. Martin, 497 P.2d 426 (Okla. 1972).

39. Spidle v. State, 446 S.W.2d 793 (Mo. 1969).

40. Chaffin v. State, 180 S.E.2d 741 (Ga. 1971).

41. Chaffin v. Stynchcombe, 412 U.S. 17 (1973).

42. People v. Olary, 170 N.W.2d 842 (Mich. 1969).

43. Colten v. Kentucky, 407 U.S. 104 (1972).

44. Beltkowski v. State, 183 N.W.2d 563 (Minn. 1971).

45. See also People v. Cox, 255 N.E.2d 208 (Ill. 1970) (defendant's sentence of five to thirty years on a third trial was upheld though he had received only ten to thirty years after his first two trials; a longer sentence was held justified because the defendant was a fugitive from justice after his third trial was started); State v. Koehmstedt, 297 N.W.2d 315 (N.D. 1980) (a defendant's harsher sentence on a de novo trial after an appeal from a drunken driving conviction in a justice of the peace court was upheld); Cournoyer v. Sharkey, 267 A.2d 722 (R.I. 1970) (a defendant's harsher sentence after his second trial for contempt of court was upheld because he continued in contempt between the date when his original conviction was reversed on appeal and the date of his new trial).

46. United States v. Edwards, 415 U.S. 800 (1974).

47. People v. Spencer, 286 N.W. 2d 879 (Mich. 1979).

48. Commonwealth v. Hrynkow, 330 A.2d 858 (Pa. 1974).

49. Pickens v. State, 551 S.W.2d 212 (Ark. 1977).

50. People v. Young, 205 Cal. Rptr. 402 (Cal. 1984).

51. See also State v. Gonzales, 523 P.2d 66 (Ariz. 1974) (the court held valid a warrantless impounding of the defendant's clothing for evidence some time after he had been arrested and the garb taken from him); State v. Calegar, 661 P.2d 311 (Idaho 1983) (the court allowed a warrantless search of a suitcase found in the defendant's car; the case was searched in the police station—not in the car when he was arrested); State v. McClain, 533 P.2d 1277 (Kans. 1975) (the

warrantless taking of the defendant's clothing from the jail twelve hours after his arrest was held constitutional).

52. United States v. Robinson, 414 U.S. 218 (1973).

53. People v. Brisendine, 531 P.2d 1099 (Cal. 1975).

54. The case is mentioned by Peter Galie in "The Other Supreme Courts: Judicial Activism among State Supreme Courts," *Syracuse Law Review* 33 (1982): 731, 779.

55. Commonwealth v. Toole, 448 N.E.2d 1264 (Mass. 1983).

56. State v. Kaluna, 520 P.2d 52 (Hawaii 1974).

57. Zehrung v. State, 569 P.2d 189 (Alas. 1977).

58. People v. Cannon, 310 N.E.2d 673 (Ill. 1974).

59. State v. Mims, 208 S.E.2d 288 (S.C. 1974).

60. State v. Lohff, 214 N.W.2d 80 (S.D. 1974).

61. State v. Beaucage, 424 A.2d 642 (R.I. 1981).

62. Hughes v. State, 522 P.2d 1331 (Okla. 1974).

63. See also State v. Morris, 227 N.W.2d 150 (Iowa 1975) (a warrantless search of the person discovering marijuana was sustained when the defendant had been arrested for intoxication—or disorderly conduct; the report does not make this distinction clear); State v. Harris, 286 N.W.2d 468 (N.D. 1979) (a warrantless pat-search of the person finding the gun was held valid when the defendant had been arrested for disorderly conduct); State v. Lopes, 552 P.2d 120 (Utah 1976) (a warrantless search of a person finding a pistol was held valid when the defendant had been arrested for a traffic violation).

64. United States v. Ross, 456 U.S. 798 (1982).

65. Id. at 825.

66. State v. Ringer, 674 P.2d 1240 (Wash. 1983).

67. State v. Eubanks, 355 N.W.2d 57 (Iowa 1984).

68. Commonwealth v. Duell, 451 A.2d 724 (Pa. 1982).

69. Estep v. Commonwealth, 663 S.W.2d 213 (Ky. 1983).

70. State v. Jackson, 646 S.W. 2d 369 (Mo. 1982).

71. See also Vathis v. State, 474 So.2d 423 (Fla. 1985) (a warrantless search of a garbage bag in the trunk of a car was sustained); Commonwealth v. King, 449 N.E.2d 1217 (Mass. 1983) (a warrantless search of a duffel bag and green bag in a car was upheld); State v. Maldonado, 322 N.W.2d 349 (Minn. 1982) (a warrantless search of a paper bag in a car was sustained as constitutional).

72. Aguilar v. Texas, 378 U.S. 108 (1964).

73. Spinelli v. United States, 393 (U.S. 410 (1969).

74. Illinois v. Gates, 462 U.S. 213 (1983).

75. Id. at 238.

76. State v. Jackson, 688 P.2d 136 (Wash. 1984).

77. State v. Jones, 706 P.2d 318 (Alaska 1985).

78. See also Commonwealth v. Reddington, 480 N.E.2d 6 (Mass. 1985) (the *Aguilar-Spinelli* test was required by the state constitution though that document allowed a finding of probable cause where one prong of *Aguilar-Spinelli* was not satisfied but there was independent corroboration of the informant's tip); People v. Johnson, 488 N.E.2d 439, 497 N.Y.S.2d 618 (N.Y. 1985) (New York State Constitution's search and seizure clause prevents *Gates*' "totality of the circum-

stances" test from being used to determine whether probable cause existed to make a warrantless arrest based solely on an informant's tip).

79. Wolf v. State, 664 S.W.2d 882 (Ark. 1984).

80. Tatman v. State, 494 A.2d 1249 (Del. 1985).

81. State v. Abbott, 499 A.2d 437 (Conn. 1985).

82. See also Moore v. State, 441 So.2d 1003 (Ala. 1983); State v. O'Connor, 378 N.W.2d 248 (S.D. 1985); State v. Doucette, 470 A.2d 676 (Vt. 1983) (the *Gates* test was used in all three cases to determine the existence of probable cause for issuance of a search warrant).

83. North Carolina v. Pearce, 395 U.S. 711 (1969).

84. United States v. Edwards, 415 U.S. 800 (1974).

85. Beckwith v. United States, 425 U.S. 341 (1976).

86. Illinois v. Gates, 462 U.S. 213 (1983).

87. United States v. Robinson, 414 U.S. 218 (1973).

88. North Carolina v. Pearce, 395 U.S. 711 (1969).

89. *New York Times*, November 13, 1975, p. 63.

90. State v. Sorenson, 639 P.2d 179 (Utah 1981).

91. State v. DeBonis, 276 A.2d 137 (N.J. 1971).

92. Commonwealth v. Toole, 448 N.E.2d 1264 (Mass. 1983).

93. State v. Campbell, 691 P.2d 929 (Wash. 1984).

94. Hughes v. State, 522 P.2d 1331 (Okla. 1974).

95. See his "First Things First: Rediscovering the States' Bills of Rights," *University of Baltimore Law Review* 9 (1980): 379, 383.

96. *New York Times*, November 6, 1986, p. A30.

97. *Cleveland Plain Dealer*, November 6, 1986, p. 1B.

98. *Wall Street Journal*, November 28, 1986, p. 10; *U.S. News and World Report*, November 17, 1986, p. 23.

7

Remnants of the Past: Economic Due Process in the States

SUSAN P. FINO

Substantive due process has been and remains today one of the most controversial areas of constitutional interpretation. Unlike the more familiar procedural due process, substantive due process involves judicial scrutiny of legislative ends or goals rather than the means used to reach those ends. Substantive due process requires the judicial discovery of fundamental values protected by the due process clauses of the Fifth or Fourteenth amendments to the federal Constitution or state constitutional counterparts of these amendments. Thus judges breathe meaning into the liberty and property provisions in the federal and state constitutions. Acts of the legislature are then evaluated in the light of these constitutionally protected, judicially defined liberties. If legislation, purported to be a valid exercise of the police power, is found to be an invasion of judicially defined constitutional liberties, it will be struck down. For many scholars of constitutional law and the judicial process, substantive due process results in the substitution of judicial value judgements for those of the legislature.

The original and perhaps most criticized use of substantive due process has been in the protection of property and economic liberties. Justices in the late nineteenth and early twentieth centuries developed the notion of liberty of contract, which was used to invalidate legislation said to infringe upon an individual's right to enter into voluntary agreements. Liberty of contract prevented the states and the federal government from regulating certain commercial transactions[1] and the wages[2] and hours of workers,[3] as well as from protecting collective bargaining.[4] The use of substantive due process to strike down popular legislation during the New Deal helped to bring on the court-packing crisis of 1937.[5]

Although President Franklin D. Roosevelt's proposal that the number of justices on the Supreme Court be increased to a maximum of fifteen was not approved, the plan prompted a reconsideration of the Court's stance with respect to New Deal legislation. Justice Owen J. Roberts's celebrated "switch in time that saved nine" resulted in the Court's sustaining types of economic regulation that had been found earlier to be constitutionally infirm. Chief Justice Charles E. Hughes, in effect, interred economic substantive due process in 1937 in *West Coast Hotel v. Parrish*.[6]

By 1938, the U.S. Supreme Court had indicated that a simple rational basis test was sufficient to sustain the constitutionality of economic legislation. In *United States v. Carolene Products*, Chief Justice Harlan F. Stone concluded that a presumption of constitutionality attaches to economic legislation and that facts supporting the rational basis for the legislation are to be assumed.[7] However, in *Carolene Products*, the chief justice reserved certain areas for "more exacting judicial scrutiny": legislation that appears to affect certain political rights such as the right to vote and laws affecting "discrete and insular minorities."[8] A constitutional double standard developed at the federal level. The judiciary subjected economic acts and regulations to a minimal rationality standard, while legislation that affected individual rights or minorities was scrutinized by reference to a much higher standard.[9]

Clearly, substantive due process became virtually moribund as a measure of economic enactments, although it reappeared in *Griswold v. Connecticut*[10] for the protection of personal autonomy. Although the resurgence of substantive due process was initially disguised as an "emanation" or "penumbra" from the Bill of Rights, the Supreme Court itself has acknowledged that substantive due process is again a part of the law.[11] The liberty provisions of the Fifth and Fourteenth amendments now protect an individual's decision to use birth control devices,[12] a woman's decision to terminate a pregnancy,[13] and family living arrangements.[14] But the federal courts, in the interpretation of the Constitution, continue to minimize any revival of such predicates in the area of economic regulation.[15]

By contrast, many state supreme courts have never forsaken *Lochner*, liberty of contract, or economic due process. Monrad Paulsen found in 1950 numerous examples of state courts clinging to pre–1937 constitutional doctrines in a number of clearly defined areas.[16] He found state court decisions invalidating state legislation under the state constitution in areas such as price regulation, the control of competition by licensing, the prohibition of certain business methods (such as the sale of ice cream from street corner wagons), and the regulation of labor unions and labor practices. A student note in the *Ohio State Law Journal* updated Paulsen's research in 1957; there were indications of the continuing judicial invalidation of statutes in the same areas.[17] John A. C. Hetherington, writing as late as 1958, found additional examples of the use of economic due process in the states.[18] For example, Hetherington noted cases striking down regulation of the barbering trade in which the Arizona Supreme Court cited *Lochner* as controlling.[19]

The commentaries generally take a dim view of the persistence of economic due process in the states, although Paulsen and Hetherington see some role for courts in the oversight of state legislation. Paulsen perceives a need for state court activity as a result of the capture of the state legislature by special interest groups. "Given the short legislative session in many states and the concentrated attention which pressure groups may devote to that session," Paulsen is moderately sympathetic to the courts' exercise of judicial review.[20] Hetherington agrees that state legislatures may not necessarily be "democratic" and adds that property rights deserve some protection.[21] Hetherington also argues that state courts are in a better position to resort to economic due process than their federal counterparts. State court decisions, grounded in state constitutional law, do not have national effect as precedents. Moreover, state courts may be particularly sensitive to local conditions and needs, and therefore they tend to be closer to existing problems than the U.S. Supreme Court.[22]

This chapter offers an examination of contemporary economic due process decisions in the states. Following a review of major cases decided since 1960, the argument will be made that there is a role for state supreme court activism in the area of economic regulation and that economic due process need not provoke a state constitutional crisis if properly limited. The cases discussed in this fifty-state survey were identified with the aid of LEXIS and represent a reasonably complete portrayal of state supreme court activism in the economic sphere.[23] It must be noted that the examples of judicial invalidation of economic regulation do not depict the usual business of state supreme courts in the area of substantive due process. More often, state supreme courts rely upon the "new" substantive due process for the protection of personal autonomy.[24] With respect to economic regulation, adherence to the federal deferential standards remains the rule.[25]

The Regulation of Advertising

Before the U.S. Supreme Court afforded commercial speech the protection of the First Amendment in 1976, two state supreme courts had struck down state bans on the advertisement of prescription drugs on state substantive due process grounds.[26] The Pennsylvania Supreme

Court, in *Pennsylvania State Board of Pharmacy v. Pastor*, declared unconstitutional a section of the pharmacy act that prohibited the advertisement of prices of "dangerous or narcotic drugs."[27] The Pennsylvania
court, speaking through Justice Samuel J. Roberts, acknowledged "that
the day has long passed when the Due Process Clause of the Fourteenth
Amendment could be used to indiscriminately strike down state economic regulatory statutes"[28] and that "deference to the legislative judgment is now the federal watchword."[29] However, Justice Roberts rejected
the argument that the same deferential standard is appropriate for state
supreme courts. State courts are in a better position to review local
legislation than is the U.S. Supreme Court. State court interpretation of
state law is not of national authority or impact and may be adapted to
local conditions.

The Pennsylvania court then reviewed all plausible reasons for the
state regulation: that advertising may lead to increased drug use; that
consumers will fail to patronize a single pharmacy, thus undermining
the pharmacist's ability to monitor drug use; and that there is a need to
prevent the deterioration of drugs with a short shelf-life. The court
concluded that the challenged regulation bore no "real substantial relationship" to the objectives of the commonwealth and therefore was
unconstitutional. Justice Roberts expressed the view that the ban on
prescription advertising probably had caused some consumers to pay
more than others for the same medication. While the legislature had
elected to be protective of pharmacists, the state court chose to be protective of consumers. Yet this substitution of the value judgments of the
judiciary for those of the legislature remains the essence of substantive
due process.

The Maryland Court of Appeals looked to *Pastor* for guidance in
deciding *Maryland Board of Pharmacy v. Sav-A-Lot, Inc.*[30] Again the issue
was a state-imposed ban on the advertisement of prices of prescription
drugs, and again the ban was held unconstitutional. The Maryland Court
of Appeals agreed with the Pennsylvania court that the appropriate test
for the legislation was "whether the statute, as an exercise of the state's
police power, provides a real and substantial relation to the public health,
morals, safety and welfare of the citizens of the state."[31] Like Pennsylvania, the Maryland court acknowledged a special role for state supreme
courts in the review of state economic legislation despite the "current
direction taken by the Supreme Court in the area of economic regulation,
as distinguished from the protection of fundamental rights."[32] The
Maryland court reviewed the reasons for the advertising ban and found
them inadequate to pass the substantial relation test. Moreover, the act
worked against the interests of consumers, particularly the elderly and
the poor. Thus, the act was held unconstitutional under the Fourteenth
Amendment and the Maryland Declaration of Rights.

Pastor and *Sav-A-Lot* are throwbacks to an earlier era; they may represent the last of their genre. The U.S. Supreme Court has accorded commercial speech the protection of the First Amendment and has set aside bans on prescription price advertising, real estate "for sale" signs, and attorney advertising on federal constitutional grounds.[33] Therefore, in cases that involve advertising bans, the First Amendment and its state constitutional counterparts may serve as a more appropriate, and perhaps less controversial, basis for analysis.

Limitations on Professions

Government regulation of private industry is an accepted fact of twentieth-century life. Since the advent of the minimal rationality test for economic regulation, courts—especially federal courts—have played a limited role in stemming the tide of increased government intervention in commercial affairs. However, a number of state supreme courts have reserved a role for the judiciary and substantive due process to strike down legislation which the courts perceive to be anticompetitive. Such invalidation has applied, in particular, to state laws limiting entry into a profession or restricting the conditions under which professions operate.

An example of such judicial scrutiny in the interests of competition may be found in the 1973 decision in *Maryland State Board of Barber Examiners v. Kuhn*.[34] At issue was a statute prohibiting cosmetologists from rendering to male patrons the same services that they may lawfully provide for female patrons. The legislation was founded in the belief that the restrictions placed on the cosmetologists would protect the male public from inadequately trained hairdressers and promote public hygiene. The Maryland Court of Appeals applied the "real and substantial relationship" test developed in *Sav-A-Lot* and found the statute constitutionally defective under the Fourteenth Amendment and the Maryland Declaration of Rights. Judge Irving A. Levine reasoned that the right to engage in a lawful occupation is protected and must not be interfered with arbitrarily or capriciously. Regulations affecting a lawful business must be limited to the protection of a real and substantial public interest.

The arguments used by the Maryland Court of Appeals parallel those of the U.S. Supreme Court in the days before the New Deal. There is little chance that such arguments would prevail in an economic regulatory case brought to a federal court and presented under the federal Constitution. Yet the Maryland court's reasoning prevailed in another barbering case decided by the West Virginia Supreme Court in 1979. In *Thorne v. Roush*,[35] the West Virginia Supreme Court issued a writ of mandamus to compel the issuance of barber's licenses to junior barber apprentices because the apprenticeship program was required under a constitutionally defective statute. The state statute was found to be arbitrary and capricious and a violation of the state constitution.

In 1974, the Supreme Court of California invalidated a state statute that prohibited the licensing of medical practitioners who possessed a doctor of osteopathy degree instead of the traditional doctor of medicine degree. *D'Amico v. Board of Medical Examiners*[36] nominally was an equal protection case that challenged the rationality of the different treatment of two types of medical practitioner. The California court acknowledged a state interest in protecting the public from poorly trained or incompetent physicians, but it found that the classification the legislature used bore no rational relationship to the achievement of that goal. The court implied that a less restrictive alternative to the absolute ban on the licensing of osteopaths existed. The examinations and examining board already in place for medical doctors could be used to screen graduates of osteopathic schools to protect the public and to guarantee a minimal standard of care. This finding led to the conclusion that an absolute ban was irrational. Once again, a state court, exercising the power of judicial review, had substituted its conception of public policy for that of the legislature.

The Supreme Court of Florida has maintained a strong tradition sustaining the rigorous review of legislation that limits the practice of certain professions. *Florida Accountants Association v. Dandelake*[37] struck down a state law that allowed only certified public accountants to call themselves accountants. All noncertified accountants had to be designated as bookkeepers and could not serve as independent contractors or engage in certain types of public accounting. The Florida Supreme Court invoked liberty of contract and found such liberty fundamental and protected from arbitrary impairment.

The Florida court also invalidated a state law prohibiting personal solicitation by public adjusters in *Larson v. Lesser*.[38] The court once again referred to liberty of contract and cited with approval the U.S. Supreme Court decision in *Adkins v. Children's Hospital*,[39] a controversial decision that had been overruled by the Court in 1937 in *West Coast Hotel*.[40] For the Florida court of the late 1950s, there was "no such thing as an absolute freedom of contract, nevertheless, freedom is the general rule and restraint is the exception."[41]

Yet liberty of contract in Florida was not merely a phenomenon of the 1950s. In 1986, in *Department of Insurance v. Dade County Consumer Advocate's Office*,[42] the Florida Supreme Court declared unconstitutional a statute forbidding insurance agents from accepting a commission less than the amount prescribed by the insurer. A majority concluded that the statute unconstitutionally limited the bargaining power of the public; it cited with pride the Florida court's tradition of economic due process.

For the majority, there was a clear role for the courts in invalidating legislation that restricts the competitive pricing of consumer services.

If there is a common thread running through these state cases, it is a preference for robust economic competition. Although none of the courts seriously suggested a return to old-style laissez faire, all sought to minimize restrictions on entry into a profession or restrictions that limit the bargaining power of the consumer, as in the advertising cases. State supreme court justices, as Hetherington pointed out, are aware of the extent to which special interests may capture state legislatures or regulatory agencies and may be tempted to second-guess decisions of lawmakers or regulators. Substantive due process provides a means of reevaluating legislation. Many observers are sympathetic to the state courts' efforts to protect the bargaining power of the public. But there is always the danger that judicial review may not be carefully limited.

Thus far, no state court has developed any explicit legal principles by which to confine a review of economic regulation. Instead, the outcome of these cases seems to depend on individual judicial conceptions of sound economic policy, and parallels drawn from *Lochner* persist. While the eradication of distinctions between barbers and hairdressers or accountants and bookkeepers is not likely to provoke the emotional public outcry against pre–1937 federal decisions, state courts may accurately be characterized as superlegislatures in these cases.

Price Regulation

Both Paulsen and Hetherington found numerous examples in the 1940s and 1950s of state supreme courts that had invalidated unfair trade practices statutes limiting the ability of wholesalers and retailers to sell items below cost. Latter-day instances of judicial disapproval of such statutes continue to appear. In 1959, the Supreme Court of Washington set aside the state's fair trade practices act in *Remington Arms Co. v. Skaggs*.[43] The Washington law prohibited the sale of brand-name products below prices set by the original seller. Under the statute, it was irrelevant whether the retailer was a party to the original price agreement. The Washington court had little difficulty finding the legislation an unconstitutional violation of liberty of contact.

The Supreme Court of North Carolina considered a similar state statute, the fair trade act of 1937, which limited the resale of certain products and established minimum prices stipulated by the seller. As in the Washington statute, the North Carolina law limited the ability of a retailer to set prices even if the retailer was not a party to the original pricing agreement. In *Bulova Watch Co. v. Brand Distributors*,[44] after acknowledging that federal decisions are persuasive but not binding on the states, the North Carolina court indicated that any statute that impairs the ability to enter into contracts may be the object of careful judicial scrutiny.

The court attempted to apply a balancing test in assessing the constitutionality of the fair trade act, weighing the benefit to the public against the infringement on a retailer's liberty of contract. The justices noted that fair trade acts had their origins in the unusual circumstances of the Great Depression and that a number of state courts, reconsidering the constitutionality of such acts in the light of a comparatively sound economy, had found them defective. The nonsigner provision of the act was nullified on liberty of contract grounds.[45]

In *Hand v. H. & R. Block, Inc.*,[46] the Arkansas court evaluated a franchising law that prohibited the charging of a royalty fee greater than the lowest fee charged franchisees in other states. The court conceded that economic legislation generally receives deferential treatment and that the police power of the state may be used to regulate private property. The court held, however, that regulations affecting property and contractual rights may be sustained only if the regulations serve a public, rather than a private, purpose. Here the court found no real, substantial, or rational relation of the statute to the public safety, health, morals, or general welfare. As such, the act was a "palpable invasion of rights secured by fundamental law" and could not be sustained as a valid exercise of the police power.[47]

The supreme courts of Washington, North Carolina, and Arkansas were persuaded that competitive pricing of goods would eventually benefit the seller and consumer despite a legislative judgment to the contrary. On the surface, the cases seem to increase the power of the consumer and to strengthen the business climate of the state though the decisions may be shortsighted. The Supreme Court of Colorado was faced with a similar challenge to the state's unfair practices act, but the court came to a different conclusion. In *Flank Oil Co. v. Tennessee Gas Transmission Co.*,[48] it offered compelling reasons for deference to the legislature in this area of the law. The legislature may find that predatory price wars may ultimately lead to monopoly uncontrolled by the forces of competition.

The arguments of the court in *Flank Oil* illustrate the potential pitfalls of economic due process guided by the simple notion that competition benefits consumers. Immediate benefits, in the form of lower prices to the consumer, may give way to the elimination of some marginal competitors. Ultimately the market in a particular good may come to be controlled by a few major vendors with the power to control prices. When courts make such policy decisions, they are faced with the same problems of unanticipated consequences faced by the legislature but with limited judicial resources to undo the harm of their decisions. The road to monopoly may be paved with good but ill-considered intentions.

Penalties for Undesirable Actions

Since 1960, state supreme courts have disagreed with legislatures three times over penalties for conduct that the legislature finds undesirable. In each case, the court struck down a statute authorizing the penalty on substantive due process grounds, arguing that a less onerous means existed to redress the problem. This preference for a judicial, rather than a legislative, solution typifies substantive due process.

In 1978, the California Supreme Court set aside a section of the state's civil code that assessed fines of $100 per day against a landlord who willfully deprived a tenant of utilities for purposes of eviction. The court, in *Hale v. Morgan*,[49] found that the "due process shield" protects property as well as liberty and that the penalty was unreasonable and oppressive. The court pointed out that the penalty was mandatory, that it might be unlimited in duration, and that the trier of fact was permitted no discretion in fixing the amount. A six-member majority reasoned that the penalty allowed "the occasional experienced and designing tenant to ambush an unknowing landlord converting a single wrongful act of the latter into a veritable financial bonanza."[50] Therefore the section of the civil code was held to violate provisions of the California Constitution that prohibit excessive fines. Justice Frank C. Newman concurred on the ground that the section provided an appropriate means of judicial review and in the belief that the decision was not a "harbinger of a disinterred substantive-due-process review."[51]

The Georgia Supreme Court invalidated a state law that imposed criminal liability on a licensee for the sale of alcoholic beverages to a minor or for sales on Sunday. In *Davis v. City of Peachtree*,[52] the court held that due process precluded the imposition of a criminal penalty for actions taken by the licensee's employees without his knowledge, authorization, or consent. A unanimous court weighed the relative interests of the public and the individual and found that there were other, less onerous, means by which the public interest might be served.

In 1986, the Florida Supreme Court, in *State v. Saiez*,[53] struck down a state statute that prohibited the possession of embossing machines designed to reproduce credit cards. The statute was not found to be overbroad or unconstitutionally vague, yet it was held invalid on due process grounds under the federal and state constitutions. Justice Rosemary Barkett reasoned that the statute invaded a sphere of individual liberty and failed to bear a "reasonable and substantial relation" to the legitimate state goal of the prevention of credit card fraud. For the court, it was "unreasonable to criminalize the mere possession of embossing machines when such prohibition clearly interferes with the legitimate personal and property rights of a number of individuals who use embossing machines in their businesses."[54]

The penalty cases represent a form of substantive due process but one that is not comparable to the old liberty of contract standard. While liberty of contract places certain types of individual transactions outside the sphere of legitimate government activity, these cases acknowledge that government regulation is permissible though limited by specified substantive concerns. Courts will require that legislatures evaluate alternative approaches to public problems and select the means that impinge the least on individual freedom. Whether the legislature has made an acceptable choice of means will depend on the "substantial relation" test rather than the minimal rationality standard required by federal due process. Courts may also be guided by provisions in the state constitution (other than due process) that may impose specific limitations on the choice of means. In sum, the approach in the penalty cases does not eliminate judicial discretion, but it does limit the scope of review.

Issues for the Future: The Intersection of Privacy and the Economy

While judicial invalidation of legislation based upon the rationale articulated in cases such as *Lochner*[55] remains relatively rare in the states, a new form of substantive due process injects the principles of privacy or personal autonomy developed by the Supreme Court in *Griswold v. Connecticut*[56] and *Roe v. Wade*[57] into the review of traditional exercises of the police power. State supreme courts have found that the constitutional right to privacy limits the reach of the legislature in areas as diverse as zoning,[58] the regulation of insurance companies,[59] massage parlors[60] and outpatient clinics,[61] the protection of trade secrets,[62] employment[63] and blood donation records,[64] and the operation of ethics acts for government employees.[65] A few recent examples will illustrate the nature of these new constitutional challenges and the problems that they pose for state courts.

The U.S. Supreme Court determined in *Moore v. East Cleveland*[66] that strict scrutiny of a zoning ordinance was required since the ordinance involved the intrusive regulation of the living arrangement of blood family members. The justifications offered for the ordinance, such as the prevention of overcrowding and parking congestion, were found to be insufficient to sustain the ordinance's narrow definition of a family. Yet for the federal Court in *Belle Terre v. Boraas*,[67] a zoning ordinance affecting unrelated groups was judged by reference to a simple rational basis test, and it was upheld.

State supreme courts have not uniformly followed the federal Court's distinction between related and unrelated groups in reviewing zoning regulations measured against due process and privacy challenges. The New Jersey Supreme Court specifically rejected *Belle Terre* and in *State v. Baker*[68] found that, under the state constitution, the means chosen by the legislature must bear a substantial relationship to the effectuation of a goal. The California court in *Santa Barbara v. Adamson*[69] went a step further and held that the privacy rights of a group of unrelated individuals sharing a large house may be invaded only upon a showing of a compelling state interest. Consequently a zoning ordinance limiting occupancy of a house to persons related by blood, marriage, or legal adoption was held unconstitutional. The Ohio court also selected the compelling interest standard to review a similar zoning ordinance with similar results in *Saunders v. Clark County Zoning Department.*[70]

The Supreme Court of Michigan invalidated another such zoning ordinance, although the court did not resort to the compelling interest standard. In *Delta Charter Township v. Dinolfo,*[71] the court recognized that a community has a valid interest in the prevention of overcrowding and the preservation of the residential character of the neighborhood; yet distinctions between groups must not be arbitrary or unreasonable. The court noted that the ordinance operated to exclude a small group of communitarian Christians, but it could not exclude Ma Barker and her sons. The ordinance lacked a reasonable relationship between legislative means and ends and thus was unconstitutional.

In 1977, the U.S. Supreme Court was asked to extend the constitutional right to privacy to prevent the State of New York from creating a computerized data bank of the names and addresses of patients prescribed certain drugs. In *Whalen v. Roe,*[72] the Court noted that earlier cases had demonstrated that the right to privacy encompassed two dimensions: an individual's interest in disclosing certain personal matters and an individual's interest in making important personal decisions. Despite the Orwellian overtones of the New York program, the Court found that neither privacy interest was sufficiently impaired to render the data collection unconstitutional.

A number of state supreme courts have extended the constitutional right of privacy to areas yet unexplored by the federal Court. For example, in *Lopez v. Fitzgerald,*[73] the Illinois court ruled that the right to privacy under the federal and state constitutions prevented the disclosure of building inspection reports to tenants' groups concerned with the condition of their dwellings. The Colorado court, in *Augustin v. Barnes,*[74] found the right to privacy under the federal Constitution broad enough to invalidate a regulation that required a disclosure statement to be filed with the original insurer when a client changed to a new insurer.

The Supreme Court of Montana has been particularly active, undoubtedly aided by a provision in the state constitution declaring that the right to privacy is "essential" and shall not be infringed without the showing of a "compelling state interest."[75] The Montana court noted that a telephone company was entitled to a protective order to prevent the public disclosure of certain trade secrets in the course of a rate hearing.[76] It employed a balancing test weighing the government's interest on behalf of the public against the constitutional protections of privacy and private property. Although the regulatory agency argued that constitutional protections of privacy adhere to individuals, not to corporations, the supreme court looked to the state constitution and found that the distinction between individuals and corporations with respect to privacy was not supported by a compelling state interest. To like effect, in *Missoulian v. Board of Regents*,[77] the Montana court held that the constitutional right to privacy prevented the public disclosure of performance evaluations for the presidents of the six state universities.

Although many of these hybrid cases present novel questions, the constitutional resolution of the cases may be easier than the old liberty of contract issues. Every state constitution has a counterpart to the Fourth Amendment that protects persons, their homes, papers, and effects. Some contain explicit privacy provisions, and still others, such as the Montana document, set out the appropriate standard of review for the court. State judges in deciding privacy-economy cases need not create a new fundamental right as the Supreme Court did in *Lochner* or *Griswold*; thus they may avoid charges of usurpation of legislative authority.

Some of the new privacy cases carry with them an emotional element absent in the review of purely economic regulation. This may arouse public sentiment against the courts and precipitate recall efforts, constitutional amendments, or statutory limitations on judicial authority. In *People v. Privitera*,[78] the California Supreme Court refused to extend the right of privacy to a licensed physician's decision to prescribe laetrile for terminally ill cancer patients. More recently, the Florida court has held that the right to privacy protects the confidentiality of blood donation records; therefore, discovery was unavailable to a sufferer of AIDS attempting to show that he or she had contracted the disease in the course of hospital blood transfusions.[79] In such emotionally charged settings, the most carefully crafted decisions may not prevent a public backlash against the judiciary.

Conclusions

Economic due process remains a vital part of the constitutional order in a number of states. However, contemporary cases reveal relatively few instances of its explicit use. This conclusion contrasts with the earlier findings of Paulsen and Hetherington, who during the 1940s and 1950s, cited numerous examples of substantive due process in the areas of price regulation, licensing, the regulation of business methods, and labor relations.

For the most part, state supreme courts have adopted the deferential posture of the federal courts with respect to economic regulation. Paulsen and Hetherington wrote in the era before *Griswold v. Connecticut* signaled the return to substantive due process in the interests of privacy and personal autonomy.[80] It is possible that state supreme courts may have abandoned scrutiny of economic affairs to devote their resources to this emerging area of the law. Such states as Florida, Georgia and North Carolina, which have not been notably creative in relation to privacy or personal autonomy, have remained within the old economic due process tradition.

Strong arguments can be made in favor of retaining substantive due process as a restraint on legislative power. Bernard H. Siegan has offered four reasons for the revitalization of economic review. For him, a major objective of the framing of the Constitution was the protection of property rights; thus, judicial review is said to be embedded in the framework of the Constitution.[81] Second, Siegan sees no justification for a failure to protect economic liberties; that is, he finds no principled reason for distinguishing among protected constitutional freedoms.[82] Third, Siegan notes that regulation ultimately may be harmful to society if it is the product of interest groups' capture of the legislature or the bureaucracy.[83] Fourth, because of the capture phenomenon, legislation is not necessarily democratic and, consequently, courts should reserve final authority over the protection of economic freedoms.[84]

While Siegan is a partisan of an extreme version of laissez faire, his points are well taken and should not be ignored. A constitutional double standard is difficult to justify in any principled fashion. Moreover, the survey of state cases demonstrates a strong anticompetitive strain in some state legislation. It is not difficult to discern the influence of established barbers in some cases or the work of the insurance lobby in others. The great gains of the New Deal—minimum wage and maximum hour requirements and the protection of collective bargaining—are now settled law. If these accomplishments are ever threatened, it will not be at the hands of the state judiciary. What is left for state courts to review is an odd hodgepodge of economic legislation—some protectionist, some excessive, and some poorly drafted. A review of cases such as those cited in this chapter will hardly provoke another 1937-style institutional crisis for the judiciary.

State supreme courts serve as useful laboratories for experiments with a revitalized economic due process. As Hetherington and the Pennsylvania Supreme Court have pointed out, decisions grounded in state constitutional law do not have national precedential value. Poorly conceived decisions or ones that have unfortunate unanticipated consequences need not spill over into the law of other states. In addition, most state courts are more accountable to the electorate than are the federal courts. The partisan or nonpartisan election of judges remains the dominant means of judicial recruitment. If states that operate under a Missouri plan, with its requirement for a retention election on the judge's record, are added, a majority of state supreme court judges will face the voters sometime during their careers. What is more, most state supreme court justices serve terms of office ranging from six to eight years. Judicial election, coupled with short terms of office, make state judges sensitive to majoritarian pressures. While a lack of insulation from popular opinion may be undesirable for some areas of law, it provides a way to check excessive uses of economic due process without resort to a court-packing plan or other court-curbing techniques.

In both the traditional economic cases and the newer, hybrid economic-privacy cases, judges have resorted to a balancing test to determine the constitutionality of legislation. While a balancing test may be criticized as a standardless weighing of competing values in which the values favored by the court prevail, a carefully articulated test makes explicit the factors that enter into a decision and provides guidance for the legislature and lower courts. The Supreme Court of Alabama, in *Mount Royal Towers v. Alabama Board of Health*,[85] developed such a test that attempts to outline the factors that the court will consider in scrutinizing economic legislation under the state constitution. It weighs the nature of the economic interests affected against the public purpose to be served in the light of the degree of impairment of individual interests and the degree of burden that the legislation imposes. Neither this test nor any other balancing test can eliminate judicial discretion; judges will need to decide the definition of "important" or the degree of impairment. But as case law develops, the meaning of such concepts will become clearer as courts look to specific applications of the concepts to concrete cases.

State supreme court judges also may limit the use of economic due process by their own devices and formulas. The most effective check on any court remains the judges' sense of self-restraint. State courts can develop guidelines for substantive due process. The "real and substantial" relation test, as well as the insistence that legislatures adopt the least restrictive means of approaching a problem, are an improvement over the judicial abdication embodied in the minimal rationality standard. In turn, legislatures may limit judicial discretion by carefully drafting statutes that contain explicit findings justifying legislative means and ends. Finally, state supreme courts may be guided by other provisions in state constitutions—ones that specifically limit the means selected by legislatures. To this end, the California Supreme Court, in *Hale v. Morgan*,[86] found the civil fines imposed to be a violation of the excessive fines provision of the California Constitution. Thus, reliance on explicit provisions of the state constitution can provide a sound basis for the exercise of judicial review without the appearance of a substitution of judicial value judgements, based on vague conceptions of natural law, for those of the legislature.

Notes

1. See, for example, Allegeyer v. Louisiana, 165 U.S. 578 (1897), and New State Ice Company v. Liebmann, 285 U.S. 262 (1932).

2. Adkins v. Children's Hospital, 261 U.S. 525 (1923).

3. Lochner v. New York, 198 U.S. 45 (1905).

4. Adair v. United States, 208 U.S. 161 (1908), and Coppage v. Kansas, 236 U.S. 1 (1915).

5. For a detailed history of substantive due process that focuses on the protection of property and economic interests, see Bernard H. Siegan, *Economic Liberties and the Constitution* (Chicago: University of Chicago Press, 1980). It should be noted that substantive due process alone was not responsible for the Court-packing crisis.

6. West Coast Hotel v. Parrish, 300 U.S. 379, 391 (1937).

7. United States v. Carolene Products, 304 U.S. 144 (1938).

8. Id. at note 4.

9. For examples of minimal rational basis scrutiny under the Fourteenth Amendment for economic legislation, see Day-Brite Lighting, Inc. v. Missouri, 342 U.S. 421 (1952), and Williamson v. Lee Optical, 348 U.S. 483 (1955).

10. Griswold v. Connecticut, 381 U.S. 479 (1965). For a description of the "new" use of substantive due process, see Richard A. Epstein, "Substantive Due Process by Any Other Name: The Abortion Cases," *Supreme Court Review 1976*: 159–85.

11. See, in particular, the concurrence of Justice Potter Stewart in Roe v. Wade, 410 U.S. 113 (1973), and the majority opinion of Justice Lewis F. Powell in Moore v. East Cleveland, 431 U.S. 494 (1977).

12. Griswold v. Connecticut, 381 U.S. 479 (1965).

13. Roe v. Wade, 410 U.S. 113 (1973).

14. Moore v. East Cleveland, 431 U.S. 494 (1977).

15. Professor Stanley H. Friedelbaum has argued that the contemporary Court has carefully scrutinized economic legislation but not explicitly under substantive due process standards. See Stanley H. Friedelbaum, "Reprise or Denouement: Deference and the New Dissonance in the Burger Court," *Emory Law Journal* 26 (1977): 337–78. See also Robert G. McCloskey, "Economic Due Process and the Supreme Court: An Exhumation and Reburial," *Supreme Court Review 1962*: 34–62.

16. Monrad G. Paulsen, "The Persistence of Substantive Due Process in the States," *Minnesota Law Review* 34 (1950): 91–118.

17. Comments, "Substantive Due Process in the States Revisited," *Ohio State Law Journal* 18 (1957): 384–401.

18. John A. C. Hetherington, "State Economic Regulation and Substantive Due Process of Law," *Northwestern University Law Review* 53 (1958): 226–51.

19. Id., p. 239. The Arizona decision is Edwards v. State Board, 258 P.2d 418 (Ariz. 1951).

20. Paulsen, "Persistence," p. 117.

21. Hetherington, "State Economic Regulation," p. 248.

22. Id., p. 250.

23. A variety of LEXIS searches were used to locate all recent substantive due process decisions in the area of personal autonomy as well as of economic regulation. The cases discussed in this chapter represent those in which a state supreme court struck down an economic regulation on explicit substantive due process grounds.

24. Examples of state supreme court decisions in the areas of privacy and personal autonomy include: Right to Choose v. Byrne, 450 A.2d 925 (N.J. 1982) (abortion funding) and Sterling v. Cupp, 625 P.2d 123 (Or. 1981) (privacy rights of male prisoners monitored by female guards).

25. Cases in which the state supreme courts invoked the traditional deferential standard of Williamson v. Lee Optical, 348 U.S. 483 (1955) are legion. A number of state courts have been more deferential than the federal standard requires. The Supreme Court of Rhode Island, in upholding the denial of a building permit in Santini v. Lyons, 448 A.2d 124, 126 (R.I. 1982), despite equal protection and substantive due process arguments, held that "a legislative enactment is presumed constitutional until the party challenging the statute proves the contrary beyond a reasonable doubt." This standard of proof, usually associated with criminal prosecutions, places an almost impossible burden on the challenger.

One area of economic regulation is beyond the scope of this chapter. Numerous state courts have heard challenges to Sunday closing laws, and the grounds for decision and the outcomes are mixed. Although some challenges to these laws involved substantive due process, the resolution of most of the cases turned on equal protection analysis. For a comprehensive discussion of Sunday closing laws in the states, see the opinion of the Supreme Court of Connecticut in Caldor's Inc. v. Bedding Barn, Inc., 417 A.2d 343 (Conn. 1979).

26. Virginia Pharmacy Board v. Virginia Consumer Council, 425 U.S. 748 (1976).

27. Pennsylvania State Board of Pharmacy v. Pastor, 272 A.2d 487 (Pa. 1971).

28. Id. at 490.

29. Id.

30. Maryland Board of Pharmacy v. Sav-A-Lot, 311 A.2d 242 (Md. 1973).

31. Id. at 244.

32. Id. at 251.

33. Virginia Pharmacy Board v. Virginia Consumer Council, 425 U.S. 748 (1976), Linmark Associates, Inc. v. Willingboro, 431 U.S. 85 (1977), and Bates v. State Bar, 433 U.S. 350 (1977).

34. Maryland State Board of Barber Examiners v. Kuhn, 312 A.2d 216 (Md. 1973). The statute was also challenged successfully on equal protection grounds under the Fourteenth Amendment and the Maryland Declaration of Rights.

35. Thorne v. Raush, 261 S.E.2d 72 (W. Va. 1979).

36. D'Amico v. Board of Medical Examiners, 520 P.2d 10 (Cal. 1974). Chiropractors have not fared as well as osteopaths in state supreme courts. Two state courts have upheld limitations on the practice of chiropractic despite equal

protection and substantive due process challenges. See Kentucky Association of Chiropractors v. Jefferson County Medical Society, 549 S.W.2d 817 (Ky. 1977) and State ex rel. Iowa Department of Health v. Van Wyk, 320 N.W.2d 599 (Iowa 1982).

37. Florida Accountants Association v. Dandelake, 98 So.2d 323 (Fla. 1957).

38. Larson v. Lesser, 106 So. 2d 188 (Fla. 1958).

39. Adkins v. Children's Hospital, 261 U.S. 525 (1923).

40. West Coast Hotel v. Parrish, 300 U.S. 379 (1937).

41. Larson v. Lesser, 106 So.2d 188, 191 (Fla. 1958).

42. Dept. of Insurance v. Dade County Consumer Advocate's Office, 492 So.2d 1032 (Fla. 1986). The three-member minority was dismayed by the holding of the court. Id. at 1040.

43. Remington Arms Co. v. Skaggs, 345 P.2d 1085 (Wash. 1959).

44. Bulova Watch Co. v. Brand Distributors, 206 S.E.2d 141 (N.C. 1974).

45. The court also found that the statute delegated legislative regulatory power to private businesses in violation of the state constitution.

46. Hand v. H.&R. Block, Inc., 528 S.W.2d 916 (Ark. 1975).

47. Id. at 923.

48. Flank Oil Co. v. Tennessee Gas Transmission Co., 349 P.2d 1005 (Colo. 1960).

49. Hale v. Morgan, 584 P.2d 512 (Cal. 1978).

50. Id. at 522.

51. Id. at 524.

52. Davis v. City of Peachtree, 304 S.E.2d 701 (Ga. 1983).

53. State v. Saiez, 489 So.2d 1125 (Fla. 1986).

54. Id. at 1129.

55. Lochner v. New York, 198 U.S. 45 (1905).

56. Griswold v. Connecticut, 381 U.S. 479 (1965).

57. Roe v. Wade, 410 U.S. 118 (1978).

58. Charter Township of Delta v. Dinolfo, 351 N.W.2d 831 (Mich. 1984).

59. Augustin v. Barnes, 226 P.2d 625 (Colo. 1981).

60. Ok Yop Myrick v. Board of Pierce County Commissioners, 677 P.2d 140 (Wash. 1984). A county resolution that regulated the operation of massage parlors by requiring overhead sprinklers, two-way viewing, unlocked doors, and uniform and educational requirements for masseuses was found to infringe on federal constitutional rights of privacy and association.

61. Village of Oak Lawn v. Marcowitz, 427 N.E.2d 36 (Ill. 1981). An ordinance that heavily burdened ambulatory surgical clinics that performed even a single abortion was struck down on federal and state constitutional grounds.

62. Mountain States Telephone and Telegraph v. Department of Public Service Regulation, 634 P.2d 181 (Mont. 1981).

63. Missoulian v. Board of Regents of Higher Education, 675 P.2d 962 (Mont. 1974).

64. Rasmussen v. South Florida Blood Service, 500 So.2d 533 (Fla. 1987).

65. City of Carmel-by-the-Sea v. Young, 466 P.2d 225 (Cal. 1970); Falcon v. Alaska Public Offices Commission, 570 P.2d 469 (Alas. 1977); Denoncourt v. State Ethics Commission, 470 A.2d 945 (1983). In each case, the court struck down aspects of financial disclosure requirements of state ethics acts.

66. Moore v. East Cleveland, 431 U.S. 494 (1977).

67. Belle Terre v. Boraas, 416 U.S. 1 (1974).

68. State v. Baker, 405 A.2d 368 (N.J. 1979).

69. Santa Barbara v. Adamson, 610 P.2d 436 (Cal. 1980).

70. Saunders v. Clark County Zoning Department, 421 N.E.2d 152 (Ohio 1981). The Ohio court avoided invalidating the ordinance by reading the definition of family to include any social unit that performs the function of child rearing. The court found this definition necessary in order to protect rights guaranteed under the due process clause of the Fourteenth Amendment.

71. Delta Charter Township v. Dinolfo, 351 N.W.2d 831 (Mich. 1984). Not all challenges to the regulation of living arrangements for unrelated persons have been upheld. See, for example, Rademan v. Denver, 526 P.2d 1325 (Colo. 1974).

72. Whalen v. Roe, 429 U.S. 589 (1977).

73. Lopez v. Fitzgerald, 390 N.E.2d 835 (Ill. 1979).

74. Augustin v. Barnes, 626 P.2d 625 (Colo. 1981).

75. Montana Const., Art. II, sec. 10. An example of a compelling state interest may be found in Montana Human Rights Division v. City of Billings, 649 P.2d 1283 (Mont. 1982). After reviewing the history of the privacy provision in the state constitution and noting how the state standard for the protection of privacy is more stringent than the federal standard, the court nevertheless found a compelling state interest in the disclosure of employment records as part of an investigation of discrimination.

76. Mountain States Telephone and Telegraph v. Department of Public Service Regulation, 634 P.2d 181 (Mont. 1981).

77. Missoulian v. Board of Regents, 675 P.2d 962 (Mont. 1984).

78. People v. Privitera, 591 P.2d 919 (Cal. 1979).

79. Rasmussen v. South Florida Blood Service, 500 So.2d 533 (Fla. 1987).

80. Griswold v. Connecticut, 381 U.S. 479 (1965).

81. Siegan, *Economic Liberties*, p. 318.

82. Id. at 320.

83. Id.

84. Id. at 321.

85. Mount Royal Towers v. Alabama Board of Health, 388 So.2d 1209, 1214–15 (Ala. 1980). The court upheld a denial of a certificate of need to a proposed health care facility. The court also discussed at some length the difference between federal and state standards in economic cases.

86. Hale v. Morgan, 584 P.2d 512 (Cal. 1978).

8

The Constitutional Initiative: A Threat to Rights?

JANICE C. MAY

Unique among methods of state constitutional policymaking, the constitutional initiative enables the voters to propose and to adopt constitutional amendments independently of the legislature or of a constitutional convention. First adopted in its modern form by the State of Oregon in 1902, the initiative is in use in seventeen states today. During the last two decades, the nation has witnessed an increase in the number of constitutional amendments proposed and adopted by the constitutional initiative procedure. This increase has coincided with a rediscovery of state constitutions as sources of rights and liberties. The confluence of these two developments has revived an old controversy over the constitutional initiative as an appropriate instrument for constitutional change.

Although hailed, particularly by the judiciary, as quintessentially democratic, a means whereby the people can directly exercise their reserved and sovereign power to change constitutions, the constitutional initiative has also been criticized as a threat to rights and liberties, primarily minority rights. Critics have even charged that the device imperils constitutional government and destroys the integrity of state constitutions as fundamental law. Moreover, the courts, as guardians of rights, have been criticized for their deference to direct democracy at the cost of the protection of minority rights. In this regard, state judges, who in most states must face the electorate, are said to be particularly vulnerable to voter backlash for decisions protective of rights unpopular with the populace.

In this chapter, the controversy over the constitutional initiative will be reviewed as it applies to state constitutional decisionmaking, with emphasis upon rights and liberties. There is evidence that the constitutional initiative is a relatively minor method of state constitutional change except in a few states; that its threat to rights and liberties has been exaggerated; and that, although there may be cause for concern, the constitutional initiative is probably no worse and no better than many other democratic processes or institutions in the United States.

The Constitutional Initiative

The constitutional initiative is as old as the nation. The Georgia Constitution of 1777 could be amended only by a procedure originating with the voters of the counties, but it was never utilized.[1] The modern constitutional initiative at the state level owes its origins largely to the progressive movement at the turn of the twentieth century. The initiative was part of a package of reforms designed to increase popular participation in government and political parties intended as a cure for the political ills of the day. In 1902, Oregon, a pioneer with respect to these reforms, which became known as the Oregon plan or system, was the first state to adopt the constitutional initiative.[2] By the end of 1918, twelve additional states, all in the West or Midwest except for Massachusetts and Arkansas, had approved the device The order of adoption was as follows: Oklahoma (1907), Missouri (1908), Michigan (1908), Arkansas (1909), Arizona (1910) Colorado (1910), California (1911), Nebraska (1912), Ohio (1912), Nevada (1912), North Dakota (1914), and Massachusetts (1918).[3]

Fifty years later, during a second burst of enthusiasm for direct democracy, the voters of four more states accepted the mechanism: Florida in 1968, Illinois in 1970, and Montana and South Dakota in 1972.[4] Except for South Dakota, the constitutional initiative was incorporated in new or revised constitutions ratified on the dates listed.

All but one of the seventeen states utilizing the constitutional initiative have adopted the direct model, which allows the voters to place a proposition on the ballot independently of the legislature or a constitutional convention. Massachusetts, the only eastern state among the seventeen, is also the only one to boast the indirect version, which requires petitions for initiated propositions to be submitted to the legislature. The legislature may then approve the proposition with or without amendment for placement on the ballot, or it may refuse to submit the proposition to the voters.[5]

Frequency of Use and Electoral Success

The frequency with which the constitutional initiative has been used since the first proposition was adopted in Oregon in 1906 has varied greatly over the years. Arranged by decades, the number of proposals and adoptions is as follows:[6]

1900–1909	11–7	1950–1959	45–16
1910–1919	137–50	1960–1969	41–17
1920–1929	68–14	1970–1979	63–20
1930–1939	133–47	1980–1986	67–22
1940–1949	63–28		

The most prolific period was 1910–1919, during which 137 proposals were on the ballot and 50 were approved. The 1930s were a close second. The decade of the 1980s is well on its way to becoming the third most active decade by overtaking the 1920s, currently the third. It does not seem appropriate, however, to describe the past twenty years of activity as an initiative explosion insofar as the constitutional initiative alone is concerned. The number of propositions may appear to be especially high, however, because if the truncated first period is disregarded, the 1960s produced the fewest propositions.

The total number of propositions during the eighty-year history of the constitutional initiative is 628, of which 221 passed, for a modest electoral success rate of 35.2 percent. In addition, numerous propositions have never reached the ballot stage. California data indicate that, from 1912 to 1979, about two-thirds of the propositions "titled" by the attorney general prior to the collection of signatures failed to qualify for ballot placement. Since 1960, an astounding 80 percent did not qualify.[7]

The seventeen states with the constitutional initiative differ considerably with respect to their use of and electoral success with the device. Ranking the states by the number of proposals and adoptions yields the following order:[8]

California	102–32	North Dakota	33–20
Oregon	100–32	Nebraska	17–8
Colorado	79–23	Nevada	10–6
Arkansas	55–32	Montana	5–2
Arizona	49–19	Florida	4–2
Ohio	46–9	South Dakota	3–1
Oklahoma	44–12	Massachusetts	2–2
Michigan	44–11	Illinois	1–1
Missouri	34–9		

California and Oregon are the heaviest users followed by Colorado. In five states, all but one of which have adopted the constitutional initiative

Table 1

Constitutional Initiative Propositions as a Percentage of State Constitutional Amendments Proposed and Adopted in Seventeen States (as of December 1986)

State	Total Amendments Proposals	Total Amendments Adoptions	Constitutional Initiatives Percentage of Proposals	Constitutional Initiatives Percentage of Adoptions
Arizona	191	105	25.6	18.0
Arkansas	160	73	34.3	43.8
California	768	460	18.4	06.9
Colorado	231	109	34.1	21.1
Florida	68	44	05.8	04.5
Illinois	9	4	11.1	25.0
Massachusetts	143	116	01.3	01.7
Michigan	44	15	36.3	33.3
Missouri	107	68	07.4	04.4
Montana	21	13	14.2	15.3
Nebraska	278	184	06.1	04.3
Nevada	168	103	05.9	05.8
North Dakota	214	123	15.4	16.2
Ohio	241	142	19.0	06.3
Oklahoma	264	124	16.6	09.6
Oregon	360	182	27.7	17.5
South Dakota	181	94	01.6	01.0
Total	3,448	1,959	19.1	11.3

Sources: Adapted from The Book of the States, 1986–87, p. 14, Table 1.1 and preliminary data for the 1988–89 edition; Congressional Research Service, A Compilation of Statewide Initiative Proposals Appearing on Ballots Through 1976; and National Civic Review, annual surveys on "State Constitutional Development," 1977–1985.

The number of amendments and the number of initiatives are limited to the Michigan Constitution of 1963.

The number of amendments and the number of initiatives are limited to the Missouri Constitution of 1945.

within the past twenty years, the number of proposals was five or fewer, and the number of adoptions was only one or two.

To assess the importance of the constitutional initiative as a method of constitutional change in the initiative states, a comparison of initiative usage with that of alternative methods of change is useful. Data from table 1 show that the constitutional initiative has accounted for 19 percent of the 3,449 constitutional amendments proposed and 11 percent of the 1,959 amendments adopted.[9] In only three states (Arkansas, Colorado, and Michigan) did initiatives amount to as much as one-third (34 to 36 percent) of the proposals, and in just two (Arkansas and Michigan) did initiative adoptions reach or exceed that level. Moreover, the approval rate for propositions submitted by other methods was almost twice as high as that for the initiative (61 percent compared with 35 percent). In only two states with a substantial number of initiatives did the success rate for the initiative overtake that enjoyed by other propositions: North Dakota (60.6 percent to 53.9 percent) and Arkansas (58.1 percent to 39 percent). In no state did the number of initiated measures surpass the total proposed or adopted by all other methods. It is also of interest that the constitutional initiative has accounted for only 4 percent of the total number of amendments to all state constitutions currently in effect. The vast majority of amendments (90 percent) to the fifty state charters have been proposed by state legislatures.[10] In terms of sheer volume, the constitutional initiative does not appear to pose a threat to the body politic or to representative institutions.

Constitutional Initiative Propositions on Rights

From the turn of the century to the present, critics of the constitutional initiative have expressed grave concern that the voters, yielding to prejudice and passion and indifferent to constitutional niceties, will use the procedure to tamper with rights and liberties, particularly minority rights. After eighty years of experience with the constitutional initiative, a record exists on which to make an informed judgment about such a serious charge. The record consists of initiative proposals and adoptions from the time of the first initiative proposal in 1906 to the present. Although questions may always be raised about the data, the compilation of statewide initiatives provides essential information about the number and general categories, as well as the specific content of propositions.[11]

A striking finding from the listing of propositions is that a very small proportion of the total of 628 measures pertains to rights. In fact, if the propositions were limited to traditional rights normally placed in a bill of rights, such as the fundamental freedoms of speech, press, religion, and assembly, various equality rights, and the rights of persons accused of crime, the number would be even smaller, approximately twenty-three. By adopting a broader standard to encompass nontraditional rights, such as the right to work, which is found in the bills of rights of three of the constitutional initiative states,[12] and several other provisions, relating mostly to the rights of women and minorities, the number expands to fifty-seven. Even with the larger number, only 9 percent of the 628 constitutional initiatives proposed over an eighty-year span concerned rights. Corroboration of a low number is provided by a study of initiative propositions submitted for ballot qualification, including those that failed, from 1912 to 1979 in California.[13] Measures classified under the label "civil liberties–civil rights" amounted to only 4 percent of the total. One reason is the apparent lack of public interest in civil rights issues, as demonstrated by public opinion surveys.[14]

It is also significant that only twenty-five of the fifty-seven propositions passed, an extremely low number for eighty years of activity, amounting to one every three or four years. This is only 11 percent of the 221 propositions approved by the voters. The approval rate, however, is 44.5 percent, almost ten points higher than that for all constitutional initiatives.

Another surprising finding concerns the types of rights propositions on the ballot. The most numerous category pertained to women's rights. This was accounted for principally by the nine women's suffrage and one woman-on-juries propositions early in the history of the constitutional initiative. In addition, there were three antiabortion measures and a repeal-the-ERA proposal, to bring the total to fourteen. The eleven right-to-work propositions that divorce membership in unions from hiring and firing practices constituted the second most numerous group. Nine measures related to ethnic, immigrant, racial, or low-income groups, among them the grandfather clause and property rights for aliens.[15] Seven dealt with criminal justice[16] and four with civil trials and tort reform.[17] The others were scattered among health rights (three), rights of expression and association(three), religion (three), equality of representation (one), eminent domain (one), and the right to keep and bear arms (one).

In view of the concern over the threat to liberty posed by the constitutional initiative, the fact that the device has been used to promote rights has been overlooked. Ten of the propositions pertaining to women were designed to increase their rights (nine suffrage and one jury service). Other provisions favorable to rights included one extending property rights to aliens and three criminal justice provisions (abolishing the death penalty, requiring indictment by a grand jury, and speedy arraignment). Two removed the poll tax as a requirement for voting. The right to keep and bear arms is a new but not universally acclaimed state constitutional right.

Several of the other propositions are difficult to classify as for or against an expansion of rights. The so-called right-to-work proposals, which by a triumph of public relations appear to but do not guarantee anyone the right to a job, may be regarded as conferring freedom of choice on workers or as strictly an antiunion proposition that may reduce workers' rights by discouraging unionism. Another problem is tort reform. Consumer groups and attorneys who defend low-income persons on a contingency fee basis look upon reform as a restriction on the constitutional right of access to the courts, whereas defendants in tort cases regard the proposals as essential to their rights. In a few other instances, information was lacking for a definitive classification.

There is considerable evidence that, although not numerous, more of the electorally successful constitutional initiatives have reduced rather than expanded rights. Every one of the proposals that diminished minority rights passed (grandfather clause, repeal of fair housing, antibusing, and antidesegregation), and others that are less obviously minority related have also been adopted (making English the official language and the mandatory referendum on low-rent housing). All the propositions limiting the rights of the accused were approved (restoration of the death penalty, the Victims' Bill of Rights, and allowing comment on refusal to testify). Moreover, a substantial number of pro-rights measures failed, mainly the eight women's rights propositions (seven suffrage and one jury) and the attempt to confer property rights on aliens.

In contrast, at least eight pro-rights measures passed: the two anti–poll tax suffrage proposals that are historically relevant to minority rights, three items favorable to criminal defendants (abolition of the death penalty, grand jury indictment, and speedy arraignment), two of the women's suffrage proposals, and the right to keep and bear arms. Moreover, the voters have rejected a significant number of questionable measures. Among these are the California Francis Amendment that would have denied rights to subversives, a state-aid-to-private-schools measure, two antiabortion proposals, and a repeal-the-ERA proposition. It is also significant that none of the measures pertaining to religion or expression was adopted. Most of the right-to-work proposals failed, including one that would have prohibited right-to-work laws, and the tort reform measures divided evenly.

An analysis of propositions by historical period casts a different light on the content of the initiatives. The types of propositions considered changed about 1950. Since then, an imbalance is evident in that, except for one poll tax proposal, none of the propositions has favored women, minorities, or persons accused of crime. Instead, the initiatives are antifeminist, antiminority, antiaccused, and also antiunion, with one exception. Conspicuous by their absence are modern antidiscrimination proposals (state ERAs and protection of the handicapped, elderly and other groups), rights of privacy, environmental rights, the right to know, and similar measures. These rights-expanding proposals have been submitted to the voters by legislatures and constitutional conventions.[18]

Sponsors of constitutional initiatives have apparently been marching to the beat of a different drummer. Moreover, during the past two decades, a comparatively large number of propositions are new to the constitutional initiative procedure. They include the following subjects: English as the official language, tort reform, repeal of a state ERA, antibusing, antiabortion, restoration of the death penalty, California Victims' Bill of Rights, and the right to keep and bear arms. In addition, all these proposals have a conservative cast, and many concern "morals, life style, and race."[19] Finally, the purpose of several of the propositions adopted during the past two decades has been to strike at judicial decisions favorable to rights. Restoration of the death penalty in California by initiative after the California Supreme Court had held capital punishment unconstitutional is a well-publicized example.

In sum, over an eighty-year period, the number of constitutional initiatives concerned with rights has been small, and the number adopted is very small. The prediction that the constitutional initiative would destroy rights and liberties has not been borne out, although it is true that a few proposals were designed to reduce rights. But generally there are too many checks on the process to allow radical changes in state constitutional rights should the attempt be made to employ the initiative for that purpose.

The Judicial Check

Constitutional initiative procedures and propositions are subject to judicial scrutiny, and they are not infrequently circumscribed by the federal and state courts to protect rights. In fact, the initiative, both constitutional and statutory, has spawned so many cases over so many points of contention that some commentators have warned of the danger of overloading the courts with litigation.[20] Nonetheless, the volume of cases has not quieted those who question whether the courts have adequately protected rights. Critics argue that the courts are too deferential to, even paralyzed by, the initiative because the courts are reluctant to interfere with the exercise of an instrument of popular sovereignty.[21] Other commentators claim that the courts are aggressive, perhaps even too aggressive, particularly in their enforcement of the laws governing the constitutional initiative procedure.[22] A brief analysis of the judicial check on the constitutional initiative and its effectiveness as a protector of rights follows.

Constitutionality of the Initiative

The initiative had scarcely been adopted before litigation commenced. The legal issue that threatened all devices of direct democracy in use in the United States was their constitutionality: did they destroy the representative character of the government and thereby violate the guaranty clause of Article IV of the U.S. Constitution, which reads in part: "The

United States shall guarantee to every State in this Union a Republican Form of Government."?[23] The first and still leading U.S. Supreme Court case on this question is *Pacific States Telephone and Telegraph Co. v. Oregon,* decided in 1912.[24] At issue was a licensing tax levied by a statutory initiative proposal adopted by the voters. The company refused to pay the tax on a number of grounds, including the contention that its imposition was in violation of the republican form of government clause. The nation's highest court refused to rule on the merits of the argument. It based its decision on the principle followed in *Luther v. Borden* that whether a government is republican in form is a political question to be decided by the legislative and executive branches.[25] In short, the issue was held to be nonjusticiable. Inasmuch as it had seated the Oregon congressional delegation, the Congress apparently had found no fatal objection to the initiative and referendum procedures. The Supreme Court, in like fashion, declined to rule whether the initiative and referendum violated the U.S. Constitution.

In two earlier state cases, the supreme courts of Oregon and Oklahoma did move to the merits of the issue of constitutionality.[26] In upholding the initiative and referendum, the Oregon court made three points of interest: (1) the guaranty clause fails to describe or to prohibit specific types of governmental procedures or structures; (2) the people have the power to reserve for themselves a portion of the legislative power; and (3) republican government has not been threatened or replaced by the devices of direct democracy because they are only supplemental to representative institutions. In its ruling sustaining the constitutionality of the Oklahoma initiative and referendum amendment, the Oklahoma Supreme Court followed the Oregon precedent. Since these early decisions, no court, federal or state, has struck down the devices of direct democracy on constitutional grounds. In fact, various statements by judges in cases in which the devices have been at issue have indicated their wholehearted endorsement of this "precious right" of the people.[27]

U.S. Supreme Court Decisions on Constitutional Initiative Propositions

Although the courts have not found the constitutional initiative invalid as a process or procedure, they have set aside specific constitutional initiative propositions. In four leading cases on civil rights, the U.S. Supreme Court has ruled on the merits of measures adopted by the procedure. In none of the four did the fact that the initiative procedure was the source of the proposition determine the outcome, although the contending parties and the justices considered its relevance.

In the first case, *Guinn v. United States,* decided in 1915, the Court invalidated on Fifteenth Amendment grounds a constitutional initiative that provided for the so-called grandfather clause under which white voters were sheltered from a literacy test.[28] In *Lucas v. Colorado General Assembly*, the Court overturned a constitutional initiative whose purpose was to validate the federal analogy of representation for the Colorado legislature by allowing factors other than population to be included in the base of representation for one house of the bicameral body.[29] The fact that the voters ("a majority") had approved the principle did not save the provision from running afoul of the equal protection of the laws clause of the Fourteenth Amendment.[30]

In the remaining cases, the Court considered more subtle forms of discrimination, and the results were mixed. In *Reitman v. Mulkey*, the U.S. Supreme Court reviewed a constitutional initiative that, in effect, repealed California's fair housing laws and privatized decisions on the sale, rental, or purchase of real estate.[31] The Court affirmed the California Supreme Court's ruling that the proposition was in violation of the equal protection clause of the U.S. Constitution. In dissent, Justice John M. Harlan, joined by Justices Hugo Black, Tom Clark, and Potter Stewart, argued that the state enactment was constitutional because it had been adopted in the "most democratic of processes" "on a matter left open by the federal Constitution."[32]

The only case to uphold the constitutionality of the challenged constitutional initiative proposition was *James v. Valtierra*.[33] At issue was a California proposition that required a popular referendum in cities and counties before a state public body could engage in federally aided low-rent housing projects. For the majority, Justice Hugo Black wrote that not only was the mandatory referendum racially neutral but also that it enabled the voters to take part in decisions affecting the development of their communities. "Provisions for referendums demonstrate devotion to democracy, not to bias, discrimination or prejudice," he wrote.[34]

State Limitations on the Constitutional Initiative

Constitutional initiatives must conform not only to the U.S. Constitution but also to state laws. An important difference between the limitations imposed by the U.S. Constitution and the state constitutions is that an electorally successful initiative will become part of the state charter, the highest state law, provided no U.S. or state constitutional prohibitions have been breached. State constitutional issues will be focused therefore primarily on procedural and specific content requirements of state constitutions as they apply to the initiative,[35] whereas the constitutionality of a substantive change in rights or liberties will more likely be based on the U.S. Constitution.

The constitutional initiative has been the subject of considerable litigation in state courts. In view of the volume of cases, the number of constitutional and statutory provisions applying to the initiative, and the different approaches taken by the courts to enforce the limitations, it is difficult to draw an overall conclusion about the adequacy of the state judicial check on the constitutional initiative. An analysis of major issues will contribute to this end.

Propositions Not Constitutional Amendments. One issue reaching the state courts is whether a constitutional initiative proposition is, in reality, a proposal for constitutional change. As might be anticipated, constitutional initiatives have been challenged for placing statutory material rather than fundamental law into state constitutions. In an early case, the Supreme Court of Missouri held that the constitutional initiative did not confer a right to insert "mere legislative acts" in the constitution.[36] In later cases, the courts have refused to draw distinctions between statutory and constitutional law, requiring only that initiatives comply with the procedures governing the process.[37] But the issue of whether a given proposition is a constitutional initiative is not dead. In 1984, the Montana Supreme Court struck from the ballot a proposal intended to compel the state legislature to petition the Congress to call a constitutional convention to consider adoption of the federal balanced budget amendment.[38] The state's highest court ruled that the initiative was, in reality, a legislative resolution rather than a proposed constitutional amendment. The court held that the proposal was also in violation of the U.S. Constitution because Article V, the amending article, authorized only state legislatures to petition the Congress to call a convention. In the same year, the California Supreme Court removed from the ballot for substantially the same reasons a similar proposition that was a statutory rather than a constitutional initiative.[39]

State courts have also refused to sanction proposals that are constitutional revisions rather than amendments. The leading case is *McFadden v. Jordan*, in which the California high court ruled that the constitutional initiative could not be employed to consummate extensive revision.[40] The decision was rendered before the California constitution had been amended to provide for the single-subject rule, which also precludes comprehensive revision by limiting the scope of proposals.

Single-Subject Rule. The single-subject rule, specifically incorporated in five state constitutions and applicable to others, has loomed large as a state legal issue in constitutional initiative cases.[41] In recent years, the Florida and California courts have interpreted the rule in highly important cases pertaining to individual rights as well as to other subjects.

In Florida, the state's supreme court has developed what one commentator calls a "complex and rather confusing body of law" on the single-subject limitation.[42] Applying its guidelines, the court has struck from the ballot three major propositions: a proposal for a unicameral legislature,[43] a Proposition 13–type tax-limitation measure,[44] and a tort reform proposal.[45] Although the Florida courts have upheld propositions in the face of challenges for violation of the single-subject rule,[46] the overall impression is one of judicial aggressiveness.

The California Supreme Court has assumed a more relaxed posture.[47] In two recent cases, the California court applied the rule to Proposition 13, the Jarvis-Gann property tax limitation measure, and the California Victims' Bill of Rights, adopted in 1978 and 1982, respectively. In *Amador Valley Joint Union High School District v. State Board of Equalization*,[48] the court held that the sections of Proposition 13 were "reasonably germane and functionally related to the general subject of property tax relief."[49] The Victims' Bill of Rights also passed muster under the germaneness test in *Brosnahan v. Brown*.[50] The court found that the ten sections, despite their diversity, all related to criminal justice and popular concern about victims of crime. The majority opinion stated that the court "should not prohibit the sovereign people from either expressing or implementing their own will" on such important matters as their own safety.[51] The California decisions raise questions about judicial deference to the voters and the effectiveness of the single-subject rule. According to one commentator, no initiative has failed the one-subject test in California since the 1940s.[52]

Subject Exclusions. The Illinois and Massachusetts courts have enforced their state constitutional provisions limiting the subjects that may be included in constitutional initiative proposals. In Illinois, an attempt to add an ethics reform proposal by constitutional initiative fell victim to the clear wording of a constitutional provision that restricted the initiative to legislative structures and procedures.[53] In Massachusetts, the Supreme Judicial Court ruled that the constitutional limitation on appropriations prohibited a highway fund;[54] in a second case, a proposal to reduce the size of the Massachusetts lower chamber and to change reapportionment was upheld over the objection that judicial powers had been unconstitutionally reduced.[55]

Ballot Wording. Another procedural limitation that has been an issue in several cases is the requirement that ballot titles and summaries be clear and unbiased. The tort reform measure in Florida failed not only the single-subject test but also the "clear and unambiguous language" standard as interpreted by the court from statutory regulations on ballot wording.[56] The court compared the language of the actual amendment and the ballot summary with a measure of exactitude that again suggests that judicial activism persists in Florida.

The Arkansas Supreme Court has also applied language standards to initiative propositions. In 1984 it removed from the general election ballot a constitutional initiative that prohibited public funding for abortions. The court ruled that the wording prepared by the attorney general was "biased" and had a "partisan coloring" because it referred to the fetus as an "unborn child."[57]

Preelection Judicial Review. In several cases, the courts have removed a proposition from the ballot before the election, thereby depriving the electorate of the opportunity to vote on it. The question of the propriety of preelection as opposed to postelection review by the courts has inspired a lively controversy.[58]

Preelection review of procedural and other technical requirements is defended as necessary to make the constitutional initiative process work as intended and to protect the voter and the integrity of the ballot. An additional consideration is that, following the approval of a proposition in the election, it is virtually impossible to persuade the courts to enforce violations of the requirements.[59] Called "election-cures-errors," the practice assumes that the public has spoken on the issue and that this should dispose of the matter.

In contrast, preelection review of substantive issues, including the constitutionality of the proposition, has been challenged as judicial encroachment on the legitimate powers of the electorate. It is contended that initiatives should be treated in the same manner as proposed laws before the legislature, which normally cannot be litigated until after passage.

The Constitutional Initiative as a Check on Judicial Review. Although the state courts have ample authority to enforce state constitutional and statutory limits on the constitutional initiative, the courts themselves may be trammeled by this instrument of direct democracy. A certain tension has existed between the electorate and the courts from the time of the adoption of the initiative; and attempts have been made to use the constitutional initiative to curb the courts and to overturn their decisions.[60] An early but atypical example is a constitutional initiative approved by the Colorado voters in 1912. It sought to deprive the Colorado state courts, except for the supreme court, of the power to review specified laws under the state and the U.S. Constitution. In addition, it required a popular vote on Colorado Supreme Court decisions that overturned state laws on either state or federal constitutional grounds; a "no" vote would serve to "recall" the decision. In companion cases decided in 1921, the Colorado high court held the provisions unconstitutional on federal supremacy and due process grounds.[61]

Several of the constitutional initiatives concerning rights and liberties were obviously inspired by displeasure with court decisions, both federal and state. In a contemporary setting, the 1956 Arkansas initiative directing the state legislature to oppose desegregation by all lawful means was clearly a response to *Brown v. Board of Education.*[62] The antibusing proposition, approved by the Colorado voters in 1974, was a reaction to *Keyes v. School District No. One*[63] and other busing decisions of the federal courts. The antiabortion funding proposals of 1984 and 1986 were indirectly responsive to *Roe v. Wade.*[64] Dissatisfaction with the state civil justice system has led to tort reform measures in Arizona, Montana, and Florida; and concern about state criminal justice has resulted in the initiatives on the death penalty and the Victims' Bill of Rights. In addition, several of the initiatives were designed to reverse specific court decisions. Three California constitutional initiatives are in point, and a recent Oregon proposition is relevant.

The first of the three California measures was adopted in 1950 to reverse the decision in *Housing Authority for the City of Eureka v. Superior Court*.[65] The California Supreme Court had held that the referendum process could not be invoked to overturn a decision of local authorities to apply for federal aid for low-rent housing projects; the decision was said to be administrative rather than legislative. In the same year, a proposition to require a referendum before such projects could be approved was qualified for the ballot and accepted by the voters. (This constitutional initiative was upheld in *James v. Valtierra*.) In 1972, California voters adopted by initiative a constitutional amendment to restore the death penalty after capital punishment had been held in violation of the cruel or unusual punishment clause of the California bill of rights by the California Supreme Court in *People v. Anderson*.[66] The third proposition is the California Victims' Bill of Rights, Proposition 8, ratified in 1982. Although less differentiated, sweeping, and policy oriented than the other two California initiatives, Proposition 8 also targeted specific court decisions for overrule, the most publicized of which, perhaps, were those imposing the exclusionary rule.[67] One commentator has estimated that as many as fifty cases may be affected by the passage of the initiative, but its full impact will not be known for some time.[68]

The constitutional initiative that in 1984 resurrected the death penalty in Oregon represents a somewhat different approach to changing state court decisions. In *Oregon v. Quinn*, the Oregon Supreme Court invalidated a 1978 statutory initiative that permitted the judge to impose capital punishment in given circumstances.[69] The court held that the law violated the state constitutional right to a trial by jury "on all essential elements of an offense."[70] The constitutional initiative of 1984 was designed not only to remedy the constitutional infirmity found by the court in *Quinn* but also to prevent the Oregon courts from invalidating the death penalty on other state constitutional grounds not yet litigated. In other words, its purpose was to immunize the proposition from state constitutional objections.

The use of the constitutional initiative to dilute rights needs to be placed in perspective. The number of initiatives actually overturning decisions expanding rights is not large. It is a smaller subset of a small group of initiative propositions that have been proposed and a very small group of initiatives that have been adopted to curb rights. Moreover, even when a constitutional amendment is adopted, the state courts have the power to interpret and apply the new provision. As James K. Fischer has written: "It must not be forgotten that successful ballot propositions become part of the state constitution and ultimately are subject to state court construction and interpretation. This judicial scrutiny can alter the results achieved by ballot propositions."[71] Fischer also writes that "majoritarian use of ballot propositions to change state constitutional law from that wrought by state courts has been notoriously ineffective."[72]

The California Supreme Court's interpretation of the constitutional initiative restoring the death penalty is instructive on this point. In *People v. Superior Court of Santa Clara County (Engert)*, the court struck down, on due process grounds for vagueness, a state law applying the death penalty in aggravating circumstances.[73] The court noted that the death penalty might be held unconstitutional in a future case should the penalty be wholly disproportionate to the crime to which it was applied.

The complex and loosely worded California Victims' Bill of Rights will undoubtedly be revised as courts attempt to enforce its provisions. As Judge Stanley Mosk of the California Supreme Court has said, it "contains more enigmas than any recent enactment."[74] In one case decided soon after its adoption, the California high court held that the truth-in-evidence section did not apply to juvenile cases with respect to the use of incriminating statements as substantive evidence at trial.[75]

In sum, the state and federal courts have enforced procedural and substantive limitations upon the constitutional initiative. Ballot propositions have been invalidated for violations of rights protected by the U.S. Constitution and for noncompliance with a host of state procedural and other requirements. The courts have reviewed, with varying degrees of aggressiveness, sometimes to the point of criticism for undue interference with the voters' rights to use the constitutional initiative. In short, the judicial check on the constitutional initiative is a force to be reckoned with.

The Electoral Check

The author of the most recent and comprehensive empirical study of the initiative (constitutional and statutory) is critical of the device as a method of policymaking and is concerned about its threat to civil rights and liberties.[76] Generally his description is one of low and unrepresentative voting turnouts; irrational, uninformed, and prejudiced voters; costly campaigns with access to the ballot and to the media restricted to the few people with resources; and special-interest and single-issue confrontational politics that exacerbates factional divisions in the United States. But this characterization of the initiative is overdrawn; other democratic institutions and processes suffer from many of the same flaws when judged by empirical standards.

Studies of voter turnout on initiative propositions reveal a number of findings surprisingly favorable to the initiative. Although ballot propositions typically draw fewer voters than do candidates for public office,[77] initiative propositions are more likely to capture the voters' interest than other propositions. Significantly, proposals placed on the ballot by the initiative outpoll those submitted by the legislature.[78] Moreover, at least in California and Colorado, the turnout for initiatives is comparable to that for the "down ballot" candidate races. In seven California elections from 1970 to 1983, the average drop-off rate from the total vote in the election was 8 percent on initiatives. This was about the same as the turnout for controller (7 percent), attorney general (6 percent), and general assembly (8 percent) and better than that for the board of equalization (12 percent) and the supreme court (32 percent).[79] In the 1976 general election, the drop-off for initiatives was less than that for all the candidate races except for president.[80] In the Colorado general election of 1976, voter participation was higher for the ten initiatives than for the legislative and judicial retention elections; more votes were cast for six of the initiatives than the statewide vote for Congress; and, in at least four counties, the vote on a given initiative exceeded that for president of the United States.[81] Moreover, in California, voter fatigue is usually not a factor with initiatives; voters seek them out wherever they are on the ballot, as was the case with last-placed Proposition 13.[82]

Moreover, critics of the initiative may well have overestimated the effectiveness of elitist groups with substantial organizational capabilities and financial resources. Passage of initiatives cannot be bought with large campaign contributions,[83] and citizen groups with modest means, including those outside the political mainstream, have enjoyed a measure of success, particularly in certain policy areas such as nuclear power and environmental protection. It has been estimated that as many as one-fourth of the initiatives in California in recent years have originated with short-term groups lacking ties to the established political structures.[84] Additionally, "virtually every type of interest group . . . has utilized the initiative process in California," according to V. O. Key, Jr., and Winston W. Crouch.[85]

On the basis of empirical research, it can be assumed that the constitutional initiative has proved to be less than a perfect method for democratic participation in constitutional change; but studies of the actual operation of the device fail to demonstrate that the procedure has been dangerous to our institutions or rights or without positive merit. One reason is that the voters behave in a manner that adds yet another check on any potential threats to rights that the device might engender: their pronounced tendency to reject ballot propositions. About two-thirds of all initiatives and 60 percent of those concerned with rights have been defeated. This negative bias in voting behavior may not be the same as perfect rationality but, insofar as rights are concerned, support of the status quo is generally a vote to preserve rights. State constitutions have been traditionally protective of rights and, if no change occurs, the constitutional shield will remain. New rights may be desirable, but civil libertarians would probably have preferred a "no" vote on some of those adopted in recent years.

Moreover, experience with the initiative over an eighty-year period points up the fact that propositions concerned with governmental structures and processes far outnumber those on rights and liberties.[86] Among these have been major reforms, including Nebraska's unicameral legislature, Missouri's merit selection of judges, Illinois' reduction in the size of the lower house of the state legislature and the substitution of single-member districts for the unique cumulative voting system, Florida's "sunshine amendment" on ethics and financial disclosure, Ohio's county home rule amendment, and countless others. Many citizens and scholars regard these reforms as contributing to better government.

Furthermore, though the constitutional initiative may be less than a perfect instrument of democracy, other processes and institutions are also flawed. Relatively low and unrepresentative turnouts have been characteristic of American elections in the twentieth century. State legislatures suffer from some of the same electoral problems that plague the initiative, not the least of which is the influence of well-organized and well-financed interest groups on access to legislators and the quality of representation.[87] Additionally, rational decisionmaking models scarcely apply to the legislature or other institutions. But perhaps most important is the fact that, historically, the state legislature has not been in the forefront of racial progress. The handful of antiracial propositions adopted by the initiative pales in significance when compared with segregation, racial gerrymandering, disenfranchisement, and other discriminatory laws enacted by state legislatures in the not-so-distant past.

Summary and Conclusions

The constitutional initiative has proved to be a relatively minor method of state constitutional policymaking in all but a few of the seventeen states in which it is available to the voters. Even in the heavy user states, the constitutional initiative accounts for a lesser number of proposals and adoptions than do other methods of state constitutional amendment. Moreover, the adoption rate of initiative proposals is half that of the alternate procedures. In five initiative states, or 30 percent of the seventeen, the number of constitutional initiatives is minuscule, ranging from a maximum of five proposals to a high of only two adoptions.

Although commonly indicted as a threat to rights and liberties, the constitutional initiative has been utilized infrequently to reduce or to terminate them. Under a broad and generous definition of rights, less than 10 percent of the proposals submitted to the voters have even concerned rights, and less than half of these have been adopted, for a grand total of twenty-five in eighty years. Three of these were later declared unconstitutional by the U.S. Supreme Court. No more than ten of the electorally successful propositions sought to reduce the rights of racial minorities or of persons accused of crime. In contrast, at least eight were designed to expand rights.

One reason for the low volume of constitutional initiative activity in civil rights is the network of checks that restrict its use. Initiatives must conform to U.S. constitutional standards protective of rights. Numerous state constitutional and statutory requirements, most of them governing the initiative process, have been enforced by state courts. Moreover, patterns of voter behavior operate as a restraint because the electorate rejects approximately two-thirds of the ballot propositions.

Although resorted to sparingly to alter civil rights, the constitutional initiative has been utilized far more frequently to change governmental structures and processes, including a number of major reforms. Moreover, voter turnout on initiatives has been respectable in comparison with proposals submitted by the legislature and with "down ballot" candidate races; and a variety of citizen groups has been engaged in the process with a measure of success.

Inasmuch as the threat to rights has been exaggerated, state constitutional reforms have been adopted, and citizen participation has been encouraged, it appears that condemnation of the constitutional initiative for its shortcomings as a democratic procedure is excessive. None of our institutions, including elections and the state legislature, is free from defects. The constitutional initiative, which may be regarded as an ancillary procedure that offers but does not guarantee effective popular participation in state constitutional policymaking, is no better and no worse than other democratic procedures and institutions in the United States. Furthermore, elite behavior is not so exemplary that outlets for public expression and power should be abandoned.

Notes

1. Walter Fairleigh Dodd, *The Revision and Amendment of State Constitutions* (Baltimore: Johns Hopkins University Press, 1910), p. 42.

2. Id., p. 127. Oregon sec. 1(2)(a).

3. David B. Magleby, *Direct Legislation: Voting on Ballot Propositions in the United States* (Baltimore and London: Johns Hopkins University Press, 1984), pp. 38–40, table 3.1. The voters of Nevada adopted the referendum in 1904 and added the initiative in 1912.

4. Id. Florida Const., Art. XI, sec. 3; South Dakota Const., Art. XXIII, sec. 1, sec. 2. (These sources differ from Magleby's.)

5. Massachusetts Const., Art. XLVIII, sec. 1, sec. 2.

6. The source for initiatives from 1906 through 1976 was the Congressional Research Service. See Virginia Graham, *A Compilation of Statewide Initiative Proposals Appearing on Ballots through 1976* (Washington, D.C.: Library of Congress, 1978). Sources for initiatives from 1977 through 1986 were the *National Civic Review*, annual surveys on "State Constitutional Developments," and preliminary data collected for the forthcoming edition of *The Book of the States, 1988–89* by Albert L. Sturm.

7. Magleby, *Direct Legislation*, p. 67, table 4.1

8. Graham, *Compilation; National Civic Review*; annual surveys; preliminary data for *The Book of the States*.

9. The percentage of constitutional initiatives would be somewhat higher if the calculations included only the total number of constitutional amendments proposed and adopted beginning with the effective date of the adoption of the constitutional initiative in each state. These data are not readily obtainable for all states. Data collected for California from 1912, when the initiative was authorized, through 1976 indicate that the percentage of initiatives was 16 percent of the total constitutional amendment proposals and 18 percent of adoptions, figures comparable to those in the text that includes all amendments from the date of the initial adoption of the California constitution in 1879. The calculations for California from 1912–1976 are drawn from Eugene C. Lee, "California," in *Referendums: A Comparative Study of Practice and Theory*, ed. David Butler and Austin Ranney (Washington, D.C.: American Enterprise Institute for Public Policy Research, 1978), p. 90, table 5.1.

10. Janice C. May, "Constitutional Amendment and Revision Revisited," *Publius: The Journal of Federalism* 17 (Winter 1987): 159, table 1.

11. Information about each proposition was drawn from Graham, *Compilation, National Civic Review*, and preliminary data for *The Book of the States, 1988–89*. Space considerations prevented the inclusion of a four-page table that organized the propositions by state, date, topic, and electoral outcome. Problems arose from the reliance on captions or titles rather than complete descriptions of the proposals and from missing data. Scholars may well differ with my decisions on inclusion of a proposition as a rights measure and its classification in the text that follows.

12. Florida Const., Art. I, sec. 8; Missouri Const., Art. I, sec. 29; South Dakota Const., Art. VI, sec. 2.

13. Magleby, *Direct Legislation*, p. 204, Appendix B.

14. Id., pp. 74–76.

15. The remaining seven were two anti–poll tax measures and one each of the following: mandatory referendums on low-rent housing, antidesegregation, fair housing repeal, antibusing, and English as the official language.

16. Three were on the death penalty and one each on allowing comments on failure to testify, speedy appearance before magistrate, grand jury indictment, and the California Victims' Bill of Rights.

17. Two provided for jury verdicts by three-quarters of the jurors, but one was joined with a proposal to allow women to serve on juries, which was counted as a women's rights measure only. One proposal to define contempt of court and to provide a jury trial for contempt was classified as civil because it was

probably directed at contempt for failure to comply with injunctions during labor disputes.

18. May, "Constitutional Amendment and Revision," pp. 173–75.

19. Magleby, *Direct Legislation*, p. 191. Magleby comments on the conservative nature of recent initiatives.

20. Id., pp. 47, 194.

21. See Comment, "Judicial Review of Laws Enacted by Popular Vote," *Washington Law Review* 55 (December 1979): 183.

22. Richard Briffault, "Distrust of Democracy," book review, *Texas Law Review* 63 (March-April 1985): 1365.

23. U.S. Constitution, Art. IV, sec. 4.

24. Pacific States Telephone and Telegraph Co. v. Oregon, 223 U.S. 116 (1912).

25. Luther v. Borden, 7 How. 1 (1849).

26. Kadderly v. City of Portland, 94 P.710 (Ore. 1903) and Ex parte Wagner, 95 P.435 (Okla. 1908).

27. For example, see comments in Brosnahan v. Brown, 651 P.2d 274, 281 (Cal. 1982), and James v. Valtierra, 402 U.S. 137, 141 (1972).

28. Guinn v. United States, 238 U.S. 347 (1915). U.S. Constitution, Amend. XV, reads in part as follows: "The right of citizens of the United States to vote shall not be denied or abridged by the United States or any State on account of race, color, or previous condition of servitude."

29. Lucas v. Colorado General Assembly, 377 U.S. 713 (1964).

30. U.S. Constitution, Amend. XIV, sec. 1 reads in part as follows: "nor shall any State...deny to any person within its jurisdiction the equal protection of the laws."

31. Reitman v. Mulkey, 387 U.S. 368 (1067).

32. Id. at 391, 396.

33. James v. Valtierra, 402 U.S. 137 (1967).

34. Id. at 141. Black dismissed the argument that low-income persons were discriminated against, an issue pursued by the court minority.

35. The constitutions of a few states expressly exclude certain subjects from inclusion in a constitutional initiative. Of these, Illinois is the most restrictive because all topics are off limits except "structural and procedural subjects" contained in the legislative article (Art. XIV, sec. 3). The Massachusetts document excludes four types of subjects: religion and most other civil rights and liberties; the judiciary, including court decisions, which may not be reversed; local and special laws; and appropriations Art. XLVII, Sec. 2). The Missouri charter excludes appropriations (Art. III, sec. 51), and the California document contains two prohibitions: no proposition may name a person to hold public office or identify a private corporation to exercise a power or to perform a function (Art. II, Sec. 12).

36. State ex rel. Halliburton v. Roach, 130 S.W. 689, 696 (Mo. 1910).

37. The Nebraska Supreme Court considers this point at some length in Omaha National Bank v. Spire, 389 N.W.2d 269 (Neb. 1986). See cases cited by the court.

38. State ex rel. Harper v. Waltermire, 691 P.2d 836 (Mont. 1984).

39. AFL-CIO v. Eu, 686 P.2d 609 (Cal. 1984).

40. McFadden v. Jordan, 196 P.2d 787 (Cal. 1948).

41. The single-subject rule is expressly incorporated in the following state constitutional provisions: California (Art. IV, sec. 22 (d)); Florida (Art. XI, sec. 3); Missouri (Art. III, sec. 49), Oregon (Art. IV, sec. 1(4)); and Oklahoma (Art. XXIV, sec. 1).

42. Comment, "Amendment Nine and the Initiative Process: A Costly Trip to Nowhere," *Stetson Law Review* 14 (Spring 1985): 356.

43. Adams v. Gunter, 238 So.2d 824 (Fla. 1970). The decision was reached before the passage in 1972 of a constitutional amendment that specifically incorporated the single-subject rule.

44. Fine v. Firestone, 448 So.2d 984 (Fla. 1984).

45. Evans v. Firestone, 457 So.2d 1351 (Fla. 1984).

46. Floridians against Casino Takeover v. Let's Help Florida, 363 So.2d 337 (Fla. 1978) (private casinos); Weber v. Smathers, 338 So.2d 819 (Fla. 1976) ("sunshine amendment"); Carroll v. Firestone, 497 So.2d 1204 (Fla. 1986) (state lottery).

47. For a discussion of the single-subject rule in the California courts, see Daniel H. Lowenstein, "California Initiatives and the Single-Subject Rule," *UCLA Law Review* 30 (1983): 936–75.

48. Amador Valley Joint Union High School District v. State Board of Equalization, 583 P.2d 1281 (Cal. 1978).

49. The words quoted are those of California Supreme Court Justice Stanley Mosk, taken from his dissenting opinion in Brosnahan v. Eu, 641 P.2d 200, 204 (Cal. 1982).

50. Brosnahan v. Brown, 651 P.2d 274 (1982).

51. Id. at 281.

52. Comment, "New Limits on the California Initiative: An Analysis and Critique," *Loyola of Los Angeles Law Review* 19 (May 1986): 1054.

53. Coalition for Political Honesty v. State Board of Elections, 359 N.E.2d 138 (Ill. 1976).

54. Opinion of the Justices, 9 N.E.2d 186 (Mass. 1937).

55. Cohen v. Attorney General, 237 N.E.2d 657 (Mass. 1957).

56. Evans v. Firestone, 457 So.2d 1351, 1353–1355.

57. Arkansas Women's Political Caucus v. Riviera, 677 S.W.2d 846 (Ark. 1984).

58. Among the numerous articles on the subject are the following: Note, "The Judiciary and Popular Democracy: Should Courts Review Ballot Measures Prior to Elections?" *Fordham Law Review* 53 (March 1983): 928; Comments, "Preelection Judicial Review: Taking the Initiative in Voter Protection," *California Law Review* 71 (July 1983): 1216–38.

59. Comments, "Preelection Judicial Review": 1217, n. 5.

60. James M. Fischer, "Ballot Propositions: The Challenge of Direct Democracy to State Constitutional Jurisprudence," *Hastings Constitutional Law Quarterly* 11 (Fall 1983): 47. His observation is limited to California.

61. People v. Max, 198 P. 150 (Colo. 1921) and People v. Western Union Tel. Co., 198 P. 146 (Colo. 1921).

62. Brown v. Board of Education, 347 U.S. 483 (1954).

63. Keyes v. School District No. One, 413 U.S. 189 (1973).

64. Roe v. Wade, 410 U.S. 113 (1973).

65. Housing Authority for the City of Eureka v. Superior Court, 219 P.2d 457 (1950).

66. People v. Anderson, 493 P.2d 880, cert. den. 406 U.S. 958 (1972).

67. Early cases on the California exclusionary rule, such as People v. Cahan, 282 P.2d 905 (Cal. 1955) have been overruled. See In re Lance, 694 P.2d 744 (Cal. 1985).

68. K. Connie King, "Brown's Court Legacy: Crusaders Against Social Injustice," *California Journal* 13 (September 1982): 311.

69. Oregon v. Quinn, 623 P.2d 639 (Or. 1981).

70. See Katherine H. Waldo, "The 1984 Death Penalty Initiative: A State Constitutional Analysis," *Willamette Law Review* 22 (Winter 1986): 285–353.

71. Fischer, "Ballet Propositions," p. 80.

72. Id., p. 45.

73. People v. Superior Court of Santa Clara County, 647 P.2d 76 (Cal. 1982).

74. A. D. Ertuckel, "Debating Initiative Reform: A Summary of the Second Annual Symposium on Elections at the Center for the Study of Law and Politics," *Journal of Law and Politics* 2 (Fall 1985): 329.

75. Ramona R. v. Superior Court, 693 P.2d 789 (Cal. 1983).

76. Magleby, *Direct Legislation*.

77. Id., p. 100. From 15 to 18 percent fewer voters participate in elections on ballot propositions than for candidates.

78. Id., p. 84, table 5.2

79. Id.

80. Id., p. 91, table 5.6.

81. John S. Shockley, *The Initiative Process in Colorado Politics: An Assessment*, Bureau of Governmental Research and Service (Boulder, Colo.: University of Colorado, August 1980), pp. 2–3, table 1.

82. Magleby, *Direct Legislation*, pp. 90–92.

83. Id., pp. 147–48. See table 8.1.

84. Briffault, "Distrust of Democracy," p. 1358.

85. V. O. Key, Jr., and Winston W. Crouch, *The Initiative and Referendum in California* (Berkeley: University of California Press, 1939), p. 447.

86. Magleby, *Direct Legislation*, p. 74. Referring to a "categorization of more than twelve hundred initiatives voted on since 1898," Magleby observes that the "subject areas most apt to result in initiatives are governmental processes and taxes." The numerical dominance of propositions concerning governmental structures and processes was borne out by my analysis of the 628 constitutional initiatives in the study for this chapter. Approximately 220 constitutional initiatives proposed changes in governmental organization and procedures, exclusive of women's suffrage and poll tax provisions, that were placed in the category of rights; 256 were related to fiscal policy.

87. Briffault, "Distrust of Democracy" pp. 1361–64. In succinct fashion, Briffault reviews legislative shortcomings when measured against ideal standards of representation, deliberation, and sensitivity to minority interests.

Selected Bibliography

———————— STANLEY H. FRIEDELBAUM

The revival of state constitutional law during the past two decades has resulted in a notable expansion of the available literature. Symposia have been undertaken in the political science journals and in the law reviews, as well as in a variety of book collections. The principal lacunae relate to one of the most elemental tools in the study of public law: the traditional casebook that has long served as the benchmark of legal education. It is doubtful that this omission will long remain, though state case selections pose more vexing problems than the more conventional products emanating from the U.S. Supreme Court.

Perhaps the most significant contributions have occurred in the treatment of civil rights issues. Much of this development was predictable in view of judicial efforts to counteract the perceived conservatism of the Burger and Rehnquist courts by a resort to state predicates. Yet there is more to the return to state constitutions than an attempt to evade unwelcome federal decisions. State common law questions have arisen with respect to such issues as reproductive technology in general and surrogate parenthood in particular. Nor is it appropriate, as one of the contributors to this collection demonstrates, to assume that concepts of economic liberty may be treated apart from human rights. The attempt to do so will not survive long-standing tests associated with the American constitutional tradition.

The listings that follow do not include individual state studies. These studies may be useful and enlightening in describing the status of human rights within a particular state culture. However, the coverage at times may be uneven when judged as public law essays. Nor are individual state studies readily accessible through standard literature guides.

Abrahamson, Shirley S. "Criminal Law and State Constitutions: The Emergence of State Constitutional Law." *Texas Law Review* 63 (1985): 1141–93.

Advisory Commission on Intergovernmental Relations. "American Constitutions: 200 Years of Federalism." *Intergovernmental Perspective* 13 (Spring 1987).

Brennan, William J., Jr. "The Bill of Rights and the States: The Revival of State Constitutions as Guardians of Individual Rights." *New York University Law Review* 61 (1986): 535–53.

———. "State Constitutions and the Protection of Individual Rights." *Harvard Law Review* 90 (1977): 489–504.

Collins, Ronald K. L., and Peter J. Galie. "Models of Post-Incorporation Judicial Review: 1985 Survey of State Constitutional Individual Rights Decisions." *Publius: The Journal of Federalism* 16 (Summer 1986): 111–39.

Collins, Ronald K. L., Peter J. Galie, and John Kincaid. "State High Courts, State Constitutions, and Individual Rights Litigation since 1980: A Judicial Survey." *Publius: The Journal of Federalism* 16 (Summer 1986): 141–61.

"Comment: The Independent Application of State Constitutional Provisions to Questions of Criminal Procedure." *Marquette Law Review* 62 (1979): 596–621.

Countryman, Vern. "Why a State Bill of Rights?" *Washington Law Review* 45 (1970): 454–73.

The Courts: The Pendulum of Federalism. Washington, D.C.: Roscoe Pound–American Trial Lawyers Foundation, 1979.

"Developments in the Law—The Interpretation of State Constitutional Rights." *Harvard Law Review* 95 (1982): 1324–1502.

Douglas, Charles G., III. "State Judicial Activism—The New Role for State Bills of Rights." *Suffolk University Law Review* 12 (1977): 1123–50.

Driscoll, Dawn-Marie, and Barbara J. Rouse. "Through a Glass Darkly: A Look at State Equal Rights Amendments." *Suffolk University Law Review* 12 (1977): 1282–1311.

Fischer, James M. "Ballott Propositions: The Challenge of Direct Democracy to State Constitutional Jurisprudence." *Hastings Constitutional Law Quarterly* 11 (1983): 43–89.

Force, Robert. "State 'Bills of Rights': A Case of Neglect and the Need for a Renaissance." *Valparaiso University Law Review* 3 (1969): 125–82.

Hetherington, John A. C. "State Economic Regulation and Substantive Due Process of Law." *Northwestern University Law Review* 53 (1958): 226–51.

Howard, A. E. Dick. "State Courts and Constitutional Rights in the Day of the Burger Court." *Virginia Law Review* 62 (1976): 874–944.

Hudnut, Paul S. "State Constitutions and Individual Rights: The Case for Judicial Restraint." *Denver University Law Review* 63 (1985): 85–108.

Kelman, Maurice. "Foreword: Rediscovering the State Constitutional Bill of Rights." *Wayne Law Review* 27 (1981): 413–33.

Keyser, David R. "State Constitutions and Theories of Judicial Review: Some Variations on a Theme." *Texas Law Review* 63 (1985): 1051–80.

Kirby, James C., Jr. "Expansive Judicial Review of Economic Regulation under State Constitutions: The Case for Realism." *Tennessee Law Review* 48 (1981): 241–82.

Linde, Hans A. "E. Pluribus—Constitutional Theory and State Courts." *Georgia Law Review* 18 (1984): 165–200.

―――. "First Things First: Rediscovering the States' Bills of Rights." *University of Baltimore Law Review* 9 (1980): 379–96.

Maltz, Earl M. "The Dark Side of State Court Activism." *Texas Law Review* 63 (1985): 995–1023.

Nettik Simmons, Dennis. "Towards a Theory of State Constitutional Jurisprudence." *Montana Law Review* 46 (1985): 261–88.

Neuborne, Burt. "The Myth of Parity." *Harvard Law Review* 90 (1977): 1105–31.

"Note: Expanding Criminal Procedural Rights under State Constitutions." *Washington and Lee Law Review* 33 (1976): 909–33.

"Note: Of Laboratories and Liberties: State Court Protection of Political and Civil Rights." *Georgia Law Review* 10 (1976): 533–64.

"Note: The New Federalism: Toward a Principled Interpretation of the State Constitution." *Stanford Law Review* 29 (1977): 297–321.

"Note: Private Abridgement of Speech and the State Constitutions." *Yale Law Journal* 90 (1980): 165–88.

"Note: State Economic Substantive Due Process: A Proposed Approach." *Yale Law Journal* 88 (1979): 1487–1510.

"Note: Toward a Right of Privacy as a Matter of State Constitutional Law." *Florida State University Law Review* 5 (1977): 633–745.

Paulsen, Monrad G. "The Persistence of Substantive Due Process in the States." *Minnesota Law Review* 34 (1950): 91–118.

―――. "State Constitutions, State Courts and First Amendment Freedoms." *Vanderbilt Law Review* 4 (1951): 620–42.

Pollock, Stewart G. "State Constitutions as Separate Sources of Fundamental Rights." *Rutgers Law Review* 35 (1983): 707–22.

Porter, Mary Cornelia, and G. Alan Tarr, eds. *State Supreme Courts: Policymakers in the Federal System*. Westport, Conn.: Greenwood Press, 1982.

"Project Report: Toward an Activist Role for State Bills of Rights." *Harvard Civil Rights–Civil Liberties Law Review* 8 (1973): 271–350.

Sedler, Robert. "The State Constitutions and the Supplemental Protection of Individual Rights." *University of Toledo Law Review* 16 (1985): 465–505.

Spaeth, Harold J. "Burger Court Review of State Court Civil Liberties Decisions." *Judicature* 68 (1985): 285–91.

Sturm, Albert L., and Kaye M. Wright. "Civil Liberties in Revised State Constitutions." In *Civil Liberties: Policy and Policy Making*, pp. 179–89. Edited by Stephen L. Wasby. Lexington, Mass.: D. C. Heath and Co., 1976.

Tarr, G. Alan, and Mary Cornelia Porter. "Gender Equality and Judicial Federalism: The Role of State Appellate Courts." *Hastings Constitutional Law Quarterly* 9 (1982): 919–73.

―――, eds. "New Developments in State Constitutional Law." *Publius: The Journal of Federalism* 17 (Winter 1987).

Treadwell, Lujuana W., and Nancy W. Page. "Equal Rights Provisions: The Experience under State Constitutions." *California Law Review* 65 (1977): 1086–1112.

Welsh, Robert. "Whose Federalism? The Burger Court's Treatment of State Civil Liberties Judgments." *Hastings Constitutional Law Quarterly* 10 (1983): 819–75.

Wilkes, Donald E., Jr. "More on the New Federalism in Criminal Procedure."
    Kentucky Law Journal 63 (1975): 873–94.
————. "The New Federalism in Criminal Procedure: State Court Evasion of
    the Burger Court." *Kentucky Law Journal* 62 (1974): 421–51.
————. "The New Federalism in Criminal Procedure Revisited." *Kentucky Law
    Journal* 64 (1976): 729–52.
Williams, Robert F. "Equality Guarantees in State Constitutional Law." *Texas Law
    Review* 63 (1985): 1195–1224.
————. "In the Supreme Court's Shadow: Legitimacy of State Rejection of Su-
    preme Court Reasoning and Result." *South Carolina Law Review* 35 (1984):
    353–404.

Index

Contributors

SUE DAVIS is Assistant Professor of Political Science at the University of Delaware. Her articles have appeared in *American Politics Quarterly, , Polity, Publius* , and the *Western Political Quarterly*. Her book, *Justice William H. Rehnquist: The Quest for a "New" Federalism* is forthcoming.

SUSAN P. FINO is Assistant Professor of Political Science at Wayne State University. She is the author of articles and papers relating to the new judicial federalism. She is the author of *The Role of State Supreme Courts in the New Judicial Federalism* (Greenwood Press, 1987).

STANLEY H. FRIEDELBAUM is Professor and Vice-Chairperson in the Department of Political Science at Rutgers University, New Brunswick, New Jersey. He is the author of *Contemporary Constitutional Law: Case Studies in the Judicial Process* and of monographs on judicial deference and state constitutional law. His articles have appeared in *The Supreme Court Review, University of Chicago Law Review, Emory Law Journal, Dickinson Law Review, Publius,* and as chapters in *Civil Liberties: Policy and Policy Making, Politics in New Jersey,* and *State Supreme Courts: Policymakers in the Federal System* (Greenwood Press, 1982). His current essay on Justice William J. Brennan, Jr. will appear in a volume of Burger Court profiles.

PETER J. GALIE is Professor and Chairperson in the Department of Political Science at Canisius College. He has written numerous articles relating to various aspects of state constitutional law. He is currently preparing a commentary on the New York State Constitution.

DANIEL C. KRAMER is Professor of Political Science at the College of Staten Island, CUNY. His articles relate to a variety of topics in the areas of constitutional law and civil liberties. He is the author of *Participatory Democracy: Developing Ideals of the Political Left* and of *Comparative Civil Rights and Liberties*. He is currently preparing a book on the interface between government and business in the United Kingdom as well as articles on Justice Byron White and the Takings Clause.

JANICE C. MAY is Associate Professor of Government at the University of Texas at Austin. She has published numerous articles and monographs on state constitutions, election law, and judicial reform, and is coauthor of *Texas Government* and of the biennial survey of state constitutions in *The Book of the States*. She served as member of two Texas Constitutional Revision Commissions and the Texas State Bar's Board of Directors.

ROBYN MARY O'NEILL is a practicing attorney on the staff of the Cook County, Illinois legal assistance office. Currently she is serving as a public advocate in defense of the rights of senior citizens.

MARY CORNELIA PORTER is Visiting Professor of Political Science at Northern Illinois University, De Kalb, Illinois. Her articles have appeared in *The Supreme Court Review*, *Women and Politics*, *Baylor Law Review*, *Hastings Constitutional Law Quarterly*, *Ohio State Law Journal*, and *Publius*. She is coeditor of *State Supreme Courts: Policymakers in the Federal System* (Greenwood Press, 1982) and has contributed essays to *Women in Politics* and *Women in the World*.

G. ALAN TARR is Associate Professor and Chairperson in the Department of Political Science at Rutgers University, Camden, New Jersey. He is the author or coauthor of *Judicial Impact and State Supreme Courts*, *State Supreme Courts: Policymakers in the Federal System* (Greenwood Press, 1982), *American Constitutional Law*, and *State Supreme Courts in State and Nation* as well as of numerous articles on state constitutional law. He is currently serving as series editor for "State Constitutions of the American States."